Joan Fisher's Guide to Knitting

Triune Books

Guide to Knitting

by Joan Fisher

Photography by Rex Bamber

ISBN 0 85674 021 7
Published by
Triune Books, London, England
© Trewin Copplestone Publishing Ltd 1973
Printed in Italy by
Istituto Italiano d'Arti Grafiche
Bergamo
Mohn Gordon Ltd, London

Contents

Introduction

'Besides its utility, knitting is an agreeable recreation which those who favour it can take up to fill in odd moments, and carry on even while conversing or reading.' The lines come from an encyclopedia of needlework published in the 19th century, but are as true today as they were then. Ever since it was discovered that two long needles could be used to loop a continuous single strand of thread into a strong fabric many women – and men too – in all parts of the world have found pleasure, satisfaction and relaxation in knitting. It is an infinitely versatile craft, a creative hobby, and a soothing pastime.

Throughout the centuries attempts have been made to knit most items of personal and house-hold adornment – in England in the 16th century, the boy king Edward was presented with a pair of knitted silk stockings from Spain. In Turkey it is reputed the scarlet fez hats were at one time knitted. During the Victorian era when needle-work of all kinds was so universally popular, every conceivable item was knitted – from sofa rugs, counterpanes and antimacassars to fine lacy insertions and edgings, collars and shawls.

Many countries and communities have evolved their own traditional knitting . . . there are the complex colour designs of Scandinavian work, the beautiful symmetry and muted shades of Fair Isle patterns, the cobwebby delicacy of Shetland lace. A traditional Shetland shawl, knitted from the finest hand-spun wool, measures six feet square. It is wonderfully warm, but so light it can be easily passed through a wedding ring.

From the Aran Isles off the west coast of Ireland, come creamy, richly-textured sweaters with intricate cabling worn by the local fishermen. The Aran stitches originated about 500 years ago when knitting was done with goose quills by the menfolk from wool spun by their women. In time each family adopted its own particular pattern based on the traditional stitches. Each stitch has a name and a meaning. Some are of religious significance, others relate to the sea or country-side.

Today knitting is as popular – if not more so – than it has ever been. But just as fashions in dress, furnishings and art change, so have fashions in knitting. The stitches, techniques and traditional patterns remain the same, but the

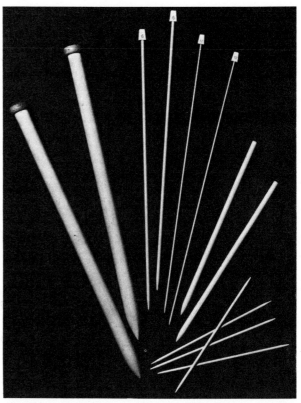

way we use them, and the new exciting yarns and colours available to us, mean that knitting has taken on a completely new look: a look of today, reflecting modern trends in fashion and design.

In this book I introduce you to the stitches and techniques of the craft of knitting, I give you a dictionary of stitch patterns to show just a few of the ways in which the two basic stitches can be used to give an infinite variety of effects. And in the pattern chapters you will find attractive new designs to make up for yourself, your home and your family. These designs have been carefully chosen to represent as many facets of knitting as possible: some patterns are quick and easy, some are more complex; some are in classic style, some in lively modern style. Some use traditional wools, others the newest 'novelty' yarns – fine floating Mohair, sparkling goldfingering, colour-ful random-dyed wool . . . There are formal designs, casual designs, dramatic designs, pretty designs, in plain colours, stripes, patterns, checks . . . Something, surely, to please everyone.

JOAN FISHER

Chapter one
THE FACTS ABOUT KNITTING

BASIC EQUIPMENT

The only two essentials for knitting are a pair of knitting needles and a ball of yarn, although a few additional items will help to make life easier.

Needles

Knitting needles are available in various thicknesses, the sizes being denoted by a series of numbers (see chart below). In the British range of sizes, the lower numbers indicate the thickest needles, the high numbers the fine needles. In the USA the system is reversed, with the high numbers used for thick needles, low numbers for fine ones. Needles may be of metal, nylon, plastic or wood, and each size is usually available in a choice of lengths. Which length you choose is a matter of personal preference, although a pattern involving a great number of stitches will be more comfortably worked on long needles.

Needles should always be clean, smooth and rigid – never use needles which show an inclination to bend easily. It is well worth while always buying the best-quality needles.

GUIDE TO KNITTING NEEDLE SIZES

British Sizes	Continental Sizes	USA Sizes
14	2	0
13	–	–
12	2.50	1
11	3.00	2
10	3.25	3
–	3.50	4
9	4.00	5
8	4.50	6
7	4.75	7
6	5.00	8
5	5.50	9
4	6.00	10
3	7.00	10½
2	8.00	11
1	9.25	13

Cable needles

These are very short needles with points at both ends used for taking stitches to the front or back of the knitting when working a cable pattern. Choose a cable needle as near as possible to the size of the needles being used for the main pattern.

Stitch holder

Frequently a pattern will instruct you to leave a number of stitches aside while others are knitted, then the first stitches are returned to later. Some patterns suggest keeping these stitches on a spare needle until required, but a stitch holder is more satisfactory as there is then no danger of any stitches slipping off and unravelling. Small numbers of stitches can be kept on a safety pin.

Also useful

A **tape measure** – to measure the garment as you knit it. Always measure your work on a flat surface, taking care not to pull at the edges. Measure along the straight line of the work.

A **row counter** – this is a small tube placed on the end of the knitting needle; it has numbers which are turned after each row in order to keep count of the number of rows worked.

A **crochet hook** – to work a crochet border round a finished knitted garment; it is also useful for picking up dropped stitches.

For finishing garments you will need pins for pinning out to the right size, an iron, ironing board and cloth for pressing, and sewing needles for joining seams.

YARNS

Wool is the traditional yarn for knitting, but there are excellent synthetic yarns available now, and also mixtures of wool and synthetics which combine the advantages of each. Cotton yarns are good for knitting summer clothes and babies' wear. Most yarns are available in different thicknesses – 2, 3 or 4-ply, double knitting and so on – your pattern will tell you which to use. As the colour of yarn may vary slightly between dye lots, it is important to buy all the yarn you need for a particular design from the same dye lot (a dye lot number is usually marked on the label of each ball). Most shops will put the yarn aside for you for a period of time so you can buy it a few balls at a time if you do not want to buy the whole amount at the beginning.

The following gives a guide to the principal yarn types available for knitting.

Acrylic yarns. These are man-made fibres, marketed under trade names such as Acrilan, Orlon, Courtelle and so on. Because of the way in which the yarns are manufactured there is usually more yardage in a ball of acrylic fibre than there is in a ball of natural yarn in the same weight. Acrylic yarns produce lightweight garments which are soft to the touch and are quick and easy to launder.

Angora. A fluffy yarn available in its pure natural form and also as a synthetic mixture in which the natural yarn is mixed with nylon. Both versions of the yarn are attractive for pretty, delicate knitwear.

Baby yarns. These are usually made from the finest, softest botany wool, or sometimes from man-made fibres. Available in 2, 3 and 4-ply weights, and also in a softly-twisted bulky 'quickerknit' form, which is quick to knit, and works to a 4-ply tension.

Bainin wool. The traditional wool used for Aran knitting. In its natural form the wool is a creamy, pale oatmeal colour, but it can be successfully dyed to any shade.

Bouclé. A textured yarn in which a normal smoothly-spun yarn is interspersed with tight clusters. A garment knitted in bouclé has a two-tone effect because of the raised clusters in the fabric.

Cashmere. A luxury natural fibre, soft and fine to the touch, which is ideal for classic sweaters and cardigans.

Chunky yarns. These are extra thick yarns which are quick to knit, and warm for outdoor and sports wear. Although thick, they can also be used successfully for well-tailored, fitting garments.

Cotton. A natural yarn available in many weights which is good for summer and light-weight clothes. Cotton is a 'harder' yarn than wool, therefore the finished fabric has a crisper look, with stitch detail clear and uniform.

Crêpe. This is another textured yarn, in which a multi-ply yarn in natural or synthetic fibres is tightly twisted. A smooth fabric with a slightly crinkled surface is produced.

Double knitting yarns. These are ideal, everyday yarns suitable for most purposes. They may be produced from natural or synthetic fibres, or a mixture of both. The yarns are quick to work with but the finished fabric is not too bulky.

Linen. A natural fibre which is frequently spun into yarns suitable for both knitting and crochet work. Sometimes the yarns are given a textured or novelty finish.

Marls. Marl yarns combine several strands of different colours twisted together after the spinning.

Mohair. A soft yarn spun from the hair of the Angora goat. Despite its lightweight, 'floating' fluffy appearance, the yarn is very strong. Ideally, it should be knitted on fairly big needles.

Novelty yarns. These yarns are intended to give special effects – sparkling, glitter and 'jewelled' yarns can all be termed novelty. So can most of the textured yarns. Often natural and man-made fibres are combined to give the particular effect required, or different colours are mixed. Glitter yarns are usually a combination of a natural yarn with a metal thread. Some novelty yarns can be successfully washed, others have to be dry-cleaned – be guided by the instructions on the label of each yarn type.

Nylon. A very strong and hardwearing fibre made from chemicals found in coal, air and water. It is resistant to bacteria and mildew, and is mothproof, also as it is a very white fibre it can be dyed successfully to brilliant white and vivid fluorescent shades. It can be used on its own, or combined with wool to give the advantages of both fibres.

Tricel. This is another man-made fibre good for both knitting and crochet work. It is hard-wearing and easy to launder.

Wool. A natural yarn available in many different weights and thicknesses, from the finest and softest baby yarns, usually of botany wool, to the sturdiest triple knitting weights which are good for chunky heavy sports sweaters.

HOLDING YOUR NEEDLES AND YARN

English method

Pass the yarn round the little finger of the right hand, then take it under the third and middle fingers and then over the first finger. The right-hand needle rests between the thumb and the first finger (like holding a pencil) and the finger stays close to the work. The left-hand needle is held with the fingers and thumb above it and the needle firmly against the palm. During work the left hand pushes the stitches along the needle towards the point, and the right first finger moves the yarn to work each stitch.

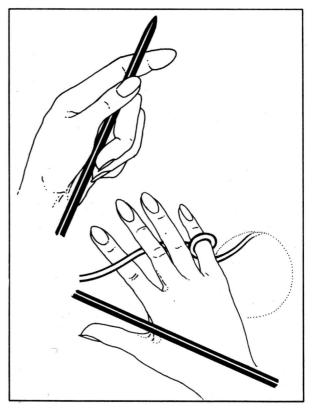

Continental methods

In the French method both hands hold the needles from on top. The yarn goes round the little finger, then over the two middle fingers and the first finger. The first finger moves the yarn as in the English method. Another method used on the continent has the yarn held by the first finger of the left hand. The needles are held as in the French method, but the yarn goes over the little finger of the left hand, under the middle two fingers then round the first finger.

Left-handed workers

If you are left-handed, then the above procedures are merely reversed – i.e. for the English method, the left hand controls the yarn, and the right hand controls the stitches.

CASTING ON

Thumb method

Undo a length of yarn from the ball – about three times the finished length required.
Make a slip loop: hold yarn between thumb and first finger of left hand; take yarn from ball in right hand and make a loop by taking main yarn over other yarn and hold loop in left hand.
Now take a needle in your right hand, put it through the loop and with it draw through the main yarn from the ball, thus making a loop on the needle. Pull yarn end to draw loop tight.
Hold the needle with the loop on it in the right hand with the main yarn coming from the ball at the back; hold other yarn in left hand under all four fingers. Take this yarn round left thumb clockwise close to the needle. Insert needle into loop on thumb, pass main yarn from ball under needle point, then with needle draw yarn through loop and let loop on thumb slip off. Pull yarn to draw stitch tight. Continue making stitches in this way until the required number is reached.

Two-needle method

Draw a short length of yarn from ball then make a slip loop as described in the thumb method above. Put needle with slip loop on it into left hand with main yarn at front. Taking second needle in right hand, insert this needle into loop

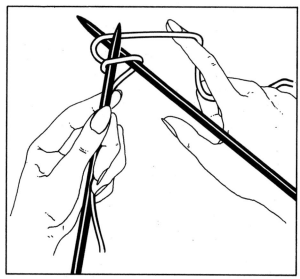

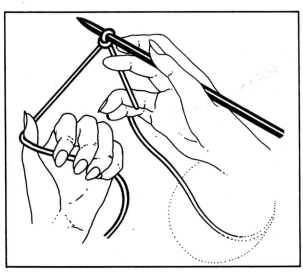

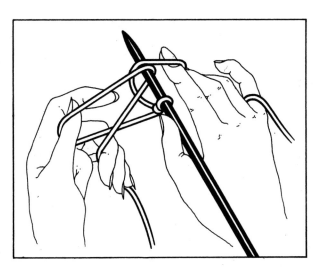

from left to right, pass main yarn under point of right-hand needle and then with this needle draw main yarn through loop to form a new loop on needle. Transfer this new loop to left-hand needle which now holds two stitches. Continue in this way until required number of stitches are formed. This method gives a 'looped' edge and if a firm edge is required the first row of knitting must be worked into the backs of the stitches.

Between-stitch method

Begin by making a slip loop and first stitch in a similar way as for the two-needle method above. Now, instead of inserting right-hand needle into stitch on left-hand needle, insert it between the two stitches, complete stitch as two-needle

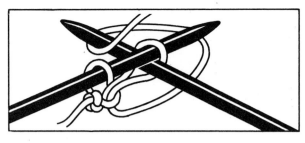

method. Continue in this way for length required. This method gives a twisted edge.

STITCHES
Knit stitch

Hold the needle with your cast-on stitches in your left hand and the empty needle and main yarn in your right hand (or vice versa if you are left-handed). Insert right-hand needle into first stitch on left-hand needle from left to right, main yarn at back of work, then take yarn under point of right-hand needle (diagram 1). With right-hand needle pull main yarn through stitch to form a loop on right-hand needle (diagram 2) and let loop on left-hand needle slip off. One stitch has been knitted on to right-hand needle. Continue along row in this way.

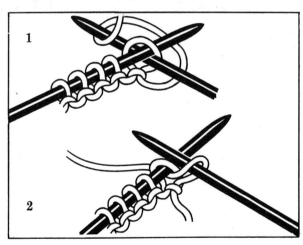

Purl stitch

Hold the needle with your cast-on stitches in your left hand and the empty needle and main yarn in right hand. Insert right-hand needle into first stitch from right to left, main yarn at front

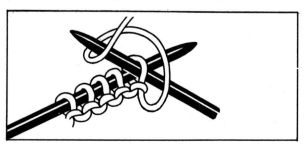

of work. Take yarn over and then under point of right-hand needle. Turn right-hand needle away from you to draw loop through on to needle and then drop loop from left-hand needle. Continue along row in this way.

INCREASING

At the beginning or end of a row increases of several stitches can be made by casting on. Increases of a single stitch made by one of the following methods are usually worked within the main body of the work, and not at the end of a row.

Work twice into one stitch

This is the most usual method. Start to knit or purl the stitch in the usual way but do not drop the loop from the left-hand needle; now insert

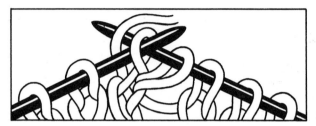

right-hand needle into back of loop from right to left for a knit stitch or from left to right for a purl stitch, and work into it again. The diagram above shows a knit stitch being worked into for the second time.

Yarn round needle or yarn over needle

This method of increasing leaves a small hole in the knitting so is usually used in lacy patterns (see page 12). In every case the strand which goes over the needle is worked as a stitch on the next row. In lacy patterns where a hole in the work is required but no increase in the number of stitches, then two stitches are usually worked together either just before or just after the 'made' stitch. Where an increase is required then the yarn is simply taken over or round the needle at the point where you want to increase the width of your work. See full instructions on page 13.

Lifting loop from previous row

Another method of making an extra stitch is to lift the loop lying between the last stitch and the next stitch on to the left-hand needle and then to knit it through the back of the loop.

DECREASING

At the beginning of a row decreases of several stitches can be made by casting off (see below). Decreases of one or two stitches made by any of the following methods are usually worked within the main body of the work and not at the end of a row.

Working two stitches together

Two stitches, sometimes three, are knitted or purled together as one stitch. When two stitches are knitted together the decreased stitch slopes to the right, so if lines of decreases are being worked at each end of the work – such as on a skirt – decreases at the end of the row are often worked by knitting two stitches together through the backs of the loops as this makes the decreased stitch slope to the left. The reverse happens when two stitches are purled together.

Pass slipped stitch over

This is worked by slipping one stitch on to the right-hand needle without working into it, then knitting the next stitch; the slipped stitch is then passed over the knitted stitch and dropped off the needle.

CASTING OFF

Never cast off too tightly, unless the pattern specifically instructs you to do so, as there is much less 'give' in this last row than in ordinary knitting.

Work the first two stitches of the row in the usual way, keeping pattern correct. With the point of the left-hand needle lift the first stitch worked over the second stitch and let it fall. Work another stitch on to the right-hand needle then lift the first stitch over the second again. Work all along the row until only one stitch remains. Draw up this stitch to make it a long one, remove needle, break yarn and thread yarn end through stitch. Draw up tightly.

TENSION

Every pattern gives a tension measurement which refers to the number of stitches and rows and should be equal to one square inch for that particular pattern. Different sizes of needles will give different tension measurements with the same yarn. To achieve the correct size of finished article it is essential to work to the tension given in the pattern. Before starting work on any garment test your tension by working a small square, of 3 or 4 in., using the yarn and needle size recommended by the pattern, and the correct stitch pattern. Press this square then mark off with pins a 2-in. square in the middle of it. Count the number of stitches and rows in this square and check them with the tension given in the pattern. If the stitches and rows are fewer than those given, try again with needles a size smaller; if they are too many, try again with needles a size larger. Only start to knit the garment when you have found the right needles to achieve the correct tension.

BASIC STITCH PATTERNS

Garter stitch

Every row is a knit row. An elastic, ridged piece of work results. If every row is worked in purl stitches a similar fabric is produced.

Stocking stitch

This consists of one row of all knit stitches, and one row of all purl stitches worked alternately. It gives a smooth surface on the right (knit) side. Sometimes the reverse side is used as the right side and this is called reversed stocking stitch.

Ribbing

In single ribbing each row consists of one stitch knit followed by one stitch purl all along; in double ribbing two knit stitches are alternated with two purl. On the second row stitches which were knitted on the first row are purled and vice versa.

Example of single rib (k.1, p.1) pattern.

Example of double rib (k.2, p.2) pattern.

Example of wide rib (k.6, p.2) pattern.

Moss stitch

This is worked in a similar way to single rib, but stitches which were knitted on the first row are again knitted on the second row, and the purl stitches are purled. Double moss stitch is two stitches knitted followed by two stitches purled.

FANCY STITCH PATTERNS

Lacy patterns

The principle of working lacy patterns is that holes, or open stitches, are set at regular intervals into a solid fabric. These holes are created by taking the yarn round the needle between two stitches to form an extra stitch. The extra stitch is usually compensated for by working two stitches together either before or after the extra stitch. Sometimes however stitches will be added in one row, and taken off in the next. The way in which the yarn is taken round the needle to form the new stitch will depend on the stitch pattern you are using.

Above: a selection of different lacy patterns.

If you want to make the new stitch between two knit stitches, then bring the yarn forward between the needles and take it back over the top of the right-hand needle so the yarn is then in the correct position for knitting the next stitch on the left-hand needle. This is usually called 'yarn forward' (y.fwd.).

If you want to make the new stitch between two purl stitches, then take the yarn over the top of the right-hand needle, then bring it back under it to the front of the work again ready to purl the next stitch on the left-hand needle. This is usually called 'yarn round needle' (y.r.n.).

If you want to make the new stitch between a purl and a knit stitch, take the yarn over the top of the right-hand needle ready to knit the next stitch on the left-hand needle. This is usually called 'yarn on needle' (y.o.n.).

If you want to make the new stitch between a knit and a purl stitch, then first bring the yarn forward between the needles, then take it over the top of the right-hand needle and bring it back under it to the front of the work again, as for 'yarn round needle'. The yarn is then in position ready to work the next purl stitch on the left-hand needle. This is also usually called 'yarn on needle' (y.o.n.).

Cable patterns

Simple 'twisted' stitch patterns can be achieved by working in the backs of stitches, instead of into the fronts as usual. Diagram 1 shows a stitch being knitted through the back loop.

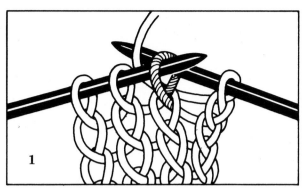

1

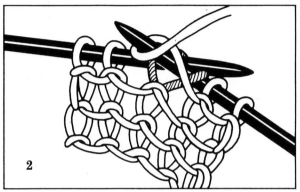

2

Diagram 2 shows a stitch being purled through the back loop.

Alternatively, a 'mock' cable effect can be achieved by knitting the second or third stitch on the left-hand needle before the first one or two. To produce a proper cable pattern however, with the traditional twisted rope-like rib, it is necessary to use a cable needle (see page 7). Two, three or more stitches are slipped from the left-hand needle on to the cable needle before being worked and then the cable needle is held either at the front of the work or the back, depending on which direction you wish the cable to twist. The corresponding number of stitches are then worked from the left-hand needle in the usual way, and then the stitches are knitted from the cable needle.

Blarney Kiss, a traditional cable pattern used in Aran knitting.

Above: a selection of different cable patterns.

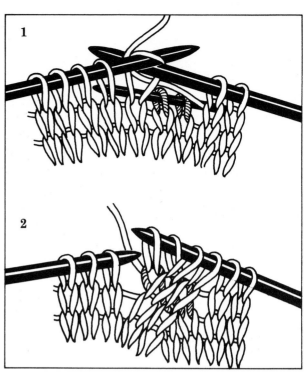

Diagrams 1 and 2 show a 'cable 4 back' pattern being worked: i.e. two stitches are slipped on to the cable needle and held at the back of the work while the next two stitches on the left-hand needle are worked, then the stitches on the cable needle are worked.

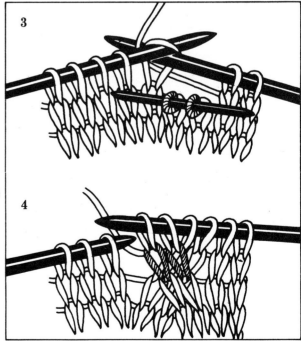

Diagrams 3 and 4 show a 'cable 4 front' pattern being worked: i.e. two stitches are slipped on to the cable needle and held at the front of the work while the next two stitches on the left-hand needle are worked, then the stitches on the cable needle are knitted.

Colour work

Any type of knitting using more than one colour of yarn, from a simple regular stripe pattern to a complex Fair Isle design, is termed colour knitting. Normally colour patterns are worked in stocking stitch, and although a particular design may use several different colours, as a general rule no more than two colours are ever in use at the same time. The easiest way to manipulate the two yarns is to hold one colour in your left hand, the other in your right. When yarn is not in use it is carried across the back of your work by one of the following methods:

Stranding. This method is suitable if each colour is used for only a few stitches. Take the yarn not in use across the back of work and pick it up when required. Cross the yarns at each colour change, and take care neither to pull the yarns too tightly, nor to leave them hanging too slackly.

Weaving. This method is suitable for patterns where each colour is used over a fairly large area. The yarn not in use should be woven under the colour in use.

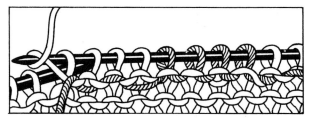

Sometimes, where large areas of colour are required, it is possible to combine these two methods to give a really professional finish to your work – i.e. strand over not more than three or four stitches then weave in the colour not in use when working the next stitch.

When joining vertical sections of colour (in a checked pattern, for instance) the colours must be twisted on the wrong side of the work where they meet, the colour to be used being twisted round the colour to be dropped.

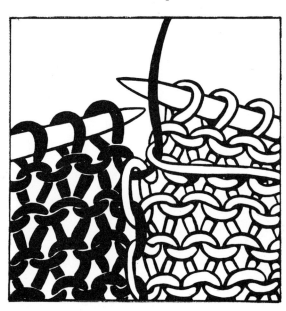

Working from a chart. Colour knitting patterns are often given in chart form. The chart is usually set out on tiny squares similar to graph paper, and each of these squares represents one knitted stitch: the squares reading across represent the number of stitches in the row (or one repeat of the pattern); the squares reading vertically represent the number of rows in the pattern. The odd-numbered (knitted) rows are worked from right to left, the even-numbered (purl) rows from left to right.

CIRCULAR KNITTING

Sometimes it is wished to knit a continuous seamless tube – for a sock or polo collar, for example. This can be done either by using a set of four needles with points at both ends or one long flexible circular needle with points at both ends. With four needles, it is best to cast all stitches on to one needle, and then divide them among three needles – the fourth is used for the knitting.

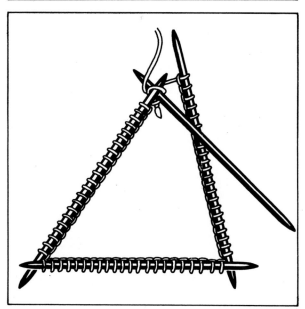

USEFUL TECHNIQUES

Joining yarn

This has to be done either when a ball of yarn is running out and a new one has to be joined in, or when you need to change to a different colour of yarn.

If you are in doubt about whether the remaining yarn from a ball will complete a row, measure it against the width of the work. If the thread is about four times as long as the width, you will probably have enough. If not, break the yarn about four inches from the work, and join the new ball with a loose knot close up to the work. These ends can be taken into the seam when you are sewing the garment up. If possible, never join in a new yarn in the middle of a row. In tubular knitting, however, there is no alternative. A knot should not be used as it will make an ugly lump in your work. Instead splice the yarn in the following way: unravel the yarn for a few inches at the end of the old ball and at the beginning of the new one and cut away a few strands of each. Twist the two ends together (by rubbing them between your palms). You should now have a join that is no thicker than the original basic yarn. Any loose ends should be carefully run into the back of the fabric when the garment is finished, using a darning needle.

Work the first and last stitches of each needle tightly to avoid a gap. When working in rounds in this way the right side will be facing on every round.

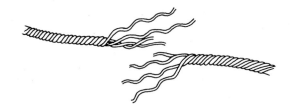

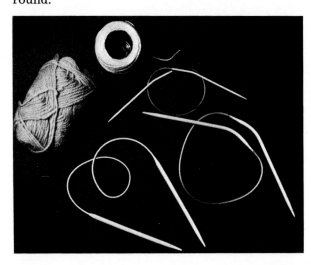

When working with a circular needle, it is important to choose the correct length of needle for the pattern you are working. Stitches should reach from point to point without stretching.

Pressing and blocking

Pressing is a very important part of the finishing process when you have made a knitted garment. Properly done, it can be slow work, but should not be skimped on this account. A good press can not only make sewing up much easier, it also makes a difference to the look of the finished garment. Pressing should be done to the individual knitted pieces, before sewing them together. Read any pressing instructions on your pattern, or on the label of the balls of yarn, since some yarns (especially synthetics) should not be pressed at all. If pressing is recommended, this is the way to do it: thread any loose ends on to a

Pretty smock dress with a lacy-patterned yoke (see page 44).

large-eyed darning needle and run them into the wrong side of the knitted fabric. Lay each piece right side down on a thick blanket, and carefully pull it out to the correct size and shape (check against measurements given in the pattern). Be sure to keep the fabric straight all the time. Do not stretch ribbed sections such as welts and cuffs.

Now pin the piece to the blanket, putting pins close together all round the edges of the garment, working from the outer edge inwards. This process is called blocking.

Lay a damp cloth across the piece and press lightly with a moderately hot iron. Too heavy a press can spoil a fancy pattern; far better to press lightly twice. A completely ribbed garment should be only very lightly pressed once. When pressing once, remove the damp cloth and allow the steam to evaporate. Remove pins. If you are using a yarn that requires no pressing, block the garment pieces as described above, then lay a damp cloth over the fabric and leave it until the fabric is quite dry. The pieces are now ready to be sewn together.

Dropped stitches

There is no need to panic if you drop a stitch. An experienced knitter can use a spare needle to repair a 'ladder', but you will probably find the job easier if you use a fine crochet hook. Slip the hook into the dropped stitch and take it up the knitting, looping through each row as if it had been knitted (remember to reverse the action if you have to pick up across knitted and purled rows).

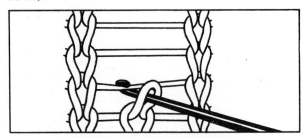

SEWING UP GARMENTS

If possible, when sewing pieces together, use the yarn which was used for knitting up the garment. If the yarn is very thick, it may be possible to strand it (i.e. to pull out a single strand of the yarn) and use this. If not, then a carefully matched yarn should be used.

There are two seams to choose from when sewing up edges: flatstitched seam and backstitched seam.

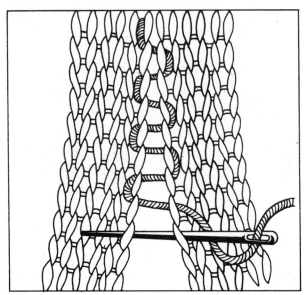

Flatstitched seam. This is used for putting on an edging, or joining ribbed sections. With right sides of work facing each other, place the two

pieces edge to edge. Using an overcasting stitch, draw the edges together, but do not draw the thread too tightly or it may snap (especially as this stitch is used for parts of garments such as welts and cuffs which have to take considerable strain).

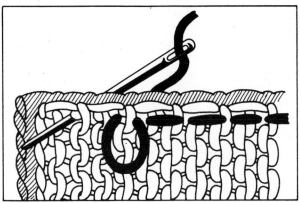

Backstitched seam. This should be used for all main seams. With right sides of work together, backstitch with small stitches as close to the edge as possible.

Seams should be pressed again lightly when they are finished. The normal order of seam stitching is as follows: shoulder seams, sew in sleeves, then sew sleeve and side seams as one long continuous seam. Edgings and pockets should be stitched in place last.

If you are working with an exceptionally heavy yarn, or making a very big garment (a car coat, for instance, or a man's thick sweater), it is sometimes wise to tape shoulder and armhole seams. This prevents sagging and stretching. When the seam is complete, enclose it with binding tape and stitch through. Heavy garments should never be hung up, but always stored flat.

Waistbands. The waistbands on skirts, trousers and shorts can be finished with rows of shirring elastic. On the wrong side of work, run the elastic through every knit stitch on every alternate row to depth of waistband required.

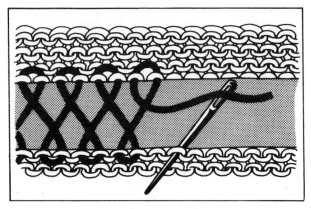

Alternatively a casing can be made on the wrong side of work and elastic, usually 1 in. wide, threaded through this casing. The casing can be formed by working herringbone stitches to depth of waistband, as shown in the diagram above.

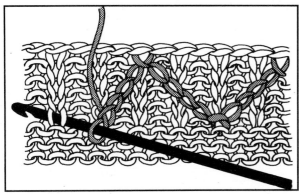

If preferred, a crochet casing can be made: insert hook into the top of one ribbed section on the knitted fabric, work one slip stitch, then work chain to depth of casing required, miss one ribbed section, and work one slip stitch into bottom of next rib. Work number of chain as before, then one slip stitch, miss one ribbed section, and one slip stitch into top of next rib. Continue in this way to form a zigzag casing of crocheted chains.

Grafting

This is a process by which two pieces of knitting can be joined without casting off and without making a seam. Place the two needles with the stitches on them together and then using a tapestry needle and length of yarn, 'sew' a new row of knitted stitches between the two groups. The diagram below shows how this is done, and how two stitches are slipped off each needle alternately. This diagram shows grafting being worked in a stocking stitch pattern, but grafting may be worked in any stitch pattern.

Picking up stitches

After the main parts of a garment have been worked and stitched together, stitches sometimes have to be picked up round a neckline or armhole edge and a collar, neckband or edging worked on these.

To pick up stitches, have the right side of work towards you and put the point of the needle through a whole loop at the edge or through both loops of a cast-off stitch. Put the yarn round the needle and draw a loop through, thus making a loop on the needle. Continue in this way across the edge until the required number of stitches are picked up. Work collar or edging on these stitches. Always make sure stitches are spaced

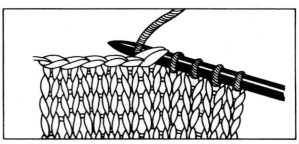

out evenly. If necessary measure across the edge first and use pins to mark the correct positions for picking up the stitches.

It is sometimes easier to use a fine needle or a crochet hook to pick up stitches and then to slip them on to the correct size needle for the edging.

Buttonholes

Small buttonholes, suitable for ball-type buttons and baby garments, can be made simply by taking the yarn over or round the needle and then knitting together the next two stitches (see lacy patterns, page 12). Larger buttonholes are usually made by casting off a number of stitches on one row and replacing them by casting on a similar number on the following row immediately over the cast-off stitches. The exact number of stitches cast off will depend on the size of button being used.

CROCHET STITCHES

A crochet edging worked round neck, sleeve and hem edges of a completed garment will give a decorative and neat finish to almost any knitted garment. A row of single crochet (slip stitch) worked all round the edge of a garment will be virtually invisible but will give a firm neat finish to edges which might otherwise droop or look uneven.

If a decorative border or edging is required, then further rows of crochet in any pattern are worked into the foundation row of single crochet.

Crochet and knitting can also be effectively combined in the same design – for instance, by using inset crochet motifs in a knitted fabric. It is as well therefore to be familiar with a few basic crochet stitches.

Chain

Make a slip loop as described on page 9, but use a crochet hook instead of knitting needle to draw yarn through loop. Pull yarn ends gently to tighten loop on hook. Now take the hook under the yarn and pull the yarn and hook through the loop on the hook. This is one chain. Continue making chain in this way until you have the number you want.

1

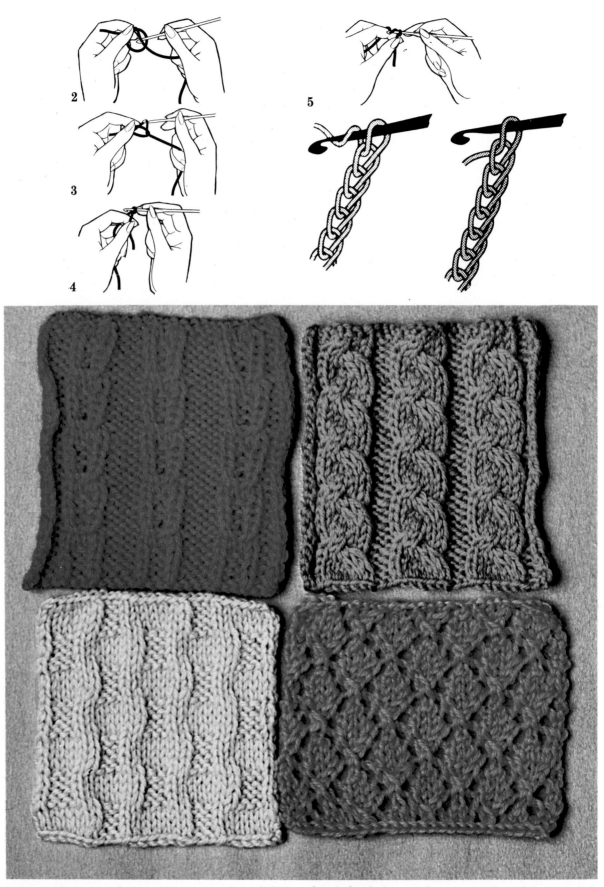

Four traditional stitch patterns: top line, left to right—lattice rib (see page 30) and alternating cables (see page 23); bottom line, left to right— *classic basketweave (see page 26) and fancy trellis (see page 27).*

Slip stitch or single crochet

Work from right to left. Insert the hook under top two loops of the first chain or stitch (or into a stitch along edge of knitting if working an edging), take yarn over hook and pull yarn through the stitch and through the loop on the hook. Insert hook into the next stitch and repeat. Continue in this way.

Three-piece pram set of dress, jacket and pram cover (see page 35).

Double crochet

Insert hook into chain or stitch (or into a stitch along edge of knitting), take yarn over hook and draw through the stitch. This makes two loops on the hook. Take yarn over the hook again and draw through the two loops on the hook. Continue in this way along row.

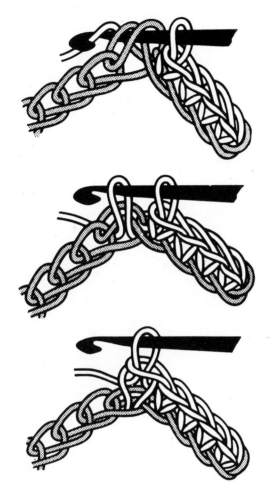

ABBREVIATIONS

The following are the abbreviations normally used in knitting patterns:

alt.	alternate
beg.	beginning
cont.	continue
dec.	decreas(e)(ed)(ing)
foll.	following
g.st.	garter stitch
in.	inch(es)
inc.	increas(e)(ed)(ing)
k.	knit
m.1	make one stitch (usually by taking yarn over or round the needle – see lacy patterns, page 12)
m.st.	moss stitch
p.	purl
patt.	pattern
p.s.s.o.	pass slipped stitch over
rem.	remain(ing)(der)
rep.	repeat
sl.	slip
st(s).	stitch(es)
st.st.	stocking stitch
t.b.l.	through back of loop
tog.	together
y.b.	yarn back
y.fwd. (or y.f.)	yarn forward
y.o.n.	yarn over needle
y.r.n.	yarn round needle

Crochet abbreviations

ch.	chain
d.c.	double crochet
sl.st.	slip stitch
tr.	treble

Pattern sizes

If a pattern gives a range of different sizes, then normally instructions are given in size order, with the different instructions relating to larger sizes in brackets. Where only one set of figures occurs this refers to all sizes.

Treble

Pass yarn over hook then insert hook into the next stitch. Yarn over hook and draw through stitch – three loops on hook. Yarn over hook again and draw through the first two loops on the hook. Yarn over hook once more and draw through remaining two loops on hook. Continue in this way along row.

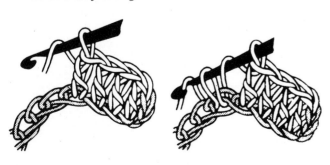

Chapter two
DICTIONARY OF STITCH PATTERNS

Alternating cables
also illustrated in colour on page 20

This is a flat version of cable rib, similar to a traditional cable but without the rope-like effect.

Cast on a multiple of 9 sts. plus 3 (e.g. 30).
1st row: * p.3, k.6; rep. from * to last 3 sts., p.3.
2nd and alt. rows: * k.3, p.6; rep. from * to last 3 sts., k.3.
3rd row: * p.3, C4 back (see Wheatear Cable pattern, page 33), k.2; rep. from * to last 3 sts., p.3.
5th row: * p.3, k.2, C4 front (see Wheatear Cable pattern, page 33); rep. from * to last 3 sts., p.3.
6th row: as 2nd row.
Rows 3-6 form pattern.

Blue, green and white Fair Isle stitch pattern
illustrated in colour on page 32

This is a decorative three-colour Fair Isle which can be used as an all-over pattern, or in bands of Fair Isle alternated with bands of plain background colour.

(chart: 27 sts. across, 17 rows. ROWS labelled at right. STS. numbered 27 26 25 24 23 22 21 20 19 18 17 16 15 14 13 12 11 10 9 8 7 6 5 4 3 2 1 along bottom)

☐ WHITE
☒ GREEN
◻ BLUE

1 SQUARE = 1 STITCH

The pattern is repeated over 24 sts., so cast on a multiple of 24 plus 1 st. to give extra st. at end of row.
Work 4 rows of st.st. in white (or number of rows wished to give band of plain colour), then cont. in st.st., work from the chart below to form the colour pattern. Each square on the chart represents one stitch, and each horizontal row of squares represents one row in the pattern.
The colour motif repeats across work from stitch 1–24 inclusive. Work the final st. in the row to correspond with the first st. in the repeat.
Work may continue in alternate bands of plain colour and Fair Isle pattern as wished.

Butterfly stitch

Small open motifs are set in stocking stitch to give lightness of texture; ideal for baby wear and summer tops.

Cast on a multiple of 10 sts. (e.g. 20).
1st row: * k.2 tog., y.fwd., k.1, y.fwd., sl.1, k.1, p.s.s.o., k.5; rep. from * to end.
2nd row: * p.7, sl.1 purlwise, p.2; rep. from * to end.
3rd and 4th rows: as first and 2nd rows.
5th row: k.
6th row: p.
7th row: * k.5, k.2 tog., y.fwd., k.1, y.fwd., sl.1, k.1, p.s.s.o.; rep. from * to end.
8th row: * p.2, sl.1 purlwise, p.7; rep. from * to end.
9th row: as 7th row.
10th row: as 8th row.
11th row: as 5th row.
12th row: as 6th row.
These 12 rows form pattern.

Above: coat and leggings with smocked effect yoke (see page 38). Opposite: bonnet and muff worked in a looped pattern (see page 58).

Classic basketweave stitch
also illustrated in colour on page 20

This gives a firm texture with an interesting surface; good for coats, jackets, skirts and trousers.

Cast on a multiple of 10 plus 7 (e.g. 27).
1st row: * p.7, k.3; rep. from * to last 7 sts., p.7.
2nd row: * k.7, p.3; rep. from * to last 7 sts., k.7.
3rd and 4th rows: as first and 2nd rows.
5th row: p.2, * k.7, p.3; rep. from * to last 5 sts., k.3, p.2.
6th row: k.2, * p.3, k.7; rep. from * to last 5 sts., p.3, k.2.
7th and 8th rows: as 5th and 6th rows.
These 8 rows form pattern.

Diagonal rib

A closely-textured stitch which is used most effectively with a heavy yarn where it gives a three-dimensional effect.

Cast on a multiple of 5 sts. (e.g. 30).
1st row (wrong side): * p. 2, (k. into front and back of next st.) 3 times; rep. from * to end.
2nd row: * (k.2 tog. t.b.l..) 3 times, k.2; rep. from * to end.
3rd row: * p.1, (k. into front and back of next st.) 3 times, p.1; rep. from * to end.
4th row: * k.1, (k.2 tog. t.b.l.) 3 times, k.1; rep. from * to end.
Continue in this way, moving the pattern one stitch along on every alt. row.

Diamond lattice

This is a firm yet open stitch which can be used with yarns of all weights, but it is probably at its best in fine yarn for a delicate design, such as an evening top or baby dress.

(Note. The extra stitch is an edging stitch but is needed in the 15th row; edging stitches at each end of the needle are recommended on all open-work designs as this makes sewing up easier.)
Cast on a multiple of 10 sts. plus 1 (e.g. 21).
1st row: k.1, * y.fwd., sl.1, k.1, p.s.s.o., k.5, k.2 tog., y.fwd., k.1; rep. from * to end.
2nd row and alt. rows: p.
3rd row: k.1, * k.1, y.fwd., sl.1, k.1, p.s.s.o., k.3, k.2 tog., y.fwd., k.2; rep. from * to end.
5th row: k.1, * k.2, y.fwd., sl.1, k.1, p.s.s.o., k.1, k.2 tog., y.fwd., k.3; rep. from * to end.
7th row: k.1, * k.3, y.fwd., sl.1, k.2 tog., p.s.s.o., y.fwd., k.4; rep. from * to end.
9th row: k.1, * k.2, k.2 tog., y.fwd., k.1, y.fwd., sl.1, k.1, p.s.s.o., k.3; rep. from * to end.
11th row: k.1, * k.1, k.2 tog., y.fwd., k.3, y.fwd., sl.1, k.1, p.s.s.o., k.2; rep. from * to end.
13th row: k.1, * k.2 tog., y.fwd., k.5, y.fwd., sl.1., k.1, p.s.s.o., k.1; rep. from * to end.
15th row: k.2 tog., * y.fwd., k.7, y.fwd., sl.1., k.2 tog., p.s.s.o.; rep. from * ending with sl.1, k.1, p.s.s.o.
16th row: p.
These 16 rows form pattern.

Embossed leaves

A shaped motif which stands away from the ground fabric. It is easier to work than it looks and is effective used in horizontal bands as well as in all-over patterns.

Cast on a multiple of 7 sts. plus 6 (e.g. 34).
1st row: p.6, * y.o.n., k.1, y.o.n., p.6; rep. from * to end.
2nd row: * k.6, p.3; rep. from * to last 6 sts., k.6.
3rd row: p.6, * k.1, y.fwd., k.1, y.fwd., k.1, p.6; rep. from * to end.
4th row: * k.6, p.5; rep. from * to last 6 sts., k.6.
5th row: p.6, * k.2, y.fwd., k.1, y.fwd., k.2, p.6; rep. from * to end.
6th row: * k.6, p.7; rep. from * to last 6 sts., k.6.
7th row: p.6, * k.3, y.fwd., k.1, y.fwd., k.3, p.6; rep. from * to end.
8th row: * k.6, p.9; rep. from * to last 6 sts., k.6.
9th row: p.6, * sl.1, k.1, p.s.s.o., k.5, k.2 tog., p.6; rep. from * to end.
10th row: * k.6, p.7; rep. from * to last 6 sts., k.6.
11th row: p.6, * sl.1, k.1, p.s.s.o., k.3, k.2 tog., p.6; rep. from * to end.
12th row: * k.6, p.5; rep. from * to last 6 sts., k.6.
13th row: p.6, * sl.1, k.1, p.s.s.o., k.1, k.2 tog., p.6; rep. from * to end.
14th row: * k.6, p.3; rep. from * to last 6 sts., k.6.
15th row: p.6, * sl.1, k.2 tog., p.s.s.o., p.6; rep. from * to end.
16th row: k.
17th row: p.
18th row: k.
19th and 20th rows: as 17th and 18th rows.
These 20 rows form pattern.

Fancy trellis
also illustrated in colour on page 20

A favourite open-work stitch for children's clothes or evening wear. It gives a regular, interesting surface with enough firmness even for outerwear if the yarn used is heavyweight.

Cast on a multiple of 7 sts. (e.g. 28).
(Note. An edge st. at each end is recommended.)
1st row: * k.2, k.2 tog., y.fwd., k.3; rep. from * to end.
2nd row: * p.1, p.2 tog. t.b.l., y.r.n., p.1, y.r.n., p.2 tog., p.1; rep. from * to end.
3rd row: * k.2 tog., y.fwd., k.3, y.fwd., sl.1, k.1, p.s.s.o.; rep. from * to end.
4th row: p.
5th row: * y.r.n., sl.1, k.1, p.s.s.o., k.5; rep. from * to end.
6th row: * y.r.n., p.2 tog., p.2, p.2 tog. t.b.l., y.r.n., p.1; rep. from * to end.
7th row: * k.2, y.fwd., sl.1, k.1, p.s.s.o., k.2 tog., y.fwd., k.1; rep. from * to end.
8th row: p.
These 8 rows form pattern.

Fleur de lis

This is one of the classic two-colour patterns which can be used for evening tops or husky sweaters, depending on the weight and type of yarn used.

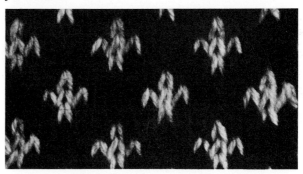

(Note. The pattern has to be reversed on completion to give the fleur de lis shape.)
Use two colours of yarn, one dark, one light (D., dark; L., light).
Cast on a multiple of 6 sts. plus 3 (e.g. 21).
1st row: k.3 D., * 1 L., 5 D.; rep. from * to end.
2nd row: p.1 L., * 3 D., 3 L.; rep. from * to last 2 sts., p.2 D.
3rd row: as first row.
4th row: p.2 D., * 1 L., 5 D.; rep. from * to last st., p.1 L.
5th row: k.2 L., * 3 D., 3 L.; rep. from * to last st., k.1 D.
6th row: as 4th row.
These 6 rows form pattern.

Houndstooth

Another favourite two-colour design which is usually associated with sporty designs – try it for the fronts of a cardigan or on a suit. Almost any colour combination looks good.

Use two colours of yarn, one dark, one light (D., dark, L., light).
Cast on a multiple of 4 sts. (e.g. 32).
1st row: k.2 L., * 1 D., 3 L.; rep. from * to last 2 sts., k.1 D., 1 L.
2nd row: p., * 1 L., 3 D.; rep. from * to end.
3rd row: k., * 1 L., 3 D.; rep. from * to end.
4th row: p.2 L., * 1 D., 3 L.; rep. from * to last 2 sts., 1 D., 1 L.
These 4 rows form pattern.

Classic sweater with centre lacy panel (see page 63).

28

Toddlers' twosome: brown pullover and trousers
(see page 50) and blue striped trouser suit (see page 51).

Lacy chevron

This stitch gives a V-shaped patterning of open-work set between open ribs. It is ideal for a light jumper or child's dress.

Cast on a multiple of 12 sts. (e.g. 48).
1st row: * k.3, y.fwd., sl.1, k.1, p.s.s.o., k.2, k.2 tog., y.fwd., k.1, y.fwd., sl.1, k.1, p.s.s.o.; rep. from * to end.
2nd and alt. rows: p.
3rd row: * k.1, k.2 tog., y.fwd., k.1, y.fwd., sl.1, k.1, p.s.s.o., k.1, k.2 tog., y.fwd., k.1, y.fwd., sl.1, k.1, p.s.s.o.; rep. from * to end.
5th row: * k.2 tog., y.fwd., k.3, y.fwd., sl.1, k.1, p.s.s.o., k.2 tog., y.fwd., k.1, y.fwd., sl.1, k.1, p.s.s.o.; rep. from * to end.
6th row: p.
These 6 rows form pattern.

Lacy rib

A firm yet open stitch which can be used by itself or as vertical bars inset between ribs of plain knitting or a different open-work stitch.

Cast on a multiple of 4 sts. (e.g. 20).
1st row: * k.2, y.fwd., sl.1, k.1, p.s.s.o; rep. from * to end.
2nd row: * p.2, y.r.n., p.2 tog.; rep. from * to end.
These 2 rows form pattern.

Lattice rib
also illustrated in colour on page 20

A raised chain on a reversed stocking stitch ground, effective in fine yarns or heavy ones.

Cast on a multiple of 8 sts. plus 4 (e.g. 28).
1st row: * p.4, cross 2 L. (i.e. with right-hand needle behind first st., k. the 2nd st. through the front loop then k. the first st. in usual way and take both off needle together), cross 2 R. (i.e. passing in front of first st. k. 2nd st. through front loop then k. first st. in usual way and take both off needle together); rep. from * to last 4 sts., p.4.
2nd row: * k.4, p.4; rep. from * to last 4 sts., k.4.
3rd row: * p.4, k.1, p.2, k.1; rep. from * to last 4 sts., p.4.
4th row: * k.4, p.1, k.2, p.1; rep. from * to last 4 sts., k.4.
5th and 6th rows: as 3rd and 4th rows.
These 6 rows form pattern.

Linked lozenges
also illustrated in colour on page 32

A two-colour pattern which has an all-over squared shape. In pastels it looks pretty for baby wear, but in solid colours and thick wool it will make a handsome sports sweater. Use two colours of yarn, one dark, one light (D., dark, L., light).

Cast on a multiple of 8 sts. plus 1 (e.g. 33).
1st row: k., * 2 D., 5 L., 1 D.; rep. from * to last st., k.1 D.
2nd row: p., * 1 L., 1 D., (2 L., 1 D.) twice; rep. from * to last st., p.1 L. **3rd row:** as first row.
4th row: p., * 2 L., 1 D., 3 L., 1 D., 1 L.; rep. from * to last st., p.1 L.
5th row: k., * 3 L., 3 D., 2 L.; rep. from * to last st., k.1 L.
6th row: p., * 1 D., 2 L., 1 D., 1 L., 1 D., 2 L.; rep. from * to last st., p.1 D.
7th row: as 5th row.
8th row: p., * 2 L., 1 D., 3 L., 1 D., 1 L.; rep. from * to last st., p. 1 L.
These 8 rows form pattern.

Medallion cables

This gives an attractive alternative to the conventional cable. The rib is kept open after each set of cabling; very effective in extremely thick yarns. A cable needle will be required.

Cast on a multiple of 11 sts. plus 3 (e.g. 36).
1st row: * p.3, k.8; rep. from * to last 3 sts., p.3.
2nd row: * k.3, p.8; rep. from * to last 3 sts., k.3.
3rd and 4th rows: as first and 2nd rows.
5th row: * p.3, C4 back (i.e. slip 2 sts. on cable needle then put to back of work, k.2, then k. sts. from cable needle), C4 front (i.e. slip 2 sts. on cable needle then put to front of work, k.2 then k. sts. from cable needle); rep. from * to last 3 sts., p.3.
6th row: as 2nd row.
These 6 rows form pattern.

Mock cable

A twisted rib which gives the effect of a narrow cabling without having to use a cable needle.

Cast on a multiple of 5 sts. plus 3 (e.g. 23).
1st row: * p.3, k.2; rep. from * to last 3 sts., p.3.
2nd row: * k.3, p.2; rep. from * to last 3 sts., k.3.
3rd and 4th rows: as first and 2nd rows.
5th row: * p.3, cross 2R (see Lattice Rib pattern, opposite); rep. from * to last 3 sts., p.3.
6th row: as 2nd row.
These 6 rows form pattern.

Open arches

A lacy stitch with pointed shapes. It is fairly firm when worked in a double knitting yarn.

Cast on a multiple of 4 sts. plus 1 (e.g. 25).
1st row: k.1, * y.fwd., k.3, y.fwd., k.1; rep. from * to end.
2nd and alt. rows: p.
3rd row: k.1, * k.1, sl.1, k.2 tog., p.s.s.o., k.2; rep. from * to end.
4th row: p.
These 4 rows form pattern.

Pink and white Fair Isle stitch pattern
illustrated in colour on page 32

This is an open diamond-shape motif which can be used in a decorative band above ribbing at welt and cuffs on a sweater or cardigan, or to form an all-over pattern, if preferred.

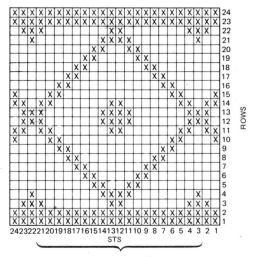

X PINK ☐ WHITE   1 SQUARE = 1 STITCH

The pattern is repeated over 19 sts., so cast on a multiple of 19 plus 5 sts. to give 2 extra sts. at beg. of row, 3 extra sts. at end of row.
Work 6 rows of st.st. in white, then cont. in st.st., work from the chart above to form colour pattern. Each square on the chart represents one stitch, and each horizontal row of squares represent one row in the pattern. The colour motif is repeated from stitch 3–21 inclusive across work. Work the final 3 sts. in the row to correspond with the 3 sts. at beg. of row (i.e. sts. 3, 2 and 1 on chart).
Work may continue in alternate bands of plain colour and Fair Isle pattern as wished.

Raised diamonds

A firm stitch with a raised surface which is interesting without being obtrusive, and is a pleasant variant on any garment where stocking stitch is appropriate.

Cast on a multiple of 8 sts. (e.g. 32).
1st row: * p.1, k.7; rep. from * to end.
2nd row: * k.1, p.5, k.1, p.1; rep. from * to end.
3rd row: * k.2, p.1, k.3, p.1, k.1; rep. from * to end.
4th row: * p.2, k.1, p.1, k.1, p.3; rep. from * to end.
5th row: * k.4, p.1, k.3; rep. from * to end.
6th, 7th and 8th rows: as 4th, 3rd and 2nd rows.
These 8 rows form pattern.

Red, white and blue Fair Isle stitch pattern

This is a geometric pattern of squares which is equally effective repeated across work, or used as a single motif set in a plain background.

The pattern is repeated over 26 sts., so cast on a multiple of 26 plus 1 st. to give extra st. at end of row.

Work 2 rows of st.st. in white (or number of rows wished to give band of plain colour), then cont. in st.st., work from the chart, right, to form the colour pattern. Each square on the chart represents one stitch and each horizontal row of squares represents one row in the pattern. The colour motif repeats across work from stitch 1–26 inclusive. Work the final st. in the row to correspond with the first st. in the repeat. Work may continue in alternate bands of plain colour and Fair Isle pattern as wished.

26	25	24	23	22	21	20	19	18	17	16	15	14	13	12	11	10	9	8	7	6	5	4	3	2	1	ROW
X	X		X		X			X	X	X	X	X			X		X			X	X					15
X			X		X	X			X	X		X	X			X		X			X	X				14
		X		X				X		X	X						X		X				X			13
	X		X				X		X	X								X		X				X		12
X		X					X	X	X	X	X								X		X				X	11
	O				O	O	O	O	O						O	O	O	O	O				O		O	10
O				O	O		O	O					O		O	O		O	O					O		9
				O	O			O		O	O	O		O		O			O		O	O			O	8
O				O	O		O	O			O		O	O		O	O							O		7
	O				O	O	O	O	O						O	O	O	O	O				O		O	6
X		X					X	X	X	X	X								X		X				X	5
	X		X				X		X	X								X		X				X		4
		X		X				X		X	X						X		X				X			3
X			X		X	X			X	X		X	X			X		X			X	X				2
X	X		X		X			X	X	X	X	X			X		X			X	X					1

STS.

☐ WHITE
☒ RED
⊡ BLUE   1 SQUARE = 1 STITCH

32

Rib and eyelet

A fancy rib with regularly-spaced open-work, suitable for men's or women's garments, as it has a tailored look.

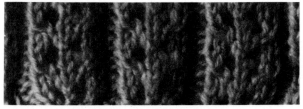

Cast on a multiple of 7 sts. plus 6 (e.g. 27).
1st row: k.2, * p.2, k.2 tog., y.fwd., k.1, y.fwd., k.2 tog. t.b.l.; rep. from * to last 4 sts., p.2, k.2.
2nd row: p.2, * k.2, p.5; rep. from * to last 4 sts., k.2, p.2.
3rd row: k.2, * p.2, k.5; rep. from * to last 4 sts., p.2, k.2.
4th row: as 2nd row.
These 4 rows form the pattern.

Two-tone tweed

A textured stitch which employs a second colour discreetly to give a tweedy effect; excellent for sporty, tailored garments.

Cast on a multiple of 2 sts. plus 1 (e.g. 21).
1st row: using dark shade, k. **2nd row:** as first row.
3rd row: using light shade, * k.1, sl.1 purlwise; rep. from * to last st., k.1.
4th row: using light shade, * k.1, y.fwd., sl.1 purlwise, y.b.; rep. from * to last st., k.1.
5th and 6th rows: as first and 2nd rows.
7th row: using light shade, * sl.1 purlwise, k.1; rep. from * to last st., sl.1.
8th row: using light shade, * sl.1 purlwise, y.b., k.1, y.fwd.; rep. from * to last st., sl.1.
These 8 rows form pattern.

Vandyke stitch

A simple but effective open stitch which gives a scalloped edge (shown here with a border of garter st.). This stitch is suitable for skirts, as the width of the panels can be adjusted to give graduated shaping.

Cast on a multiple of 12 sts. plus 1 (e.g. 25).
1st row: * k.1, y.fwd., k.4, sl.1, k.2 tog., p.s.s.o., k.4, y.fwd.; rep. from * to last st., k.1.
2nd row: p.
These 2 rows form pattern.

Wheatear cable

A narrow fanning band which is worked on the cable principle and which 'grows' in a repeating design. A cable needle will be required.

Cast on a multiple of 15 sts. (e.g. 45).
1st row: * p.1, k.13, p.1; rep. from * to end.
2nd row: * k.1, p.13, k.1; rep. from * to end.
3rd row: * p.1, C6 back (i.e. slip 3 sts. on cable needle, put to back of work, k.3, then k. sts. from cable needle), k.1, C6 front (i.e. slip 3 sts. on cable needle, put to front of work, k.3, then k. sts. from cable needle), p.1; rep. from * to end.
4th row: as 2nd row.
These 4 rows form pattern.

Wide plait

An intricate-looking piece of multiple cabling which would be an excellent centre band on a plain heavy sweater or down the sides of trousers.

Cast on a multiple of 23 sts. plus 5 (e.g. 51).
1st row: * p.5, k.18; rep. from * to last 5 sts., p.5.
2nd and alt. rows: * k.5, p.18; rep. from * to last 5 sts., k.5.
3rd row: * p.5, (C6 back—see Wheatear Cable pattern, above) 3 times; rep. from * to last 5 sts., p.5.
5th row: as first row.
7th row: * p.5, k.3, (C6 front—see Wheatear Cable pattern, above) twice, k.3; rep. from * to last 5 sts., p.5.
8th row: as 2nd row.
These 8 rows form pattern.

Chapter three
WITH BABY IN MIND

Scalloped-edge shawl (see opposite) and bobble-patterned dress (see page 40).

Baby's shawl

illustrated opposite

MATERIALS
16 oz. Twilleys Bubbly, and 3 balls (2 oz. each) Twilleys Stalite. One pair No. 6 knitting needles (USA size 8).

MEASUREMENTS
40 in. square.

TENSION
4 sts. and 6 rows to 1 in. over Bubbly.

ABBREVIATIONS
See page 22; inc. 1, increase 1 st. by p. into front then k. into back of next st.

CENTRE
Using Bubbly yarn double cast on 144 sts.
(Note. Use yarn double throughout.)
1st and 2nd rows: * k.2, p.2; rep. from * to end.
3rd and 4th rows: * p.2, k.2; rep. from * to end.
These 4 rows form patt. Continue in patt. until work measures 36 in., ending with a first or 3rd patt. row. Cast off loosely in patt.

BORDER (make 4 pieces alike)
Using Stalite yarn double cast on 140 sts.
(Note. Use yarn double throughout.)
1st row (right side): k.3, * p.6, k.2; rep. from * to last st., k.1.
2nd row: k.1, p.2, * k.6, p.2; rep. from * to last st., k.1.
3rd row: k.2, y.fwd., * sl.1, k.1, p.s.s.o., p.4, k.2 tog., y.fwd.; rep. from * to last 2 sts., k.2.
4th row: k.1, p.1, inc. 1 (see Abbreviations), * p.1, k.4, p.1, inc. 1; rep. from * to last 2 sts., p.1, k.1.
5th row: k.2, y.fwd., k.2, y.fwd., * sl.1, k.1, p.s.s.o., p.2, k.2 tog., y.fwd., k.2, y.fwd.; rep. from * to last 2 sts., k.2.
6th row: k.1, p.6, * k.2, p.6; rep. from * to last st., k.1.
7th row: k.2, y.fwd., k.2 tog., * y.fwd., sl.1, k.1, p.s.s.o., y.fwd., sl.1, k.1, p.s.s.o., k.2 tog., y.fwd., k.2 tog.; rep. from * to last 4 sts., y.fwd., sl.1, k.1, p.s.s.o., y.fwd., k.2.
8th row: p.2 tog., p.2, * inc. 1, p.6; rep. from * to last 5 sts., inc. 1, p.2, p.2 tog: 144 sts.
**9th row: sl.1, k.1, p.s.s.o., y.fwd., sl.1, k.1, p.s.s.o., k.2 tog., y.fwd., k.2 tog.; turn. Work on these sts. only.
10th row: p.6.
11th row: sl.1, k.1, p.s.s.o., k.1, y.fwd., k.1, k.2 tog.
12th row: p.2, inc. 1, p.2.
13th row: sl.1, k.1, p.s.s.o., (k.2 tog.) twice.
14th row: sl.1, p.2 tog., p.s.s.o., and fasten off.
Rejoin yarn to remaining sts. **
Work from ** to ** 17 times more: all sts. worked off.

TO COMPLETE
Press work and sew in ends. Sew border to centre, joining borders at corners. Press seams.

Pram set

illustrated in colour on page 21

MATERIALS
For pram cover: 12 balls (¾ oz. each) Hayfield Courtier Super Crimp Bri-Nylon 3-ply. One pair No. 3 knitting needles (USA size 10½). **For dress and jacket:** 7 balls (¾ oz. each) Hayfield Courtier Super Crimp Bri-Nylon 3-ply. One pair each Nos. 12, 11 and 10 knitting needles (USA sizes 1, 2 and 3). Three buttons. 2 yards baby ribbon.

MEASUREMENTS
Pram cover: approx. 24 in. by 36 in.
Dress and jacket: to fit chest size 18 (20, 22) in.; length of dress 12 (13½, 15) in. (adjustable); length of dress sleeve seam 1 in.; length of jacket 8 (9½, 11) in. (adjustable); length of jacket sleeve seam 5 (6½, 8) in. (adjustable).

TENSION
5 sts. to 1 in. with No. 3 needles and yarn double over patt.; 7½ sts. and 11 rows to 1 in. with No. 11 needles and yarn single over st.st.

ABBREVIATIONS
See page 22.

PRAM COVER
With No. 3 needles and 2 strands yarn cast on 113 sts. and, using 2 strands tog. throughout, k. 8 rows. Now beg. patt.
1st row: k.
2nd row: p.
3rd row: k.1, * y.o.n., k.2, k.3 tog., k.2, y.o.n., k.1; rep. from * to end.
4th row: p.1, * p.1, y.r.n., p.1, p.3 tog., p.1, y.r.n., p.2; rep. from * to end.
5th row: k.1, * k.2, y.o.n., k.3 tog., y.o.n., k.3; rep. from * to end.
6th row: p.
7th, 8th, 9th and 10th rows: k.
These 10 rows form patt. Cont. in patt. until work measures about 35 in. from cast-on edge, ending with a 10th patt. row. K. 3 rows. Cast off.

Edging
With right side facing, pick up along one side edge 3 sts. from each garter st. part and 7 sts. from each rep. of the 10-row patt. K. 7 rows. Cast off.
Rep. along other side edge.
Cast off.

DRESS
FRONT
With No. 10 needles and 1 strand yarn, cast on 81 (89, 97) sts. and k. 8 rows.
Cont. in 10-row patt. as given for Pram Cover until work measures approx. 7 (7½, 8) in. (or slightly more) from cast-on edge, ending with a 5th patt. row. Change to No. 10 needles.
Next row: p.1, * p.2 tog., p.6; rep. from * to end: 71 (78, 85) sts.
K. 4 rows. Change to No. 11 needles.
Beg. with a k. row, cont. straight in st.st. until work measures 8½ (9½, 10½) in. from cast-on edge, ending with a p. row (if necessary adjust length here).

Shape Armholes
Cont. in st.st., cast off 3 sts. at beg. of next 2 rows, then dec. 1 st. at each end of next 4 (5, 6) rows and of foll. 2 alt. rows.
Work straight in st.st. on rem. 53 (58, 63) sts. until armholes measure 2½ (3, 3½) in., ending with a p. row.

Shape Front Neck
Next row: k.20 (21, 22); turn.
Work another 5 rows on these sts. only, dec. 1 st. at neck edge on next and every foll. alt. row: 17 (18, 19) sts.

Shape Shoulder
Next row: cast off 5, k. to end.
Next row: p.2 tog., p. to end.

Rep. last 2 rows once. Cast off rem. 5 (6, 7) sts. Return to sts. still on needle, slip first 13 (16, 19) sts. on to a st. holder, then complete second side of neck to match first, reversing shapings.

BACK
Work as Front to beg. of armholes.

Shape Armholes and Buttonbands
1st row: cast off 3, k. to end.
2nd row: cast off 3, p.29 (32, 36), cast on 5 (6, 5); turn: 35 (39, 42) sts.
Keeping the 5 (6, 5) sts. at centre edge in garter st., cont. in st.st. dec. 1 st. at side edge on next 4 (5, 6) rows and on foll. 2 alt. rows: 29 (32, 34) sts. Work straight in st.st. with garter st. border until Back matches Front to beg. of shoulder shaping, ending at side edge.

Shape Shoulder
Cast off 5 sts. at beg. of next row and next alt. row, then 5 (6, 7) sts. at beg. of next alt. row.
Leave rem. 14 (16, 17) sts. on st. holder.
Using pins, mark position of 2 buttons on the garter st. buttonband allowing for a 3rd button on 2nd row of neckband.
With wrong side facing rejoin yarn to 35 (39, 42) sts. still on needle.
1st row: k.5 (6, 5), p. to end.
Cont. and complete this side of Back to match first, reversing shapings and working buttonholes to correspond with button marks as follows, beg. first buttonhole rows at side edge.
1st buttonhole row: k. to last 4 sts., cast off 2, k.1.
2nd buttonhole row: k.2, cast on 2, patt. to end.

SLEEVES (make 2 alike)
With No. 12 needles cast on 41 (49, 57) sts. and k. 4 rows.
Change to No. 11 needles and work the 10-row patt. once. (For a longer Sleeve, add extra st.st. rows here.)

Shape Top
Cont. in st.st., cast off 3 sts. at beg. of next 2 rows, 1 st. at beg. of next 6 rows and 2 sts. at beg. of foll. 8 (10, 12) rows. ** Cast off.

TO COMPLETE
Sew shoulder seams.
Neckband
With right side facing and No. 12 needles, beg. at centre edge of left side of Back and pick up all sts. from holders round neck, and also 10 sts. from one side of front neck and 10 (11, 11) sts. from other side: 61 (69, 74) sts.
1st row: k.5 (6, 5), p. to last 5 (6, 5) sts., k. to end.
2nd row: k.7 (7, 5), * y.o.n., k.2, k.3 tog., k.2, y.o.n., k.1; rep. from * to last 6 (6, 5) sts., k.2 (2, 1), cast off 2, k.1.
Casting on 2 sts. over those cast off on previous row, and always keeping the 5 (6, 5) sts. at each end of needle in garter st., work the 4th to 9th rows of the 10-row patt. Cast off loosely.

To Make Up
Sew side seams. Set in Sleeves and sew sleeve seams. Catch in place lower edge of button band. Press seams. Sew on buttons to correspond with buttonholes.

JACKET
MAIN PIECE
With No. 10 needles cast on 181 (197, 213) sts. and k. 6 rows.
Next 2 rows: k.6 and leave these sts. on safety pin,

k. to end: 169 (185, 201) sts.
Cont. in the 10-row patt. as given for Pram Cover until work measures approx. 3½ (4½, 5½) in. from cast-on edge, ending with a 5th patt. row.
Next row: p.1, * p.2, p.2 tog., k.4; rep. from * to end: 148 (162, 176) sts.
K. 2 rows.
Next (eyelet) row: k.3 (2, 5), * y.o.n., k.2 tog., k.2: rep. from * to last 1 (0, 3) sts., k. to end.
K. 1 row. Change to No. 11 needles.
Beg. with a k. row, work straight in st.st. until work measures 4 (5, 6) in. from cast-on edge, ending with a p. row (if necessary adjust length here).

Right Front
1st row (armhole shaping): k.36 (39, 43); turn.
2nd row: cast off 3, p. to end.
Dec. 1 st. at armhole edge on next 4 (5, 6) rows and on foll. 2 alt. rows. Work straight on rem. 27 (29, 32) sts. until armhole measures 3 (3½, 4) in. ending at centre edge.

Shape Front Neck
Next row: k.7 (8, 10) and leave these sts. on safety pin, k.20 (21, 22).
Work another 6 rows in st.st., dec. 1 st. at neck edge on every p. row: 17 (18, 19) sts.

Shape Shoulder
Next row: cast off 5, p. to last 2 sts., p.2 tog.
Next row: k.
Rep. last 2 rows once. Cast off rem. 5 (6, 7) sts.

Back
Rejoin yarn to sts. still on needle at back armhole edge.
1st row: cast off 3, k.72 (80, 86); turn: 73 (81, 87) sts.
2nd row: cast off 3, p. to end.
Complete back armhole shaping by dec. 1 st. at each end of next 4 (5, 6) rows and of foll. 2 alt. rows. Work straight on rem. 58 (64, 68) sts. until Back matches Front to beg. of shoulder shaping. Cast off 5 sts. at beg. of next 4 rows and 5 (6, 7) sts. at beg. of foll. 2 rows. Leave rem. 28 (32, 34) sts. on st. holder.

Left Front
Rejoin yarn to armhole edge of rem. 36 (39, 43) sts. then complete to match Right Front, reversing shapings.

Buttonbands

With No. 11 needles, pick up one set of 6 sts. from safety pin near lower edge and cont. in garter st. until band will fit comfortably as far as beg. of front neck. Put the 6 sts. with the 7 (8, 10) sts. on safety pin at neck and sew band in position.

Work on other set of 6 sts. in same way.

Neckband

Sew shoulder seams. With right side facing and No. 12 needles, beg. at centre edge of right front and pick up sts. from safety pin, pick up 10 sts. round front neck, pick up sts. from back st. holder, pick up 10 sts. round front neck, then sts. from safety pin: 74 (80, 86) sts. K. 1 row.

Next (eyelet) row: k.2, * y.o.n., k.2 tog., k.1; rep. from * to end.

K. 3 rows. Cast off.

SLEEVES (make 2 alike)

With No. 12 needles cast on 41 (49, 57) sts. and k. 4 rows. Change to No. 10 needles and work first 6 rows of the 10-row patt.

Next (ridge) row: p.

Change to No. 11 needles and, beg. with a p. row, cont. in st.st., inc. 1 st. at each end of 11th row from ridge row and of every foll. 8th row until there are 49 (57, 63) sts.

Work straight until sleeve measures 5 (6½, 8) in. from ridge row, ending with a p. row (if necessary, adjust length here).

Shape Top

Work as top of Dress Sleeve to **. Cast off 3 sts. at beg. of next 2 rows. Cast off.

TO COMPLETE

Sew sleeve seams and set in sleeves. Press on wrong side. Thread ribbon through eyelet holes at neckband and waist, and tie ends in bows.

Lace-trimmed matinée coat

also illustrated on page 38

MATERIALS

2 (3) oz. Emu Baby Nylon 3-ply in white. One pair each Nos. 9 and 7 knitting needles (USA sizes 5 and 7). 2½ yards lace trimming ½ in. wide in a contrasting colour. Small quantity yarn to match lace. Embroidery thread to match lace. Two small buttons.

MEASUREMENTS

To fit chest size 18 (20) in.; length 6 (7) in.; length of sleeve seam 4 (5) in.

TENSION

6½ sts. to 1 in. over garter st. with No. 7 needles.

ABBREVIATIONS

See page 22.

BACK

With No. 7 needles cast on 74 (80) sts. and work in garter st. (every row k.). Work straight for 4 (5) in.

Shape Armholes

Cast off 3 sts. at beg. of next 2 rows, then dec. 1 st. at each end of next row and every alt. row until 60 (66) sts. remain.

Shape Shoulders

Cast off 7 (8) sts. at beg. of next 4 rows. Cast off.

LEFT FRONT

With No. 7 needles cast on 37 (40) sts. and k. 8 rows. Work in patt. of squares.

1st row: k.5 (8), * k.2 tog., y.f.; rep. from * 12 times, k.6.

2nd and alt. rows: k.

3rd row: k.5 (8), * k.2 tog., y.f., k.4; rep. from * 3 times, k.2 tog., y.f., k.6.

5th row: as 3rd row.

7th row: as 3rd row.

9th row: as first row.

11th row: k.11 (14), * k.2 tog., y.f., k.4; rep. from * twice, k.2 tog., y.f., k.6.

13th and 15th rows: as 11th row.

17th row: k.11 (14), * k.2 tog., y.f.; rep. from * 9 times, k.6.

19th row: k.17 (20), * k.2 tog., y.f., k.4; rep. from * once, k.2 tog., y.f., k.6.

21st and 23rd rows: as 19th row.

25th row: k.17 (20), * k.2 tog., y.f.; rep. from * 6 times, k.6.

27th row: k.23 (26), k.2 tog., y.f., k.4, k.2 tog., y.f., k.6.

29th and 31st rows: as 27th row.

33rd row: k.23 (26), * k.2 tog., y.f.; rep. from * 3 times, k.6.

34th row: k.

These 34 rows complete patt. of squares. Cont. in garter st.

Cont. straight until work measures same as Back to armhole, ending at side edge.

Shape Armhole

Cast off 3 sts. at beg. of next row, then dec. 1 st. at armhole edge on next 4 alt. rows. Cont. straight until armhole measures 2¼ (2¾) in., ending at front edge.

Shape Neck

Cast off 12 (13) sts. at beg. of next row, then dec. 1 st. at neck edge on next 4 rows. Work straight until Front measures same as Back to shoulder, ending at armhole edge.

Shape Shoulder

Cast off 7 (8) sts. at beg. of next and next alt. row.

RIGHT FRONT

With No. 7 needles cast on 37 (40) sts. and k. 8 rows.

1st row: k. 6, * y.f., k.2 tog.; rep. from * 12 times, k.5 (8).

2nd and alt. rows: k.

3rd row: k.6, y.f., k.2 tog., * k.4, y.f., k.2 tog.; rep. from * 3 times, k.5 (8).

Cont. in patt. to match Left Front, reversing patt. and shapings.

SLEEVES (make 2 alike)

With No. 7 needles cast on 36 (38) sts. and work in garter st., inc. 1 st. at each end of 9th row and every foll. 8th row until there are 46 (50) sts. Cont. straight until Sleeve measures 4 (5) in.

Shape Top

Cast off 3 sts. at beg. of next 2 rows, then dec. 1 st. at beg. of every row until 32 sts. remain. Cast off.

TO COMPLETE
Neck Border

Join shoulders. With right side facing and No. 9 needles, pick up and k.21 (22) sts. round neck of Right Front, 32 (34) sts. round back neck and 21 (22) sts. round neck of Left Front.

K. 1 row.

Next (buttonhole) row: k.2, y.f., k.2 tog., k. to last 4 sts., k.2 tog., y.f., k.2.

K. 2 rows. Cast off.

Press very lightly with a warm iron over dry cloth.

Sew in sleeves, then sew up sleeve and side seams. Cut two 9-in. lengths of lace trimming. Join each into a circle. Gather and st. one to each sleeve edge. Join ends of rest of lace, gather and st. round coat edge — lower edge, front edges and round neck.

With 3 strands of embroidery thread work stem st. over gathering and sewing sts.

With contrasting yarn work 4 lazy daisy flowers off upper outer corners of squares on each front. Link buttons together and st. one of them to a buttonhole.

Coat and leggings

illustrated in colour on page 24

MATERIALS

9 (11, 12) balls (1 oz. each) Peter Pan Baby Quick Courtelle Double Knitting. One pair each Nos. 9 and 10 knitting needles (USA sizes 5 and 3). One crochet hook International Standard Size 3.50. One cable needle. Four small buttons.

MEASUREMENTS

To fit chest size 18 (20, 22) in.; length of coat 10½ (11, 11½) in.; length of coat sleeve seam 5 (5½, 6) in.; leggings front seam 8½ (9, 9) in.

TENSION

6 sts. to 1 in. with No. 9 needles.

ABBREVIATIONS

See page 22; cr. L. st., cross long st. (slip next 2 sts. on to cable needle and leave at back of work, k. tog. long st. and first st. on cable needle, k. into front and back of 2nd st. on cable needle, pick up left-hand side of long st. purlwise across front of work, k. tog. t.b.l. this left-hand side of long st. and next st.).

COAT BACK

With No. 9 needles cast on 81 (85, 93) sts.
Work 6 rows in garter st. (every row k.).
7th row: sl.1, k.2 (4, 3), y.r.n. twice, * k.5, y.r.n. twice; rep. from * to last 3 (5, 4) sts., k.3 (5, 4).

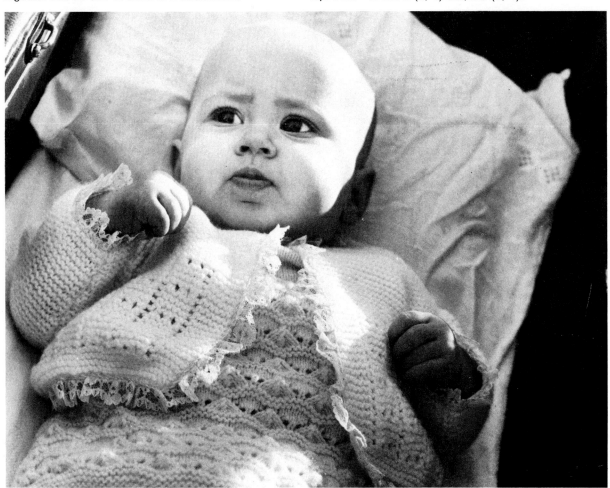

8th row: sl.1, p.1 (3, 2), sl.1, drop 2 y.r.n. loops of 7th row (long st. made), * p.4, sl.1, drop 2 y.r.n. loops of 7th row; rep. from * to last 3 (5, 4) sts., p.2 (4, 3), k.1.

9th row: sl.1, k.2 (4, 3), sl.1, * k.4, sl.1; rep. from * to last 2 (4, 3) sts., k.2 (4, 3).

10th row: sl.1, p.1 (3, 2), sl.1, * p.4, sl.1; rep. from * to last 3 (5, 4) sts., p.2 (4, 3), k.1.

11th row: sl.1, k.0 (2, 1), * cr. L st., k.1; rep. from * to last 0 (2, 1) sts., k.0 (2, 1).

12th to 16th rows: k.

Rep. 7th to 16th rows once. Cont. in st.st. until work measures 6¼ (6½, 6¾) in. from cast-on edge, ending with a p. row.

Shape Yoke

1st row: sl.1, k.1 (k.3, k.2 tog.), k.2 tog., * k.2, k.2 tog.; rep. from * to last 1 (3, 4) sts., k.1 (k.3, k.2 tog. twice): 61 (65, 68) sts.

Change to No. 10 needles. K. 5 rows.
Change to No. 9 needles.

Shape Armholes

1st row: cast off 3 sts., k.5 (7, 6), y.r.n. twice, * k.5, y.r.n. twice; rep. from * to last 8 (10, 9) sts., k.8 (10, 9).

2nd row: cast off 3 sts., p.4 (6, 5), sl.1, drop 2 y.r.n. loops, * p.4, sl.1, drop 2 y.r.n. loops; rep. from * to last 5 (7, 6) sts., p.4 (6, 5), k.1.

Working 3rd to 10th rows as 9th to 16th rows of Back, k.2 tog. at each end of 3rd and 5th rows, working extra sts. in st.st. Rep. 7th to 16th rows of Back twice more. Cont. in garter st. until armholes measure 4 (4¼, 4½) in.

Shape Shoulders

Cast off 10 sts. at beg. of next 2 rows, 8 (9, 10) sts. at beg. of next 2 rows. Cast off rem. sts.

LEFT FRONT

With No. 9 needles cast on 49 (51, 55) sts.
Work 6 rows in garter st.

7th row: sl.1, k.2 (3, 3), y.r.n. twice, * k.5, y.r.n. twice; rep. from * to last 11 (12, 11) sts., k.11 (12, 11).

8th row: k.8, p.2 (3, 2), sl.1, drop 2 y.r.n. loops, * p.4,

sl.1, drop 2 y.r.n. loops; rep. from * to last 3 (4, 4) sts., p.2 (3, 3), k.1.

Cont. in patt. as now set with 8 sts. at front edge in garter st. until the 26 patt. rows have been worked as for Back. Cont. in st.st. with 8 sts. at front edge in garter st. until work matches Back to yoke, ending with a wrong-side row.

Shape Yoke

For size 18 only. 1st row: k.2 tog. 4 times, * k.1, k.2 tog; rep. from * to last 11 sts., k.2 tog., k.9: 34 sts.

For size 20 only. 1st row: k.2 tog. 3 times, * k.1, k.2 tog.; rep. from * to last 9 sts., k.9: 36 sts.

For size 22 only. 1st row: sl.1, k.1, k.2 tog., * k.1, k.2 tog.; rep. from * to last 9 sts., k.9: 40 sts.

For all sizes. Change to No. 10 needles.

2nd to 6th rows: k.
Change to No. 9 needles.

Shape Armhole

Next row: cast off 3 sts., k.5 (6, 6), y.r.n. twice, * k.5, y.r.n. twice; rep. from * to last 11 (12, 11) sts., k.11 (12, 11).

Cont. in patt. as now set, with front border still in garter st., dec. 1 st. at beg. of 3rd and 5th rows. to match Back (10 rows of patt. worked 3 times), then work in garter st. and at the same time when armhole measures 2¾ (3, 3) in. end at front edge.

Shape Neck

Cast off 8 (8, 9) sts. at beg. of next row, 2 (2, 3) sts. at beg. of next alt. row, then dec. 1 st. at neck edge on alt. rows until 18 (19, 20) sts. remain.
Cont. straight until Front measures same as Back to shoulder, ending at side edge.

Shape Shoulder

Cast off 10 sts. at beg. of next row. K. 1 row. Cast off rem. sts.

RIGHT FRONT

Work as Left Front, reversing patt. and all shapings.
7th row will read sl.1, k.10 (11, 10), y.r.n. twice, * k.5, y.r.n. twice; rep. from * to last 3 (4, 4) sts., k.3 (4, 4).

Mark position for 4 buttons on garter-st. border of Left Front, the first 5 in. from cast-on edge, the last at top of garter-st. border, the other two evenly spaced between, then work buttonholes on Right Front to correspond with marked positions in foll. way.

Buttonhole row (right side): sl.1, k.2, k.2 tog., y.f., k.6 (7, 6), patt. to end.

SLEEVES (make 2 alike)

With No. 9 needles cast on 33 (35, 38) sts.
Work 6 rows in garter st.

7th row: sl.1, k.3 (4, 3), y.r.n. twice, * k.5, y.r.n. twice; rep. from * to last 4 (5, 4) sts., k.4 (5, 4).

Now work in patt. as set, until 16th row has been worked.

Next row: k. twice into first st., k.6 (4, 6), k. twice into next st., * k.5, k. twice into next st.; rep. from * to last 7 (5, 6) sts., k.6 (4, 5), k. twice into last st.: 39 (42, 45) sts.

Cont. in st.st., inc. 1 st. at each end of 3rd and every foll. 6th row until there are 47 (50, 53) sts. Cont. straight in st.st. until work measures 5 (5½, 6) in. from cast-on edge.

Shape Top

Cast off 3 sts. at beg. of next 2 rows. Dec. 1 st. at each end of every k. row until 23 (24, 25) sts. remain. Cast off 4 sts. at beg. of next 2 rows.
Work 1 row.
Cast off rem. sts.

COLLAR
With No. 10 needles cast on 78 (83, 85) sts.
Work 6 rows in garter st.
7th row: sl.1, k.8 (8, 9), y.r.n. twice, * k.5, y.r.n. twice; rep. from * to last 9 (9, 10) sts., k.9 (9, 10).
Keeping first and last 6 (6, 7) sts. in garter st. for borders, work 5 rows in patt. as now set.
13th row: sl.1, k.6 (9, 10), k.2 tog., * k.8, k.2 tog; rep. from * to last 9 (11, 12) sts., k.9 (11, 12).
14th row: k.
15th row: sl.1, k.6 (9, 10), k.2 tog., * k.7, k.2 tog.; rep. from * to last 8 (10, 11) sts., k.8 (10, 11).
K. 1 row. Work 1 more dec. row. K. 1 row. Cast off.

TO COMPLETE
Sew shoulder, side and sleeve seams.
Set Sleeves into armholes. Sew Collar round neck. Sew buttons on to Left Front to correspond with buttonholes.

LEGGINGS
RIGHT LEG
With No. 10 needles cast on 65 (73, 77) sts.
Work 4 rows in k.1, p.1 rib, beg. first and alt. rows sl.1, k.1, p.1.
5th (eyelet) row: sl.1, k.1, y.f., k.2 tog., * p.1, k.1, y.f., k.2 tog.; rep. from * to last st., k.1.
Work 5 more rows in rib.
Change to No. 9 needles.

Shape Back
1st row: k.
2nd row: p.
3rd row: sl.1, k.5 (6, 7); turn.
4th and every alt. row: sl.1, p. to last st., k.1.
5th row: sl.1, k.11 (13, 15); turn.
Cont. working 6 (7, 8) more sts. before each turn until the row 'sl.1, k.29 (34, 39); turn' and the foll. row have been worked.
Next row: sl.1, k.64 (72, 76).
Cont. in st.st. inc. 1 st. at beg. of next k. row and every foll 6th row until there are 75 (83, 87) sts.
Cont. straight until work measures 8½ (9, 9) in. from cast-on edge, measuring along front seams, ending with a p. row.

Shape Leg
Cast off 3 (4, 4) sts. at beg. of next 2 rows.
Cont. in st.st. dec. 1 st. at each end of next and every foll. 4th row 1 (2, 3) times, then on every k. row until 33 (37, 41) sts. remain.
Cont. straight until leg measures 5½ (5½, 6) in., ending with a p. row.
Change to No. 10 needles. Work 6 rows in k.1, p.1 rib as for beg. of Leggings, working eyelet row as at waist on 3rd row.
Change to No. 9 needles.

Shape Foot
Next row: sl.1, k.21 (24, 26); turn and leave rem. sts. on st. holder.
2nd row: sl.1, k.10 (11, 12); turn.
Cont. in garter st. on these centre (instep) sts. for 2¼ (2½, 2½) in. Leave instep sts. on safety pin. Break yarn. Starting at beg. of instep pick up 12 (13, 13) sts. along side of instep, k. instep sts., pick up 12 (13, 13) sts. along 2nd side of instep, k. 11 (12, 14) sts. from st. holder.
Next row: sl.1, k.56 (62, 66).
Work 4 (6, 6) more rows in garter st.
Next row: k.2 tog., k.20 (22, 24), k.2 tog., k.9 (11, 11), k.2 tog., k.20 (22, 24), k.2 tog.
K. 1 row.

Next row: k.2 tog., k.19 (21, 23), k.2 tog., k.7 (9, 9), k.2 tog., k.19 (21, 23), k.2 tog.
Work 1 row, then another dec. row. Rep. last 2 rows. Cast off.

LEFT LEG
Work as Right Leg, but reverse back shaping by reading k. for p. and p. for k. and inc. at end of k. rows instead of at beg.

TO COMPLETE
Sew front, back, leg, and foot seams.
With crochet hook make ch. lengths to thread through eyelet holes at waist and ankles. Make a tassel for each end of each ch. length and attach.

Baby's dress — with bobble-patterned skirt

MATERIALS
3 (4, 4) balls (23.25 gr. each) Wendy Courtelle Crêpe 4-ply. One pair each Nos. 9, 10 and 12 knitting needles (USA sizes 5, 3 and 1). Three small buttons.

MEASUREMENTS
To fit chest size 18 (20, 22) in.; length 11½ (13, 14½) in.; sleeve seam 1 in.

TENSION
8 sts. and 9 rows to 1 in. on No. 10 needles over bodice rib pattern (slightly stretched).

ABBREVIATIONS
See page 22.

FRONT
With No. 12 needles cast on 96 (108, 120) sts. and k. 8 rows.
Change to No. 9 needles and work trinity st. patt. as follows:

1st row: * (k.1, p.1 and k.1) into first st., p.3 tog.; rep. from * to end.
2nd and 4th rows: p.
3rd row: * p.3 tog., (k.1, p.1 and k.1) into next st.; rep. from * to end.
These last 4 rows form patt. Cont. in patt. until work measures 7½ (8, 8½) in. from cast-on edge, ending after a wrong-side row.
(Note. If necessary, adjust length here.)

Bodice
Change to No. 12 needles.
Next row: k.8 (4, 0), * k.2 tog., k.2; rep. from * to end: 74 (82, 90) sts.
Next row: * k.1, p.1; rep. from * to end. Rep. this last row twice more.
Change to No. 10 needles and cont. in rib until work measures 8 (9, 10) in. from cast-on edge, ending after a wrong-side row.

Shape Armholes
Cast off 4 sts. at beg. of next 2 rows; dec. 1 st. at both ends of next 5 (6, 7) rows and of foll. alt. row. Work straight on rem. 54 (60, 66) sts. to complete 2¾ (3¼, 3¾) in. from beg. of armhole, ending after a wrong-side row.

Shape Front Neck
Next row: rib 21 (23, 25); turn.
Rib another 5 rows, dec. 1 st. at neck edge every row: 16 (18, 20) sts.

Shape Shoulder
Cast off 8 (9, 10) sts. at beg. of next and foll. alt. row. Returning to sts. still on needle, slip first 12 (14, 16) sts. on to a st. holder and complete second front shoulder to match first, reversing shapings.

BACK
Work as Front to beg. of armholes.

Armholes and Buttonband
1st row: cast off 4, rib to end.
2nd row: cast off 4, rib 29 (33, 37), cast on 6 sts.; turn: 36 (40, 44) sts.
Keeping centre edge straight, complete armhole shaping by dec. 1 st. at side edge on next 5 (6, 7) rows and on foll. alt. row. Work straight on rem. 30 (33, 36) sts. until Back matches Front to beg. of shoulders, ending at side edge.

Shape Shoulder
Cast off 8 (9, 10) sts. at beg. of next row, 3 sts. at beg. of foll. row (centre edge) and 8 (9, 10) sts. at beg. of next row. Leave rem. 11 (12, 13) sts. on st. holder. Mark on this side of Back the positions for 3 equally-spaced buttons.
Returning to the 36 (40, 44) sts. on needle, join in yarn and work 1 row in rib. Cont. and complete this side of Back to match side, working buttonholes to correspond with marked button positions.
Buttonhole row (working from side edge): rib until 4 sts. rem., yarn round needle twice, k.2 tog., rib 2. Drop extra loop on the next row.

SLEEVES (make 2 alike)
With No. 12 needles cast on 48 (56, 64) sts. and work 1 in. (or length required) in k.1, p.1 rib, changing to No. 10 needles after the first 4 rows.

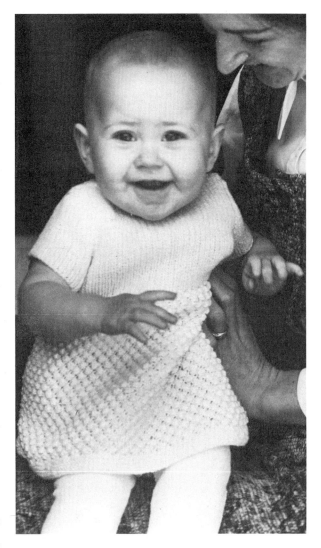

Top of Sleeve
Cast off 4 sts. at beg. of next 2 rows, 2 sts. at beg. of next 10 (12, 14) rows and 4 sts. at beg. of foll. 2 rows. Cast off.

TO COMPLETE
Sew shoulder seams.

Neckband
With right side facing and No. 12 needles start at top of left side of Back and pick up all sts. from spare needles round neck, and also 9 sts. from each side of neck. If necessary adjusting the number of sts. on first row to keep ribbing from bodice correct, work 5 rows in k.1, p.1 rib.
Cast off in rib.

To Make Up
Do not press. Sew side and sleeve seams and set in sleeves. Catch in place the lower end of first buttonband. Sew on buttons to correspond with buttonholes.

Chapter four
CHILDREN'S
CHOICE

Romper suit

MATERIALS
5 (5, 6) oz. Wendy 4-ply Nylonised. One pair each Nos. 10 and 12 knitting needles (USA sizes 3 and 1). A double-ended No. 12 needle and a cable needle. A 10 (12, 14)-in. zip fastener.

MEASUREMENTS
To fit chest size 20 (22, 24) in.; length of back from crutch to shoulder 15 (17, 19) in; sleeve seam 1½ in.

TENSION
7½ sts. and 9 rows to 1 in. on No. 10 needles over st.st.

ABBREVIATIONS
See page 22; tw.2, twist 2 (k. into front of second st. on left-hand needle, then k. into front of first st. and slip both off needle); cable 6, cable pattern 6 sts. as follows: sl. next 3 sts. on to cable needle and leave at front of work, k.3, k.3 from cable needle.

FRONT
With No. 12 needles cast on 50 (54, 58) sts.
1st row: k.2, * p.2, k.2; rep. from * to end.
2nd row (right side): p.2, * tw.2, p.2; rep. from * to end.

Rep. these 2 rows twice more and then work first row once again. **

Next row: using double-ended No. 12 needle, k.20 (22, 24), p.2, k.6, p.2, k.20 (22, 24).

This completes Right Leg. Leave these sts. on spare needle and work another identical piece as far as point marked ** for Left Leg. Change to No. 10 needles.

To Join Legs

Working sts. for Left Leg k.20 (22, 24), p.2, k.6, p.2, k.20 (22, 24); cast on 10 sts.; working from sts. for Right Leg k.4; turn.

2nd row: p.18; turn.

3rd row: k.3, sl.1 knitwise, k.1, p.s.s.o., k.8, k.2 tog., k.7; turn.

4th row: p.24; turn.

5th row: k.7, sl.1 knitwise, k.1, p.s.s.o., k.6, k.2 tog., k.11; turn.

6th row: p.30; turn.

7th row: k.11, sl.1 knitwise, k.1, p.s.s.o., k.4, k.2 tog., k.15; turn.

8th row: p.36; turn.

9th row: k.15, sl.1 knitwise, k.1, p.s.s.o., k.2, k.2 tog., k.19 (21, 23); turn.

10th row: p.42 (46, 50); turn.

11th row: k.19 (21, 23), sl.1 knitwise, k.1, p.s.s.o., k.2 tog., k.19 (21, 23), p.2, k.3; turn.

12th row: p.3, k.2, p.40 (44, 48), k.2, p.3; turn.

13th row: k.3, p.2, k.40 (44, 48), p.2, k.6, p.2; turn.

14th row: k.2, p.6, k.2, p.40 (44, 48), k.2, p.6, k.2; turn.

15th row: p.2, cable 6, p.2, k.40 (44, 48), p.2, cable 6, p.2, k.4; turn.

Working the cable twist in 21st and in every foll. 6th row, cont. to work an extra 4 sts. every row until 4 (2, 4) sts. rem. unworked at each end of needle. Carry work out to ends of needle on next 2 rows and then, keeping cable patt. correct, cont. straight on these 100 (108, 116) sts. to complete 3 in. from casting-on of crutch, ending after a p. row. (If necessary, adjust length here.)

Zip Opening

Next row: patt. 50 (54, 58); turn.

Next row: k.2, patt. to end.

Rep. these last 2 rows to complete 5½ (6½, 7½) in. from casting-on of crutch, ending after a p. row. Change to No. 12 needles.

Waist Ribbing

1st row: p.2 tog., k.2 tog., k.1, (p.2, k.2) 4 (4, 5) times, p.1 (3, 1), cable 6, p.1 (3, 1), k.2 tog., k.1, p.2 tog., p.1, (k.2, p.2) 2 (2, 3) times, k.2, p.3, k.2: 46 (50, 54) sts.

2nd row: k.3, (k.2, p.2) 4 (4, 5) times, k.1 (3, 1), p.6, k.1 (3,1), (p.2, k.2) 4 (4, 5) times, p.2, k.1.

3rd row: p.1, (tw.2, p.2) 4 (4, 5) times, tw.2, (p.1 (3, 1), cable 6, p.1 (3, 1), (tw.2, p.2) 4 (4, 5) times, p.1, k.2.

Rep. these last 2 rows 3 times more and then work 2nd row once more.

Change to No. 10 needles and, keeping cable patt. and centre edging correct, cont. in st.st. to complete 9½ (11, 12½) in. from casting-on of crutch, ending after a p. row.

Shape Armholes

Continuing in a similar way, cast off 3 sts. at beg. of next row; patt. 1 row. Dec. 1 st. at side edge on next 4 (5, 6) rows and on foll. 3 alt. rows: 36 (39, 42) sts. Work straight to complete 3 (3½, 4) in. from beg. of armholes, ending at centre edge.

Front Neck

Next row: patt. 14 (15, 16) and leave these sts. on a spare needle; patt. 22 (24, 26). Work another 8 rows for the left shoulder, dec. 1 st. at neck edge on every p. row.

Shape Shoulder

Cast off 6 (6, 7) sts. at beg. of next and foll. alt. row, and 6 (8, 8) sts. at beg. of next alt. row.

Returning to sts. still on needle, work second side of Front to match first, reversing all shapings and reading instructions for waist ribbing from end of row to beg.

BACK

Work as for Front, omitting zip opening, until Back is one row shorter than Front to beg. of waist ribbing.

Next rows: p.90 (94, 98); turn, k.80; turn, p.70; turn, k.60; turn, p.50; turn, k.40; turn, p.30; turn, k.20; turn, p. to end of row. Change to No. 12 needles.

Waist Ribbing

1st row: p.2 tog., k.2 tog., k.1, (p.2, k.2) 4 (4, 5) times, p.1 (3, 1), cable 6, p.3, k.2 tog., k.1, p.2 tog., p.1, (k.2, p.2) 6 (7, 8) times, k.2, p.1, p.2 tog., k.1, k.2 tog., p.3, cable 6, p.1 (3, 1), (k.2, p.2) 4 (4, 5) times, k.1, k.2 tog., p.2 tog.: 92 (100, 108) sts.

2nd row: k.1, p.2, (k.2, p.2) 4 (4, 5) times, k.1 (3, 1), p.6, k.3, (p.2, k.2) 8 (9, 10) times, k.3, p.6, k.1 (3, 1), (p.2, k.2) 4 (4, 5) times, p.2, k.1.

3rd row: p.1, tw.2, (p.2, tw.2) 4 (4, 5) times, p.1 (3, 1), cable 6, p.3, (tw.2, p.2) 8 (9, 10) times, tw.2, p.3, cable 6, p.1 (3, 1), (tw.2, p.2) 4 (4, 5) times, tw.2, p.1.

Rep. these last 2 rows 3 times more and then rep. 2nd row once more.

Change to No. 10 needles and keeping cable patt. correct, cont. in st.st. until Back matches Fronts to beg. of armholes (check measurements at side edges).

Shape Armholes

Cast off 3 sts. at beg. of next 2 rows; dec. 1 st. at both ends of next 4 (5, 6) rows and of foll. 3 alt. rows. Work straight until Back matches Fronts to beg. of shoulders.

Shape Shoulders

Cast off 6 (6, 7) sts. at beg. of next 4 rows and 6 (8, 8) sts. at beg. of foll. 2 rows. Leave rem. 36 (38, 40) sts. on a spare needle.

SLEEVES (make 2 alike)

With No. 12 needles cast on 54 (62, 70) sts. Work first 7 rows as given for Front. Change to No. 10 needles and, starting with a k. row, work 14 rows in st.st. (If necessary, adjust length here.)

Cast off 3 sts. at beg. of next 2 rows and 2 sts. at beg. of next 12 (16, 18) rows. Cast off.

TO COMPLETE

Press st.st. sections lightly. Sew shoulder seams. Set in sleeves and sew side, sleeve and inner leg seams.

Neckband

With right side facing and No. 12 needles, start at centre edge of right side of Front and pick up all sts. from spare needles round neck, and also 7 sts. from each side of neck: 78 (82, 86) sts.

1st row: k.2, * p.2, k.2; rep. from * to end.

2nd row: k.2, * tw.2, p.2; rep. from * until 4 sts. rem., tw.2, k.2.

Rep. these last 2 rows twice more. Cast off in patt.

To Make Up

Sew zip fastener into zip opening. Press all seams.

Smock dress

illustrated in colour on page 17

MATERIALS
6 (7, 8) balls (25 gr. each) Hayfield Diane in main shade and 1 (1, 2) balls in a contrasting shade. One pair each Nos. 10, 8 and 7 knitting needles (USA sizes 3, 6 and 7).

MEASUREMENTS
To fit chest size 22 (24, 26) in.; length 16 (18, 21) in. (adjustable); length of sleeve seam 2 in. (adjustable).

TENSION
$6\frac{1}{2}$ sts. and 8 rows to 1 in. over st.st. with No. 8 needles.

ABBREVIATIONS
See page 22; M., main shade; C., contrasting shade.

FRONT AND BACK (make 2 alike)
With No. 10 needles and M. cast on 88 (98, 108) sts. and, beg. with a k. row, work 8 rows in st.st.
9th (picot) row: k.2, * y.f., k.2 tog.; rep. from * to end. Change to No. 8 needles and, beg. with a p. row, cont. in st.st., dec. 1 st. at each end of 10th row from picot edge and every foll. 8th row until 78 (84, 90) sts.

Cont. straight until work measures $11\frac{1}{2}$ (13, $15\frac{1}{2}$) in. from picot edge, ending with a p. row. (adjust length here, if necessary).

Shape Armholes
Cast off 4 sts. at beg. of next 2 rows.
Next row: k.2 tog., k. to last 2 sts., k.2 tog.
Next row: p.
Rep. last 2 rows once. Leave rem. 66 (72, 78) sts. on st. holder.

SLEEVES (make 2 alike)
With No. 10 needles and M. cast on 45 (50, 55) sts. and, beg. with a k. row, work 4 rows in st.st.
5th row: k.1 (2, 3), * y.f., k.2 tog.; rep. from * to end. Change to No. 8 needles and, beg. with a p. row, work 5 rows in st.st.
11th (eyelet) row: as 5th row.
12th row: * p.4, p. twice into next st.; rep. from * to end: 54 (60, 66) sts.
Beg. with a k. row, cont. straight in st.st. until work measures 2 in. (or required length) from 5th row, ending with a p. row.

Shape Top
Work as Front and Back armholes.
Leave rem. 42 (48, 54) sts. on st. holder.

TO COMPLETE
Yoke
Sew raglan seams, leaving seam between Back and left sleeve unsewn. Then, with right side facing, No. 7 needles and C., k. across sts. of left sleeve, sts. of Front, sts. of right sleeve and Back sts.: 216 (240, 264) sts.
2nd row: * k.2, p.2, k.2; rep. from * to end.
3rd row: * p.1, k.2 tog., y.f., sl.1, k.1, p.s.s.o., p.1; rep. from * to end: 180 (200, 220) sts.
4th row: * k.1, p.3, k.1; rep. from * to end.
5th row: * p.1, k.3, p.1; rep. from * to end.
6th row: as 4th row.
Rep. last 2 rows 1 (2, 3) times.
Next row: p.1, * k.2 tog., y.f., k.1, p.2 tog.; rep. from * to last 4 sts., k.2 tog., y.f., k.1, p.1: 145 (161, 177) sts.
Next row: k.1, * p.3, k.1; rep. from * to end.
Work another 4 (6, 8) rows straight in rib patt. as set.

Next row: k.1, * k.2 tog., y.f., sl.1, k.1, p.s.s.o.; rep. from * to end: 109 (121, 133) sts.
Cont. in st.st. until work measures $4\frac{1}{2}$ (5, $5\frac{1}{2}$) in. from beg. of armholes, ending with a p. row.

Neck Ribbing
Change to No. 10 needles and M.
1st row: k.1, * k.2 tog., k.1; rep. from * to end.
Work 5 rows in k.1, p.1 rib.
With No. 8 needles cast off very loosely in rib.

To Make Up
Press dry, using a cool iron. Sew seam between Back and left sleeve, joining sides of neck ribbing as well. Sew side and sleeve seams. Turn up hems at lower edge and on Sleeve on the picot rows and catch lightly in position on wrong side. Press seams. With C. make 2 twisted cords each 22 in. long and thread one through each sleeve eyelet row, tying ends in bows.

Toddler's motif-patterned suit

MATERIALS
7 (7, 8) balls (2 oz. each) Twilleys Stalite in main colour, 2 balls in a contrasting shade. One pair each Nos. 10 and 11 knitting needles (USA sizes 3 and 2), and a set of four No. 11 needles (USA size 2) with points at both ends. One crochet hook International Standard Size 2.50. A waist length of narrow elastic.

MEASUREMENTS
To fit chest size 24 (26, 28) in.; length of top 14 ($14\frac{1}{2}$, 15) in.; sleeve seam $8\frac{1}{2}$ (9, $9\frac{1}{2}$) in.; length of trousers 17 ($17\frac{1}{2}$, 18) in.

TENSION
6 sts. and 8 rows to 1 in.

ABBREVIATIONS
See page 22; M., main colour; C., contrasting colour.

TOP
BACK
With No. 11 needles and M. cast on 74 (80, 86) sts. and work 1 in. in k.1, p.1 rib.
Change to No. 10 needles and work $1\frac{1}{2}$ in. in st.st.; change to C. and work 3 in. in st.st. Change to M. and continue in st.st. until work measures $9\frac{1}{2}$ (10, $10\frac{1}{2}$) in.

44

Shape Raglan

Cast off 6 sts. at beg. of next 2 rows.
Next row: k.2, sl.1, k.1, p.s.s.o., k. to last 4 sts., k.2 tog., k.2.
Next row: p.
Rep. these 2 rows until work measures 4¼ (4½, 4¾) in. from the beg. of raglan shaping. Now dec. each end of every row until 30 (32, 34) sts. remain. Cast off.

FRONT

Work as for Back until work measures 11¾ (12½, 13¼) in.

Shape Neck

Continue with the decs. for raglan as for Back and at the same time cast off the centre 12 (14, 16) sts. Finish each side separately, dec. 1 st. at neck edge on every alt. row until all sts. are worked off. Rejoin yarn at other side of neck and finish this side to match the first.

SLEEVES (make 2 alike)

With No. 11 needles and M. cast on 42 (46, 50) sts. and work 1¾ in. in k.1, p.1 rib.
Change to st.st., inc. 1 st. at the beg. and end of the 3rd row and then every 6th row until there are 62 (64, 66) sts.
When sleeve measures 8½ (9, 9½) in. shape raglan as given for Back until there are 36 sts. Now dec. each end of every row until there are 4 sts. Cast off.

TO COMPLETE

Press the pieces under a damp cloth. Sew the shoulder, side and sleeve seams. Set the sleeves into the armholes. Make crochet motifs as described on page 46, and sew eight evenly round band of C.

Neckband

With the set of four No. 11 needles and M., pick up and k. 92 (94, 96) sts. round the neck and work in k.1, p.1 rib for 1 in. Cast off loosely in rib.

LEGGINGS

With No. 11 needles and M. cast on 76 (80, 84) sts. and work ¾ in. in k.1, p.1 rib.
Next row: rib 2 (4, 6), * make 1, k.2 tog., rib 8; rep. from * to last 2 (4, 6) sts., rib to end.
Work ¾ in. in k.1, p.1 rib. Change to No. 10 needles and continue in st.st. Work 2 rows.

Shape Back

Next row: k.22 (24, 26); turn, p. back.
Next row: k.34 (36, 38); turn and p. back.
Next row: k.46 (48, 50); turn and p. back.
Cont. in st.st. across all the sts. and inc. 1 st. at beg. and end of 3rd row and each foll. 8th row until there are 90 (94, 98) sts.
Work straight until front seam measures 8 (8½, 9) in. Then dec. at the beg. and end of the 7th and then each 4th row until there are 56 (60, 64) sts.
Next row: make 6 decs. evenly along this row. Change to No. 11 needles and work 1½ in. in k.1, p.1 rib. Cast off in rib.
Work the other leg in the same way but reverse the shapings.

TO COMPLETE

Join the back and front seams. Join the leg seams. Thread elastic through the holes in ribbing.

CAP

With No. 11 needles and C. cast on 111 sts. and work in st.st. for 3 (3, 3¼) in. Change to No. 10 needles and M. K. 1 row. Continue in st.st. beg. with a k. row for 3 (3¼, 3½) in.

Shape Crown

Next row: k.3, k.2 tog., k.20, * sl.1, k.1, p.s.s.o., k.3, k.2 tog., k.20: rep. from * to last 5 sts., sl.1, k.1, p.s.s.o., k.3.
Next row: p.
Continue dec. in this way keeping the decs. over each other, and dec. the number of sts. between the shaping. When work measures 9¾ (10, 10¼) in. from cast-on edge break yarn and thread through the remaining sts., pull together and sew off the end.

TO COMPLETE
Fold the band of C. to the right side and press. Join seam. Make crochet motifs and sew four evenly round band of C. Make a 3-in. pompon in C. and sew to top of cap.

MOTIFS (make 12 in M.)
With the crochet hook make 6 ch. and join into a ring with s.s.
Next round: 3 ch., * yarn round hook, hook into ring, yarn round hook, draw through, yarn round hook, pull through 1 loop, yarn round hook and pull through 2 loops; rep. from * once, yarn round hook and pull 3 loops on hook, 2 ch., ** yarn round hook, hook into ring, yarn round hook, draw through, yarn round hook, draw through 1 loop, yarn round hook and draw through 2 loops; rep. from ** twice, yarn round hook and draw through all loops on hook, 2 ch., ***, work from ** to *** until 7 bobbles are in ring, s.s. last 2 ch. to 3rd of starting ch.; turn.
Next round: 5 ch., * 1 tr. into space, 2 ch., 1 tr. into top of bobble, 2 ch.; rep. from * to end of round, s.s. last 2 ch. to 3rd of starting ch., turn.
Next round: work 2 d.c. into each sp. and 1 d.c. over each tr. to end of round, end with a s.s. into first d.c.

Rabbit-patterned skirt and cap

MATERIALS
7 (8) oz. Hayfield Gaylon Double Knitting in main shade and 1 oz. in a contrasting shade. One pair each Nos. 10 and 8 knitting needles (USA sizes 3 and 6). Waist length elastic, 1 in. wide. Short length black thread.

MEASUREMENTS
Skirt: to fit waist size 22 (24) in.; length 8 (10) in. (adjustable). **Cap:** to fit child's average-sized head.

TENSION
5½ sts. and 7½ rows to 1 in. over st.st. with No. 8 needles.

ABBREVIATIONS
See page 22; M., main shade; C., contrasting shade.

SKIRT
FRONT
With No. 10 needles and M. cast on 112 (122) sts. and work 7 rows in st.st.
8th row (hemline): k.
Change to No. 8 needles and k. 1 row then p. 1 row. Beg. colour patt., still working in st.st.
1st row: k.: 1 C., * 5 C., 5 M.; rep. from * to last st., 1 M.
2nd row: p.: 1 M., * 2 M., 1 C., 2 M., 5 C.; rep. from * to last st., 1 C.
3rd row: k.: 1 C., * 5 C., 1 M., 1 C., 1 M., 1 C., 1 M.; rep. from * to last st., 1 M.
4th row: as 2nd row. **5th row:** as first row.
6th row: p.: 1 C., * 5 C., 5 M.; rep. from * to last st., 1 M.
7th row: k.: 1 M., * 2 M., 1 C., 2 M., 5 C.; rep. from * to

last st., 1 C.
8th row: p.: 1 C., * 5 C., 1 M., 1 C., 1 M., 1 C., 1 M.; rep. from * to last st., 1 M.
9th row: as 7th row.
10th row: as 6th row.
With M., k. 1 row then p. 1 row. **
13th row: k.38 (43) M., 8 C., 9 M., 1 C., 9 M., 9 C., 38 (43) M.
14th row: p.40 (45) M., 5 C., 11 M., 2 C., 9 M., 5 C., 40 (45) M.
15th row: k.40 (45) M., 6 C., 10 M., 1 C., 1 M., 1 C., 7 M., 6 C., 40 (45) M.
16th row: p.40 (45) M., 6 C., 7 M., 1 C., 1 M., 1 C., 10 M., 6 C., 40 (45) M.
17th row: k.40 (45) M., 7 C., 3 M., 1 C., 2 M., 1 C., 1 M., 1 C., 5 M., 1 C., 3 M., 7 C., 40 (45) M.
18th row: p.40 (45) M., 9 C., 1 M., 1 C., 3 M., 2 C., 5 M., 1 C., 1 M., 9 C., 40 (45) M.
19th row: k.41 (46) M., 10 C., 3 M., 2 C., 1 M., 1 C., 3 M., 10 C., 41 (46) M.
20th row: p.42 (47) M., 7 C., 4 M., 1 C., 1 M., 1 C., 1 M., 1 C., 5 M., 7 C., 42 (47) M.
21st row: k.40 (45) M., 1 C., 2 M., 6 C., 6 M., 1 C., 1 M., 2 C., 4 M., 6 C., 2 M., 1 C., 40 (45) M.
22nd row: p.40 (45) M., 2 C., 2 M., 5 C., 6 M., 2 C., 6 M., 5 C., 2 M., 2 C., 40 (45) M.
23rd row: k.41 (46) M., 9 C., 12 M., 9 C., 41 (46) M.
24th row: p.42 (47) M., 9 C., 10 M., 9 C., 42 (47) M.
25th row: k.44 (49) M., 7 C., 10 M., 7 C., 44 (49) M.
26th row: p.47 (52) M., 4 C., 10 M., 4 C., 47 (52) M.
Cont. straight with M. in st.st. until work measures 7 (9) in. (or 1 in. less than required length) from hemline, ending with a p. row. Change to No. 10 needles.

Waistband
Next row: k.1, * k.2 tog., k.1, k.2 tog.; rep. from * to last st., k.1: 68 (74) sts.
Beg. with a p. row, work 8 rows in st.st. K. 1 row for ridge.
Beg. with a k. row, work 8 rows in st.st. Cast off very loosely.

BACK
Work as Front to **. Working in st.st. with M. only, complete as Front.

TO COMPLETE
Press well, blocking hem and waistband. Sew side seams. Catch hem lightly in position at lower edge. Turn over waistband at ridge and hem loosely on inside, leaving opening for insertion of elastic. With black thread, embroider an eye on each rabbit. Press seams. Thread elastic into waistband and join. Finish each rabbit with a white pompon.

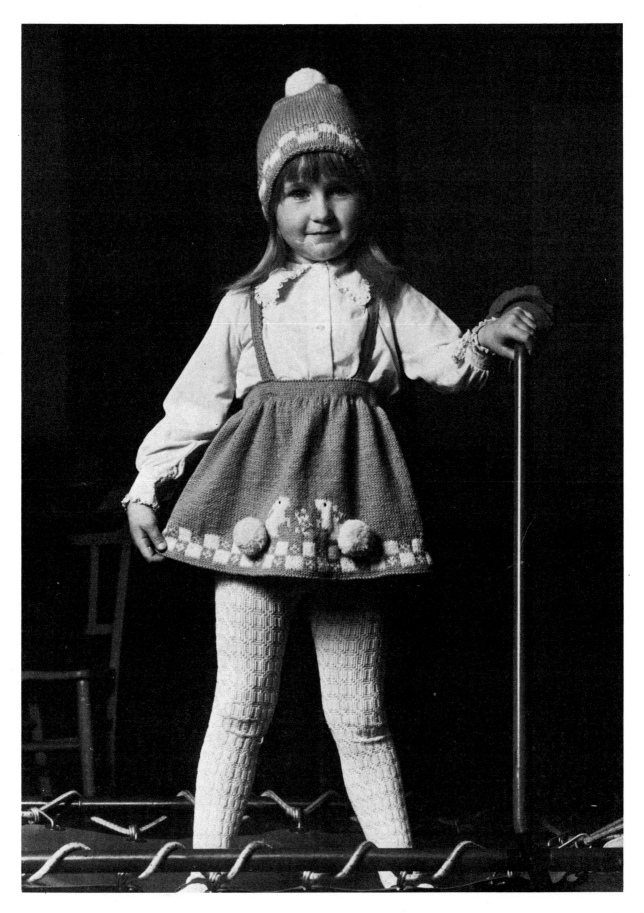

Straps (make 2 alike)
With No. 10 needles and M. cast on 11 sts.
1st row: k.
2nd row: p.5, keeping y.f., sl.1 purlwise, p.5. Rep. last 2 rows until strap is required length, probably about 16 (18) in. allowing 2 in. for sewing strap to waistband. Cast off.
Fold straps double on the sl.st. and press. Sew sides tog., using an edge-to-edge seam, and press.
Sew straps to waistband.

CAP
With No. 10 needles and M. cast on 92 (102) sts. and work 2 rows in k.1, p.1 rib.
Change to No. 8 needles and work the first 10 rows of the colour patt. as given for Skirt.
With M. k. 2 rows (2nd row forms ridge).
Change to No. 10 needles.
Work 9 rows in k.1, p.1 rib.
Change to No. 8 needles and work 24 (28) rows in st.st. dec. 1 st. at each end of first and every foll. 4th row: 80 (88) sts.

Shape Crown
1st row: * k.2 tog., k.6 (7), k.2 tog. t.b.l.; rep. from * to end.
P. 1 row then k. 1 row, p. 1 row.
5th row: * k.2 tog., k.4 (5), k.2 tog. t.b.l.; rep. from * to end.
P. 1 row.
7th row: * k.2 tog., k.2 (3), k.2 tog. t.b.l.; rep. from * to end: 32 (40) sts.
P. 1 row.
9th row: * k.2 tog.; rep. from * to end.
Thread rem. sts. on to 2 strands yarn, pull tight and knot on inside.

To Make Up
Press st. st. sections well. Sew seam at back of head and press, blocking turn-back brim in position. Make a white pompon and sew to centre of crown.

Dressing-gown
illustrated opposite

MATERIALS
10 balls (25 gr. each) Sirdar Courtelle Random. One pair each Nos. 10 and 9 knitting needles (USA sizes 3 and 5). Six buttons ½ in. in diameter.

MEASUREMENTS
To fit chest size 22 in.; length 24 in.; sleeve seam 8 in.

TENSION
7 sts. to 1 in. with No. 9 needles.

ABBREVIATIONS
See page 22.

MAIN PIECE
With No. 10 needles cast on 182 sts. and k. 8 rows.
Change to No. 9 needles and cont. in st.st. with a garter-st. border (every row k.) at each end of 8 sts.
Work 8 rows (adjust length here).
For Girl's Dressing-Gown
Next (buttonhole) row: k.3, cast off 2, k. to end.
Next row: k.8, p. to last 8 sts., k.3, cast on 2, k.3.
For Boy's Dressing-Gown
Next (buttonhole) row: k. to last 5 sts., cast off 2, k. to end.
Next row: k.3, cast on 2, k.3, p. to last 8 sts., k.8.

For Girl's or Boy's Dressing-Gown
Cont. in st.st. keeping borders correct for 148 rows, making 4 more buttonholes in same way as before with 34 rows between each buttonhole.

Shape Armholes
Next row: k.47, cast off 8, k.72 (including st. on needle used in casting off), cast off 8, k. to end.

Left Front
Working on last set of 47 sts. only, work 1 row.
1st row: k.1, k.2 tog. t.b.l., k. to end.
2nd row: k.8, k. to last 3 sts., p.2 tog., k.1.
3rd row: as first row.
4th row: k.8, p. to last st., k.1.
Rep. last 4 rows twice.
Next row: k.1, k.2 tog. t.b.l., k. to end.
Next row: k.8, p. to last st., k.1.
Next row: k.1, k.2 tog. t.b.l., k. to end.
For Girl's Dressing-Gown
Rep. last 2 rows until 24 sts. remain.
For Boy's Dressing-Gown
Rep. last 2 rows, making a buttonhole on 6th and 7th rows, until 24 sts. remain.
For Girl's or Boy's Dressing-Gown
Shape Neck
Next row: cast off 8 sts., p. to last st., k.1.
** Cont. to dec. at armhole edge as before on foll. 5 alt. rows and **at the same time** cast off 4 sts. at neck edge at beg. of foll. alt. row, 2 sts. on next alt. row, and 1 st. on next alt. row.
Work 1 row. K. rem. sts. tog. Fasten off.

Back
Rejoin yarn to centre sts. with wrong side facing and work to end.
1st row: k.1, k.2 tog. t.b.l., k. to last 3 sts., k.2 tog., k.1.
2nd row: k.1, p.2 tog., p. to last 3 sts., p.2 tog. t.b.l., k.1.
3rd row: as first row.
4th row: k.1, p. to last st., k.1.
Rep. last 4 rows twice, then rep. last 2 rows until 30 sts. remain. Cast off.

Right Front
Rejoin yarn to rem. sts. with wrong side facing and work to end.
1st row: k. to last 3 sts., k.2 tog., k.1.
2nd row: k.1, p.2 tog., p. to last 8 sts., k.8.
3rd row: as first row.
4th row: k.1, p. to last 8 sts., k.8.
Rep. last 4 rows twice.
Next row: k. to last 3 sts., k.2 tog., k.1.
Next row: k.1, p. to last 8 sts., k.8.
For Girl's Dressing-Gown
Rep. last 2 rows making a buttonhole on 7th and 8th rows, until 24 sts. remain.
For Boy's Dressing Gown.
Rep. last 2 rows until 24 sts. remain.
For Girl's or Boy's Dressing-Gown
Shape Neck
Next row: cast off 8 sts., work to last 3 sts., k.2 tog., k.1.
Work as left front from ** to end, reversing all shapings.

SLEEVES (make 2 alike)
With No. 10 needles cast on 37 sts. and k. 6 rows.
Next row: k.3, * k. twice into next st., k.4; rep. from * 5 times, k. twice into next st., k.3: 44 sts.
Change to No. 9 needles and work in st.st., inc. 1 st. at each end of 5th row and every foll. 6th row until there are 58 sts.
Cont. straight until work measures 8 in. (or required length).

Shape Top

Cast off 4 sts. at beg. of next 2 rows.
Next row: k.1, k.2 tog. t.b.l., k. to last 3 sts., k.2 tog., k.1.
Next row: k.1, p. to last st., k.1.
Rep. last 2 rows until 8 sts. remain. Cast off.

COLLAR

With No. 9 needles, cast on 8 sts.
1st row: k. twice into first st., k. to end.
2nd row: k.
3rd to 6th rows: rep. first and 2nd rows twice: 11 sts.
7th row: k.8; turn.
8th row: k. to end.
9th to 12th rows: k. all sts.
Rep. 7th to 12th rows 22 times, then 7th and 8th rows once.
Next row: k. 2 tog., k. to end.
Next row: k.
Rep. last 2 rows once.
Next row: k.2 tog., k. to end.
Cast off.

TO COMPLETE

Do not press. Sew in Sleeves. Sew on Collar. Sew on buttons to correspond with buttonholes.
Make a 60 in. long twisted cord with tassels and st. to sides at waist level.

Brown pullover and trousers

illustrated in colour on page 29

MATERIALS

9 (10, 11, 12) oz. Wendy Double Knit Nylonised. One pair each Nos. 8 and 10 knitting needles (USA sizes 6 and 3). ¾ (⅞, ⅞, 1) yd. belt stiffening, 1 in. wide. A 1½-in. buckle. A waist length of elastic, 1 in. wide.

MEASUREMENTS

To fit chest size 20 (22, 24, 26) in.; length of pullover 12 (13½, 15, 16½) in.; inner leg seam of trousers 8 (10, 12, 14) in.; front waist to crutch 6½ (7, 7½, 8) in.

TENSION

5 sts. and 9 rows to 1 in. over patt.

ABBREVIATIONS

See page 22.

PULLOVER
FRONT

With No. 8 needles cast on 60 (68, 72, 76) sts.
1st row: * k.2, p.2; rep. from * to end.
2nd row: * p.2, k.2; rep. from * to end.
These last 2 rows form patt. Cont. in patt., dec. 1 st. at both ends of 11th row and of every foll. 16th row until you have 56 (62, 66, 70) sts.
Work straight in patt. to complete 7 (8, 9, 10) in. from cast-on edge, ending after a wrong-side row.
(Note. If necessary, adjust length here.)

Shape Armhole and Front Neck

1st row: cast off 3, patt. 22 (25, 27, 29), work 2 sts. tog. in patt.; turn: 24 (27, 29, 31) sts.
Dec. 1 st. at neck edge every 3rd row, cont. in patt., completing armhole shaping by dec. 1 st. at side edge on next 3 (4, 4, 5) rows and on foll. alt. row. Then keep side edge straight and cont. to dec. as before for neck shaping until 12 (13, 14, 15) sts. rem.
Work straight to complete 11½ (13, 14½, 16) in. from cast-on edge, ending at side edge.

Shape Shoulder

Cast off 4 (4, 4, 5) sts. at beg. of next and foll. alt. row and 4 (5, 6, 5) sts. at beg. of next alt. row.
Returning to sts. still on needle, work second shoulder to match first, reversing shapings.

BACK

Work as for Front to beg. of armholes.

Shape Armholes

Cast off 3 sts. at beg. of next 2 rows; dec. 1 st. at both ends of next 3 (4, 4, 5) rows and of foll. alt. row. Work straight in patt. on rem. 42 (46, 50, 52) sts. until Back matches Front to beg. of shoulders.

Shoulders

Cast off 4 (4, 4, 5) sts. at beg. of next 4 rows and 4 (5, 6, 5) sts. at beg. of foll. 2 rows. Leave rem. 18 (20, 22, 22) sts. on a spare needle.

NECKBAND

Sew right shoulder seam. With right side facing and using No. 10 needles, pick up 42 (46, 50, 54) sts. along each side of neck, and sts. from pin at Back. Work 1 row in k.1, p.1 rib. Cast off in rib.

TO COMPLETE

Do not press. Sew side seams and left shoulder seam, joining sides of neckband. With right side facing and No. 10 needles, pick up 80 (88, 96, 104) sts. round each armhole. Work 1 row in k.1, p.1 rib. Cast off in rib.

BELT

With No. 10 needles cast on 12 sts. and work in the 2-row patt. until work is about 26 (28, 30, 32) in. (or length required) from cast-on edge. Cast off. Fold belt lengthwise over stiffening and join sides of knitted fabric with edge-to-edge stitches. Stitch ends closed. Press lightly. Stitch one end over bar of buckle.

TROUSERS
FRONT

With No. 8 needles cast on 35 (37, 43, 45) sts.
1st row: k.1 (2, 1, 2), (p.2, k.2) 4 (4, 5, 5) times, k.1, (k.2, p.2) 4 (4, 5, 5) times, k.1 (2, 1, 2).
2nd row: k.1 (2, 1, 2), (p.2, k.2) 4 (4, 5, 5) times, y. fwd., sl.1 purlwise, y.b., (k.2, p.2) 4 (4, 5, 5) times, k.1 (2, 1, 2).
These 2 rows form the patt. Keeping the slipped st. in centre correct on all wrong-side rows, cont. in patt. as set, dec. 1 st. at both ends of 9th and of every foll. 8th row until you have 27 (29, 33, 35) sts. Cont. straight until work measures 8 (10, 12, 14) in. (or length required) from cast-on edge, ending after a wrong-side row and inc. 1 st. at inner leg edge on final row for the 22 in. and 26 in. sizes only: 27 (30, 33, 36) sts.
This completes Right Leg. Leave these sts. on spare needle and work another identical piece for Left Leg.

To Join Legs
1st row: patt. sts. for Left Leg, cast on 10 sts., patt. sts. for Right Leg.
2nd row: patt. 27 (30, 33, 36), p.10, patt. 27 (30, 33, 36).
3rd row: patt. 26 (29, 32, 35), sl.1 knitwise, k.1, p.s.s.o., k.8, k.2 tog., patt. 26 (29, 32, 35).
4th row: patt. 26 (29, 32, 35), p.10, patt. 26 (29, 32, 35).
5th row: patt. 26 (29, 32, 35), sl.1 knitwise, k.1, p.s.s.o., k.2 tog.; patt. 26 (29, 32, 35).
6th row: patt. 26 (29, 32, 35), p.8, patt. 26 (29, 32, 35).
Cont. to dec. by 2 sts. in a similar way every right-side row until 54 (60, 66, 72) sts. rem. Keeping slipped sts. correct, cont. in patt. until work measures 4½ (5, 5½, 6) in. (or 2 in. less than finished length required) from joining of legs. Change to No. 10 needles and work another 1 in. in patt., keeping slipped sts. correct as before.

Waistband
Work 1 in. in k.1, p.1 rib. Cast off in rib.

BACK
Work as for Front until Back is one row shorter than Front to beg. of waistband.
Next 2 rows: keeping slipped sts. correct patt. until 8 sts. rem.; turn.
Next 2 rows: patt. until 16 sts. rem.; turn.
Next 2 rows: patt. until 24 sts. rem.; turn.
26 in. size only. Next 2 rows: patt. until 32 sts. rem.; turn.
All sizes. Work Waistband to match Front. Cast off.

TO COMPLETE
Do not press. Sew side seams and inner leg seams. Press seams, blocking 'creases'. Make a crochet or herringbone st. casing inside waistband of trousers and thread with elastic.

Blue striped trouser suit
illustrated in colour on page 29

MATERIALS
14 (15, 16, 18) balls (20 gr. each) Wendy Tricel Nylon Double Knitting in main colour (blue), 1 ball in white and in each of two contrasting shades. One pair each Nos. 9 and 11 knitting needles (USA sizes 5 and 2). A waist length of narrow elastic.

MEASUREMENTS
To fit chest size 22 (24, 26, 28) in.; length of tunic 12 (14, 16, 18) in.; sleeve seam 7½ (9, 10½, 12) in.; inner leg seam of trousers 10 (12, 14, 16) in.; front waist to crutch 6½ (7, 7½, 8) in.

TENSION
6½ sts. and 8½ rows to 1 in. on No. 9 needles over st.st.

ABBREVIATIONS
See page 22; M., main shade; W., white; C., contrasting shade.

TUNIC
FRONT
With No. 11 needles and M. cast on 88 (96, 104, 112) sts. and work 7 rows in st.st.
8th row: k. to mark hemline. Change to No. 9 needles. Beg. with a k. row, and dec. 1 st. at both ends of 11th row from hemline, work 16 (16, 20, 20) rows in M. in st.st. Dec. 1 st. at both ends of 21st row from hemline

and of every foll. 10th row, cont. in st.st. in colour patt. as follows: work 4 (4, 6, 6) rows in W., 2 (2, 4, 4) rows in first C., 4 rows in second C, 2 rows in M., 4 rows in second C., 2 (2, 4, 4) rows in first C. and 4 (4, 6, 6) rows in W. Now cont. in M. in st.st., dec. as before every 10th row until 78 (84, 90, 96) sts. rem.
Work straight to complete 7½ (9, 10½, 12) in. from hemline, ending after a p. row.
(Note. If necessary, adjust length here.)

Shape Armholes
Cont. in st.st., cast off 3 (3, 4, 4) sts. at beg. of next 2 rows; dec. 1 st. at both ends of next 4 (5, 5, 6) rows and of foll. 2 alt. rows. Work straight on rem. 60 (64, 68, 72) sts. to complete 3 (3½, 4, 4½) in. from beg. of armholes, ending after a p. row.

Shape Front Neck
Next row: patt. 18 (19, 20, 21), k.2 tog.; turn. Patt. another 7 rows, dec. 1 st. at neck edge on next and foll. alt. rows: 15 (16, 17, 18) sts.

Shape Shoulder
Cast off 5 (5, 5, 6) sts. at beg. of next and foll. alt. row and 5 (6, 7, 6) sts. at beg. of next alt. row.
Returning to sts. still on needle, slip first 20 (22, 24, 26) sts. on to a st. holder and complete second front shoulder to match first, reversing shapings.

BACK
Work as for Front, omitting front neck opening and working straight after completion of armhole shaping until Back matches Front to beg. of shoulders.

Shape Shoulders
Cast off 5 (5, 5, 6) sts. at beg. of next 4 rows and 5 (6, 7, 6) sts. at beg. of foll. 2 rows. Leave rem. 30 (32, 34, 36) sts. on a st. holder.

SLEEVES (make 2 alike)
With No. 11 needles and M. cast on 40 (44, 48, 52) sts. and work 7 rows in st.st.
8th row: k. to mark hemline. Change to No. 9 needles.
continued on page 54

Roll-collared dress with a Fair Isle border pattern (see page 54).

Two-colour tunics for big and little sisters (see page 70).

Beg. with a k. row, cont. in st.st., inc. 1 st. at both ends of 7th row from hemline and of every foll. 10th row until you have 50 (54, 60, 66) sts. Work straight to complete 7½ (9, 10½, 12) in. (or length required) from hemline, ending after a p. row.

Top of Sleeve
Cast off 3 (3, 4, 4) sts. at beg. of next 2 rows, 1 st. at beg. of next 6 rows and 2 sts. at beg. of foll. 10 (12, 14, 16) rows. Cast off.

TO COMPLETE
Sew right shoulder seam. With right side facing and No. 11 needles, start at left front shoulder and pick up 13 sts. from each side of neck, and sts. from stitch holders: 76 (80, 84, 88) sts.
With M., work 1 in. in k.1, p.1 rib on No. 11 needles and then 2½ in. on No. 9 needles. Cast off loosely in rib. Sew left shoulder seam, joining sides of polo neck. Sew side and sleeve seams. Set in sleeves. Turn up lower hem and catch lightly in position.

TROUSERS
FRONT (Right Leg)
With No. 11 needles and M. cast on 47 (51, 53, 55) sts. and work 7 rows in st.st.
8th row: k. to mark hemline.
Change to No. 9 needles.
1st row: k.
2nd row: p. 23 (25, 26, 27), keep yarn forward and sl.1 purlwise, p.23 (25, 26, 27).
Keeping the slipped st. correct in this fashion on all p. rows, complete 16 (16, 20, 20) rows in st.st. from hemline, dec. 1 st. at both ends of 7th row from hemline and of 17th (17th, 19th, 19th) row. Continuing to dec. 1 st. at both ends of every 10th (10th, 12th, 12th) row until you have 39 (43, 45, 47) sts., now work the 22 (22, 30, 30) rows in stripe patt. as given for Front of Tunic, and then cont. in M. in st.st. until work measures 10 (12, 14, 16) in. (or length required) from hemline, ending after a p. row, and dec. 1 st. at inner leg edge on the final row for the 24 in. size only: 39 (42, 45, 47) sts.
Leave these sts. on spare needle and work another similar piece for the Left Leg, as before dec. 1 st. at inner leg edge on final row for the 24 in. size only.

To Join Legs and Work Crutch
1st row: k. sts. for Left Leg; cast on 10 sts.; k. sts. for Right Leg.
2nd and alt. rows: p., keeping slipped sts. correct as before.
3rd row: k.38 (41, 44, 46), sl.1 knitwise, k.1, p.s.s.o., k.8, k.2 tog., k.38 (41, 44, 46).
5th row: k.38 (41, 44, 46), sl.1 knitwise, k.1, p.s.s.o., k.6, k.2 tog., k.38 (41, 44, 46). Cont. to dec. by 2 sts. in same fashion every right side row until 78 (84, 90, 94) sts. remain. Keeping slipped sts. correct, work straight to complete 4 (4½, 5, 5½) in. from joining of legs, ending after a p. row.
(Note. If necessary, adjust length here.)

Shape for Waist
1st row: k.2 tog., k.30, k.2 tog., k.10 (16, 22, 26), sl.1 knitwise, k.1, p.s.s.o., k.30, sl.1 knitwise, k.1, p.s.s.o.
Patt. another 11 rows dec. 1 st. at both ends of 9th row: 72 (78, 84, 88) sts.

Waistband
Change to No. 11 needles and cont. in k.1, p.1 rib to complete 6½ (7, 7½, 8) in. from joining of legs. Cast off in rib.

BACK
Work as for Front until Back is one row shorter than Front to beg. of Waistband: 72 (78, 84, 88) sts. Keeping slipped sts. correct, work as follows:
Next rows: patt. 66 (69, 72, 74); turn, k.60; turn, patt. 54; turn, k.48; turn, patt. 42; turn, k.36; turn, patt. 30; turn, k.24; turn, patt. to end of row. Change to No. 11 needles and work Waistband to match Front.

TO COMPLETE
Press, blocking hems and 'creases' in trousers. Sew side seams and inner leg seams. Turn up hems and catch lightly in position. Press all seams. Make a herringbone casing inside waistband and thread with elastic.

Pink, brown and white dress
illustrated in colour on page 52

MATERIALS
5 (5, 6) oz. Lister Lavenda Double Knitting in pink, 2 oz. in brown and 1 oz. in white. One pair each Nos. 9 and 11 knitting needles (USA sizes 5 and 2).

MEASUREMENTS
To fit chest size 22 (24, 26) in.; length 16 (18, 21) in.; sleeve seam 2 in.

TENSION
6 sts. and 8 rows to 1 in. over st.st.

ABBREVIATIONS
See page 22; P., pink; W., white; B., brown.

FRONT
With B. and No. 11 needles cast on 84 (92, 102) sts. and work 7 rows in st.st.
8th row: k. (to mark hemline).
Change to No. 9 needles and beg. with a k. row work 5 rows in st.st.
6th row: join in W. and p. in W.
With B. k. 1 row, p. 1 row (size 26 in. only: dec. 1 st. at both ends of row): 84 (92, 100) sts.
9th row: * k.1 W., k.3 B.; rep. from * to end.
10th row: * (p.1 W., p.2 B.) twice, p.2 W.; rep. from * to last 4 sts., p.1 W., p.2 B., p.1 W.
11th row: k.2 B., k.2 W., * k.1 B., k.2 W., k.3 B., k.2 W.; rep. from * to end.
12th row: * p.3 W., p.1 B.; rep. from * to end.
With W., k. 1 row, p. 1 row. With B., k. 1 row.
Change to P. and beg. with a p. row, cont. in P. in st.st., dec. 1 st. at both ends of 19th row from hemline and of every foll. 10th row until you have 72 (78, 84) sts.
Work straight to complete 11 (12½, 15) in. (or length required) from hemline, ending after a p. row.

Shape Raglan Armholes
Cast off 4 sts. at beg. of next 2 rows.
Next row: k.2, k.2 tog. t.b.l., k. until 4 sts. rem., k.2 tog., k.2.
Next row: p.
Rep. these last 2 rows until 36 (38, 40) sts. rem., ending after a p. row.

Shape Front Neck
Next row: k.2, k.2 tog. t.b.l., k.6; turn.
Dec. 1 st. at neck edge on next and foll. alt. rows, cont. to shape armhole by dec. 1 st. every right-side row until 1 st. rem. Fasten off.
Returning to sts. still on needle, slip first 16 (18, 20) sts. on to a spare needle and complete second front point to match first, reversing shapings.

BACK

Work as for Front, omitting front neck opening and working dec. on every right-side row for armhole shaping until 26 (28, 30) sts. rem. Leave sts. on a spare needle.

SLEEVES (make 2 alike)

With B. and No. 11 needles cast on 50 (54, 58) sts. and work 5 rows in st.st.
6th row: k., inc. 1 st. at both ends of row (hemline).
Cont. with No. 11 needles and B., k. 1 row, p. 1 row, k. 1 row. Change to W. and p. 1 row. With B., k. 1 row, p. 1 row.
7th row: * k. 1 W., k.3 B.; rep. from * to end.
8th row: * p.1 W., p.1 B.; rep. from * to end.
9th row: k. in W.
10th row: p. in B.
Change to No. 9 needles and P. and, starting with a k. row, cont. in st.st. to complete 2 in. (or length required) from hemline, ending after a p. row.

Top of Sleeve

Follow instructions for shaping armholes for Front, cont. to dec. until 6 sts. rem. (all sizes). Leave sts. on a spare needle.

TO COMPLETE

Sew raglan seams, leaving seam open between Back and left sleeve.

Polo Neck

With right side facing and No. 11 needles, start at top of left sleeve and pick up all sts. from spare needles round neck, and also 8 sts. from each side of neck: 70 (74, 78) sts.
With P., and working in k.1, p.1 rib, work 1 in. on No. 11 needles and 2 in. on No. 9 needles. Cast off.

To Make Up.

Press well, blocking hems. Sew seam between Back and Left Sleeve, joining sides of polo neck. Sew side seams and sleeve seams. Turn up all hems and catch lightly in position. Press all seams.

Stocking cap

MATERIALS

5 oz. Hayfield Gaylon Double Knitting in main shade and 1 ball in each of two contrasting shades. One pair each Nos. 10 and 11 knitting needles (USA sizes 3 and 2).

MEASUREMENTS

To fit child's average-sized head; approx. 16 in. round lower edge.

TENSION

6 sts. to 1 in. with No. 10 needles.

ABBREVIATIONS

See page 22; M., main shade; A., first contrasting shade; B., 2nd contrasting shade.

TO MAKE

With No. 11 needles and M., cast on 94 sts.
Work 10 rows k.1, p.1 rib.
Next row: p.
Next row: k.
Break M. and join A.
Work in st.st. beg. with a k. row.
Work 6 rows straight.
Begin the Fair Isle patt., working in st.st. taking colour from chart on the right where stated.

Read odd-numbered rows, k. rows, from right to left and even-numbered rows, p. rows, from left to right.
1st row: k.: 7 A., work next 17 sts. as first row chart, 14 A., work next 17 sts. as first row chart, 14 A., work next 17 sts. as first row chart, 8 A.
Now working sts. between chart panels in A., complete the 16 rows from the chart, thus ending with a p. row. Work a further 6 rows in st.st. Break A. and join M.
Next row: p.
Next row: k.
Next row: * k.1, p.1; rep. from * to end.
Next row: p.
Rep. last 2 rows for patt. for rem. of Cap.
Cont. straight until work measures 16 in. ending with a p. row.
Keeping patt. correct k. 2 tog. at each end of each row until 18 sts. remain.

continued on page 58

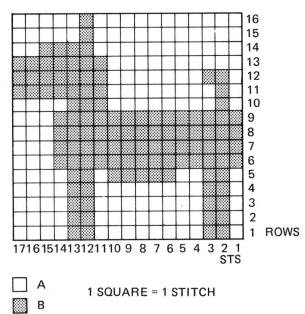

17 16 15 14 13 12 11 10 9 8 7 6 5 4 3 2 1
STS

16 15 14 13 12 11 10 9 8 7 6 5 4 3 2 1 ROWS

☐ A   ▦ B   **1 SQUARE = 1 STITCH**

Junior-style cape sets: blue cape and its teaming cream dress are both worked in traditional Aran stitches (see page 73). Little Red Riding Hood outfit has a roll-collared, cable-patterned cape, warm trousers and a smart peaked cap (see page 75).

Break yarn leaving a long end, thread yarn through needle and draw through sts. on knitting needle. Pull tightly and fasten securely.

TO COMPLETE
Press st.st. on wrong side of work under a damp cloth with a warm iron. Avoid all ribbing. Join seam. Make a pompon with M. and A. using card circles 2 in. in diameter with holes approx. 1 in. in diameter. Trim and sew to end of cap.

Bonnet and muff
illustrated in colour on page 25

MATERIALS
2 balls (50 gr. each) Patons Promise for bonnet, 1 ball for muff. One pair each Nos. 8 and 10 knitting needles (USA sizes 6 and 3). 2½ yd. ribbon, 1 in. wide.

MEASUREMENTS
Face edge of bonnet approx. 14 in.; length of muff 6½ in.; width of muff 5½ in.

TENSION
10 sts. and 16 rows to 2 in. over pattern on No. 8 needles.

ABBREVIATIONS
See page 22; m.l., make loops by knitting next st., winding yarn 3 times over needle and round first and second fingers of left hand, then over needle again, draw 4 loops through, then place loops back on left needle and knit them together with st. through back of loops.

BONNET
With No. 10 needles, cast on 65 sts. and work 4 rows st.st., starting with a k. row.
Next row: k.1, * y.fwd., k.2 tog.; rep. from * to end. Starting with a p. row, work 5 rows in st.st.
Next row: make hem by knitting tog. 1 st. from needle and 1 loop from cast-on edge all across row.
Next row: k.
Change to No. 8 needles and work in main patt. as follows:
1st row (right side): p.
2nd row: k.1, * m.l., k.1; rep. from * to end.
3rd and 5th rows: p.
4th row: k.
6th row: m.l., * k.1, m.l.; rep. from * to end.
7th row: p.
8th row: k.
These 8 rows form patt.
Continue straight in patt. until Bonnet measures 5½ in., ending with right side facing.
Next row: cast off 21, patt. to last 21 sts., cast off 21.

Break off yarn.
Rejoin yarn to remaining group of 23 sts. and continue in patt. for 4½ in. ending with right side facing. Cast off.

TO COMPLETE
Using a cool iron and dry cloth, press parts lightly on wrong side, taking care not to spoil pattern.
Using a fine backstitch seam, join cast-off sts. to sides of Bonnet.
With No. 10 needles and right side facing, pick up 57 sts. along lower edge of Bonnet leaving sides of hem free.
** Work 3 rows in st.st., starting with a p. row.
Next row: k.1, * y.fwd., k.2 tog.; rep. from * to end.
Work 3 rows in st.st., starting with a p. row. Cast off.
Fold band in half to wrong side and slip-stitch neatly in position. **
Join side of hems together. Press seams. Cut two lengths of ribbon, each 2 ft. 3 in. Make rosettes with ribbon leaving ends to tie, and stitch to sides of Bonnet.

MUFF
With No. 8 needles, cast on 29 sts. and work in patt. as for main patt. of Bonnet until piece measures 9 in. ending with right side facing. Cast off.

TO COMPLETE
Press as for Bonnet.
With No. 10 needles, pick up 51 sts. along side edges and work as for Bonnet from ** to **.
Join seam. Press seam. Attach remaining ribbon to each side of Muff.

Aran waistcoat

MATERIALS
7 (8, 8, 9) balls (50 gr. each) Mahony's Blarney Bainin (USA Blarneyspun). One pair each Nos. 7, 8 and 10 knitting needles (USA sizes 7, 6 and 3). One cable needle. 4 (4, 4, 5) buttons ⅝ in. in diameter.

MEASUREMENTS
To fit chest size 26 (28, 30, 32) in.; length 18½ (20, 21½, 23) in.

TENSION
5 sts. and 6½ rows to 1 in. over double moss st.

ABBREVIATIONS
See page 22; tw.l., twist left: pass right-hand needle behind first st. on left-hand needle, k. 2nd st. on left-hand needle through front of loop, k. first st. then slip both sts. off needle tog.; tw.r., twist right: pass right-hand needle in front of first st. on left-hand needle, k. 2nd st. through front of loop, then k. first st. and slip both sts. off needle tog.; c.4 f., cable 4 front: slip next 2 sts. on to cable needle and leave at front of work, k.2, then k.2 from cable needle; c.4 b., cable 4 back: slip next 2 sts. on to cable needle and leave at back of work, k.2 then k.2 from cable needle.
Note. The waistcoat may be made for a boy or a girl.

BACK
With No. 10 needles cast on 71 (77, 83, 89) sts. and work in rib.
1st row (right side): k.2, * p.1, k.1; rep. from * to last st., k.1.
2nd row: k.1, * p.1, k.1; rep. from * to end. Rep. these 2 rows twice more, then first row again.
Inc. row: rib 6 (8, 10, 12), * k.1, p.1, p. twice into next st., p.1, k.3, p.3, p. twice into next st., p.3, k.3, p.1, p. twice into next st., p.1, k.1, * rib 17 (19, 21, 23); rep.

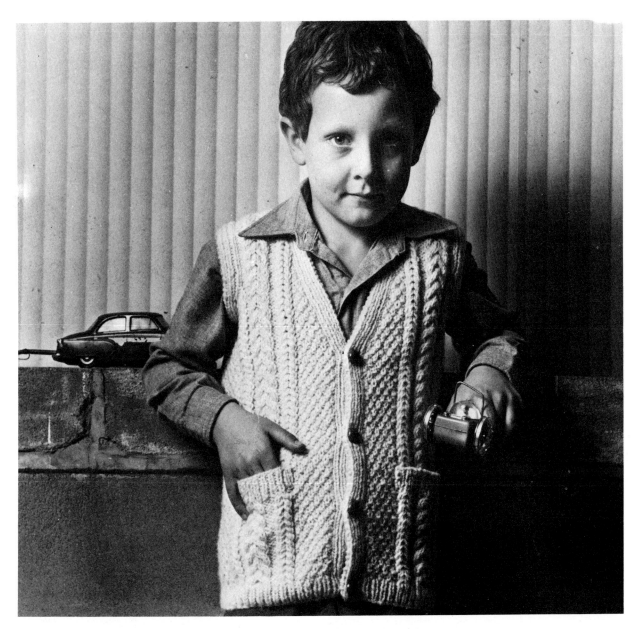

from * to *, rib 6 (8, 10, 12): 77 (83, 89, 95) sts.
Change to No. 7 needles and begin the 4-row patt.
1st patt. row: (k.1, p.1) 3 (4, 5, 6) times, * p.1, tw.l., tw.r., p.3, k.8, p.3, tw.l., tw.r., p.1, * (p.1, k.1) 8 (9, 10, 11) times, p.1; rep. from * to *, (p.1, k.1) 3 (4, 5, 6) times.
2nd patt. row: (p.1, k.1) 3 (4, 5, 6) times, * k.1, p.4, k.3, p.8, k.3, p.4, k.1 *, (k.1, p.1) 8 (9, 10, 11) times, k.1; rep. from * to *, (k.1, p.1) 3 (4, 5, 6) times.
3rd patt. row: (p.1, k.1) 3 (4, 5, 6) times, * p.1, tw.l., tw.r., p.3, c.4 f., c.4 b., p.3, tw.l., tw.r., p.1 *, (k.1, p.1) 8 (9, 10, 11) times, k.1; rep. from * to *, (k.1, p.1) 3 (4, 5, 6) times.
4th patt. row: (k.1, p.1) 3 (4, 5, 6) times, * k.1, p.4, k.3, p.8, k.3, p.4, k.1 *, (p.1, k.1) 8 (9, 10, 11) times, p.1; rep. from * to *, (p.1, k.1) 3 (4, 5, 6) times.
Continue in patt., inc. 1 st. at each end of row when work measures 6¼ (6½, 6¾, 7) in. from beginning and again when work measures 9½ (10¼, 11, 11¾) in., working the extra sts. in double moss st. as side panels. Continue straight on these 81 (87, 93, 99) sts. until work measures 13 (14, 15, 16) in. from beginning.

Shape Armholes
Cast off 4 (5, 6, 6) sts. at beginning of next 2 rows, 2 sts. at beginning of next 6 rows and 1 st. at beginning of next 6 (6, 6, 8) rows: 55 (59, 63, 67) sts. remain.
Continue straight until work is 18½ (20, 21½, 23) in.

Shape Shoulders
Cast off 5 sts. at beginning of next 4 rows and 6 (7, 8, 9) sts. at beginning of next 2 rows. Cast off remaining 23 (25, 27, 29) sts. for back neck.

POCKET LININGS (make 2 alike)
With No. 8 needles cast on 21 (21, 25, 25) sts. and work in rib as for Back for 23 (23, 27, 27) rows.
Inc. row: rib 0 (0, 2, 2) sts., work from * to * of inc. row of Back, rib 0 (0, 2, 2): 24 (24, 28, 28) sts.
Break yarn and leave sts. on a holder.

RIGHT FRONT
With No. 10 needles cast on 41 (45, 47, 51) sts.

continued on page 62

For high days and holidays—gaily-striped sweater and teaming knickerbockers (see page 82).

Roll-collar pullover is worked mainly in rib, with
a honeycomb-patterned yoke section (see page 105).

For Boy's Waistcoat: work in rib as for Back for 7 rows.
For Girl's Waistcoat: work in rib as for Back for 2 rows, then make buttonhole.
3rd (buttonhole) row: rib 3, cast off 2, rib to end.
Next row: cast on 2 sts. over cast-off sts. of previous row.
Work 3 more rows in rib.
For Girl's or Boy's Waistcoat. For size 26 only.
Inc. row: rib 6, work from * to * of inc. row of Back, rib 7, work twice into next st., slip remaining 6 sts. on to a safety pin for front border.
For size 28 only. Inc. row: rib 8, work from * to * of inc. row of Back, rib 10, slip remaining 6 sts. on to a safety pin for front border.
For size 30 only. Inc. row: rib 10, work from * to * of inc. row of Back, rib 9, work twice into next st., slip remaining 6 sts. on to a safety pin for front border.
For size 32 only. Inc. row: rib 12, work from * to * of inc. row of Back, rib 12, slip remaining 6 sts. on to a safety pin for front border.
For all sizes: change to No. 7 needles and work in patt. on the 39 (42, 45, 48) sts. of main part as follows.
1st row: p.1 (0, 1, 0), (k.1, p.1) 4 (5, 5, 6) times, work from * to * of first patt. row of Back, (p.1, k.1) 3 (4, 5, 6) times.
Continue in patt. as now set working one rep. of patt. and keeping 9 (10, 11, 12) sts. in double moss st. at front edge, until you have worked 7 (7, 8, 8) complete patts.

Pocket Opening
Next row: double moss st. 9 (10, 9, 10), slip next 24 (24, 28, 28) sts. on to a st. holder, then work on sts. of one pocket lining, double moss st. 0 (0, 2, 2), work from * to * of first patt. row, double moss st. 0 (0, 2, 2), then work remaining 6 (8, 8, 10) sts. of row in double moss st.
** Continue in patt. as before, inc. 1 st. at side edge in the same positions as the side incs. of Back, then continue on these 41 (44, 47, 50) sts. until work measures 11½ (12¼, 13, 13¾) in. from beginning, ending at front edge.

Shape Front Slope
Cast off 1 st. at beginning of next row and at same edge on every foll. 4th row 11 (12, 13, 14) times in all, and **at same time** keep side edge straight until work measures 13 (14, 15, 16) in. from beginning, ending at side edge.

Shape Armhole
Cast off 4 (5, 6, 6) sts. at beginning of next row, 2 sts. at same edge on next 3 alt. rows and 1 st. at same edge on next 3 (3, 3, 4) alt. rows.
Now keep side edge straight but continue with front decs. until all are completed, then continue straight on remaining 17 (18, 19, 20) sts. until work measures 18½ (20, 21½, 23) in., ending at side edge.

Shape Shoulder
Cast off 5 sts. at beginning of next row and next alt. row Work 1 row, then cast off remaining 7 (8, 9, 10) sts. **.

LEFT FRONT
With No. 10 needles cast on 41 (45, 47, 51) sts.
For Girl's Waistcoat: work 7 rows in rib.
For Boy's Waistcoat: work in rib for 2 rows, then make buttonhole.
3rd (buttonhole) row: rib to last 5 sts., cast off 2, rib to end.
Next row: cast on 2 sts. over 2 cast-off sts. of previous row.

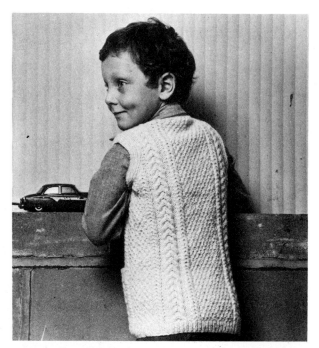

Work 3 more rows in rib.
For Boy's or Girl's Waistcoat. For size 26 only.
Inc. row: rib 6 and slip these sts. on to a safety pin for front border, work twice into next st., rib 7, work from * to * of inc. row of Back, rib 6.
For size 28 only. Inc. row: rib 6, and slip these sts. on to a safety pin for front border, rib 10, work from * to * of inc. row of Back, rib 8.
For size 30 only. Inc. row: rib 6 and slip these sts. on to a safety pin for front border, work twice into next st., rib 9, work from * to * of inc. row of Back, rib 10.
For size 32 only. Inc. row: rib 6 and slip these sts. on to a safety pin for front border, rib 12, work from * to * of inc. row of Back, rib 12.
For all sizes: change to No. 7 needles and patt. on these 39 (42, 45, 48) sts.
1st row: (k.1, p.1) 3 (4, 5, 6) times, work from * to * of first patt. row of Back, (p.1, k.1) 4 (5, 5, 6) times, p.1 (0, 1, 0).
Continue in patt. as now set with 9 (10, 11, 12) sts. in double moss st. at front edge until the 7th (7th, 8th, 8th) patt. is completed.

Pocket Opening
Next row: double moss st. 6 (8, 8, 10), slip next 24 (24, 28, 28) sts. on to a st. holder, work sts. of pocket lining as Right Front, double moss st. rem. 9 (10, 9, 10) sts.
Complete as given for Right Front from ** to **, working all shapings at opposite edges.

FRONT BORDERS
Slip the sts. of front border on which the buttonhole has been made on to a No. 10 needle with point at inner edge, join yarn, cast on 1 st., rib to end.
Continue in rib on these 7 sts. making (3, 3, 4) more buttonholes in same way as before each 3¼ (3½, 3¾, 3) in. above cast-off edge of previous one.
Continue in rib until strip is long enough to fit along front edge to shoulder when slightly stretched. Leave sts. on a pin with a few yards of yarn hanging. Work other border in a similar way omitting buttonholes.

ARMHOLE BORDERS (make 2 alike)
With No. 10 needles cast on 7 sts. and work in rib for 12 (13, 14, 15) in. Cast off.

TO COMPLETE
Pocket Tops
Slip sts. from holder at one pocket opening on to a No. 10 needle so that right side is facing for first row and join yarn.
1st row: k.2, (p.1, k.1) 5 (5, 6, 6) times, work twice into next st., (p.1, k.1) 5 (5, 6, 6) times, k.1.
Cont. in rib as given for Back, beginning with 2nd row, for 5 more rows. Cast off ribwise.
Work other pocket top in same way.

To Make Up
Do not press. Back st. shoulder and side seams. Press seams lightly on wrong side with warm iron over damp cloth. Pin front borders in place stretching them to fit as far as shoulder. Back st. as pinned to within ½ in. of shoulder, slip sts. on to a needle and continue in rib on each border until they meet at centre back neck. Cast off. Join ends of borders with a flat join and back st. remainder of inner edges in place.
Join ends of each armhole border with a flat join. Back st. borders in place stretching them to fit. Press all border seams using point of iron so as not to flatten rib. Slip st. edges of pocket linings in place on wrong side and neatly sew sides of pocket tops in place. Sew on buttons to match buttonholes.

Classic sweater
illustrated in colour on page 28

MATERIALS
7 (8, 8) balls (1 oz. each) Wendy Peter Pan Bri-Nylon Super Crimp 4-ply. One pair each Nos. 9 and 11 knitting needles (USA sizes 5 and 2). One set of four No. 11 knitting needles (USA size 2) with points at both ends.

MEASUREMENTS
To fit chest size 26 (28, 30) in.; length 15½ (16½, 17½) in.; sleeve seam 13 (14, 15) in.

TENSION
7 sts. and 9 rows to 1 in. with No. 9 needles.

ABBREVIATIONS
See page 22.

FRONT
With No. 11 needles cast on 95 (103, 111) sts.
1st row: k.2, * p.1, k.1; rep. from * to last st., k.1.
2nd row: * k.1, p.1; rep. from * to last st., k.1.
Rep. first and 2nd rows 7 times more.
Change to No. 9 needles and patt.
1st row: k.38 (42, 46) sts., p.1, (k.1, y.f., sl.1, k.2 tog., p.s.s.o., y.f., k.1, p.1) 3 times, k. to end.
2nd row: p.38 (42, 46) sts., k.1, (p.5, k.1) 3 times, p. to end.
3rd row: k.38 (42, 46) sts., p.1, (k.2, y.f., sl.1, k.1, p.s.s.o., k.1, p.1) 3 times, k. to end.
4th row: as 2nd row.
5th row: k.38 (42, 46) sts., p.1, (k.5, p.1) 3 times, k. to end.
6th row: as 2nd row.
These 6 rows form the patt. Cont. in patt. Work straight until the Front measures 9½ (10, 10½) in. from cast-on edge, ending with a wrong-side row.

Shape Raglan Armholes
Cast off 2 (3, 4) sts. at beg. of next 2 rows.
3rd row: k.2, sl.1, k.1, p.s.s.o., patt. to last 4 sts., k.2 tog., k.2.
4th row: patt.

Rep. 3rd and 4th rows until 53 (55, 59) sts. remain, ending with a wrong-side row.

Shape Neck
Next row: k.2, sl.1, k.1, p.s.s.o., patt. 16 (16, 18) sts., cast off 13 (15, 15) sts. loosely, patt. to last 4 sts., k.2 tog., k.2.
Work on last set of sts. only.
Cont. raglan shaping, dec. 1 st. at neck edge on the next 5 rows, and then on the foll. 4 (4, 5) alt. rows.
Next row: k.1, k.2 tog., k.1.
Next row: p.1, p.2 tog.
K. tog. the 2 rem. sts. and fasten off.
Rejoin yarn to rem. sts. at neck edge.
Cont. raglan shaping, dec. 1 st. at neck edge on the next 5 rows, and then on the foll. 4 (4, 5) alt. rows.
Next row: k.1, sl.1, k.1, p.s.s.o., k.1.
Next row: p.2 tog., p.1.
K. tog. the 2 rem. sts. and fasten off.

BACK
With No. 11 needles cast on 93 (101, 109) sts.
Work 16 rows in ribbing as for Front.
Change to No. 9 needles and st.st.
Work straight until Back measures 9½ (10, 10½) in. from cast-on edge, ending with a p. row.

Shape Raglan Armholes
Cast off 2 (3, 4) sts. at beg. of next 2 rows.
3rd row: k.2, sl.1, k.1, p.s.s.o., k. to last 4 sts., k.2 tog., k.2.
4th row: p.
Rep. 3rd and 4th rows until 35 (37, 39) sts. remain ending with a 4th row.
Cast off loosely.

SLEEVES (make 2 alike)
With No. 11 needles cast on 49 (53, 55) sts.
Work 20 rows in ribbing as for Front.
Change to No. 9 needles and st.st.
Work 4 rows.
Inc. 1 st. at each end of the next row, and then every 6th row until there are 71 (75, 79) sts.
Work straight until Sleeve measures 13 (14, 15) in. from cast-on edge, ending with a p. row.

Shape Top
Cast off 2 (3, 4) sts. at beg. of next 2 rows. Work 2 rows.
5th row: k.2, sl.1, k.1, p.s.s.o., k. to last 4 sts., k.2 tog., k.2.
6th to 8th rows: st.st.
Rep. 5th to 8th rows 1 (2, 3) times more.
Next row: as 5th row.
Next row: p.
Rep. last 2 rows until 15 sts. remain ending with a p. row. Cast off loosely.

TO COMPLETE
Press each piece lightly with warm iron and damp cloth. Sew raglan seams.

Neck Borders
Now using the set of 4 No. 11 needles, with points at both ends, pick up and k.33 (35, 37) sts. along back neck edge, 13 sts. from left sleeve top, 17 (17, 18) sts. down left side of front neck to the cast-off sts., 13 (15, 15) sts. from the cast-off sts. at centre front, 17 (17, 18) sts. up right side of front neck, and 13 sts. from right sleeve top.
Work 9 rounds in k.1, p.1 rib.
Cast off loosely in rib.

To Make Up
Sew side and sleeve seams. Press seams.

Chapter five
MATCHED SETS

Mother and daughter trouser suits
illustrated opposite

MATERIALS
For mother's trouser suit: 25 (27, 29) oz. Lister Lavenda Double Knitting Wool for cardigan, 20 (22, 24) oz. for trousers. One pair each Nos. 9 and 10 knitting needles (USA sizes 5 and 3). Fifteen small buttons. A waist length of elastic, ¾ in. wide. **For daughter's trouser suit:** 19 (21, 23) balls (20 gr. each) Wendy Tricel Nylon Double Knitting. One pair each Nos. 8 and 11 knitting needles (USA sizes 6 and 2). Four medium buttons. A waist length of elastic, ½ in. wide.

MEASUREMENTS
Mother's trouser suit: to fit bust size 34 (36, 38) in.; hip size 36 (38, 40) in.; length of cardigan 32 (32¼, 32½) in.; sleeve seam 18 in.; length of trousers measured down side 40 in. **Daughter's trouser suit:** to fit chest size 22 (24, 26) in.; length of coat 16 (18, 21) in.; sleeve seam 7½ (9, 10½) in.; inner leg seam of trousers 10 (12, 14) in.; front waist to crutch 6½ (7, 7½) in.

TENSION
Mother's trouser suit: 6 sts. and 8½ rows to 1 in. over patt. on No. 9 needles. **Daughter's trouser suit:** 6 sts. and 8 rows to 1 in. over st.st. on No. 8 needles.

ABBREVIATIONS
See page 22; p.g.st., purl garter stitch (i.e. purl every row); p.f.b., purl into front and back of next st.; m.1, make 1 st. by taking yarn over needle.

MOTHER'S TROUSER SUIT
CARDIGAN BACK
With No. 10 needles cast on 128 (132, 138) sts. and work 13 rows in p.g.st. (see Abbreviations).
14th row (wrong side): p.10 (3, 6), * p.f.b., p.8; rep. from * to last 10 (3, 6) sts., p.f.b., p.9 (2, 5): 141 (147, 153) sts.
Change to No. 9 needles and patt. as follows:
1st row. For size 34: p.3, * k.5, p.5; rep. from * to last 8 sts., k.5, p.3. **For size 36:** k.1, * p.5, k.5; rep. from * to last 6 sts., p.5, k.1. **For size 38:** k.4, * p.5, k.5; rep. from * to last 9 sts., p.5, k.4.
2nd row (all sizes): p.
These 2 rows form patt. Continue in patt. for 14 more rows, then dec. 1 st. at both ends of next row and every following 8th row until 127 (133, 139) sts. remain, dec. 1 st. at both ends of every following 12th row until 119 (125, 131) sts. remain, after which dec. 1 st. at both ends of every following 16th row until 111 (117, 123) sts. remain.
Continue without shaping until work measures 24 in. from beg., ending with a wrong-side row.
Now change to yoke patt. as follows:
1st row: k.1 (2, 1), * p.1, k.1; rep. from * to last 2 (3, 2) sts., p.1, k.1 (2, 1).
2nd row: p.
These 2 rows form yoke patt. Rep. them once more.

Armhole Shaping
Cast off in patt. 6 sts. at beg. of next 2 rows and 5 (6, 7) sts. at beg. of next 4 rows: 79 (81, 83) sts. Continue in yoke patt. until work measures 8 (8¼, 8½) in. from beg. of yoke section.

Shoulder Shaping
Cast off in patt. 6 sts. at beg. of next 4 rows and 9 (10, 11) sts. at beg. of next 2 rows. Cast off remaining 37 sts. for back neck.

RIGHT FRONT
With No. 10 needles cast on 70 (72, 75) sts. and work 13 rows in p.g.st.
14th row: p.10 (3, 6), * p.f.b., p.8; rep. from * to last 6 sts., p.6: 76 (79, 82) sts.
Change to No. 9 needles and work in patt. with front border in p.g.st.
1st row: p.8, * k.5, p.5; rep. from * to last 8 (1, 4) sts., then for size 34 only: k.5, p.3 (for size 36 only: k.1; for size 38 only: k.4).
2nd row: p.
These 2 rows form patt. for right front. Continue in patt. until work measures 2½ in. from beg., ending with a 2nd row and noting that **all** measurements must be taken on main patt. section, not close to border. Now make buttonhole as follows:
1st row: p.2, p.2 tog. through back of loops, wind yarn twice round right-hand needle, p.2 tog., p.2, patt. to end.
2nd row: p. until the double loop is reached, drop one loop to make a long st. and work k.1, p.1 into this st., p.3.
Make further buttonholes in a similar way when work measures 4½ in., 6½ in., 8½ in., 10½ in., 12½ in., 14½ in., 16½ in., 18½ in., 20½ in., 22½ in., 24½ in., 26½ in. and 28½ in. from beg. on main part; but at same time, when you have worked 16 rows in patt. start side shapings. Dec. 1 st. at side edge on next row and every following 8th row until 69 (72, 75) sts. remain, dec. 1 st. at same edge on every following 12th row until 65 (68, 71) sts. remain, then dec. 1 st. at same edge on every following 16th row until 61 (64, 67) sts. remain. Continue without shaping until work measures 24 in. from beg., ending with a wrong-side row. Now change to yoke patt. still keeping p.g.st. border.
1st row: p.8, * k.1, p.1; rep. from * to last 1 (2, 1) sts., k.1 (2, 1). **2nd row:** p.
Rep. these 2 rows once, then first row again, thus ending at side.

Armhole Shaping
** Cast off 6 sts. at beg. of next row and 5 (6, 7) sts. at beg. of next 2 alternate rows. Continue on remaining 45 (46, 47) sts. keeping patt. correct until work measures 6 in. from beg. of yoke patt., ending at front edge.

Neck and Shoulder Shaping
1st row: p.8, and slip off these sts. on to a safety pin for neck border, continue along row, cast off 4, work to end. Now cast off at neck edge 2 sts. at beg. of next 4 alternate rows and 1 st. at same edge on next 4 alternate rows. You have thus ended at side edge: 21 (22, 23) sts. remaining.

For size 36 only: work 2 rows straight. **For size 38 only:** work 4 rows straight. **All sizes:** cast off for shoulder 6 sts. at beg. of next row and next alternate row. Work 1 row. Cast off remaining 9 (10, 11) sts. **

LEFT FRONT
With No. 10 needles cast on 70 (72, 75) sts. and work 13 rows in p.g.st.

14th row: p.6, * p.8, p.f.b.; rep. from * to last 10 (3, 6) sts., p. to end: 76 (79, 82) sts.
Change to No. 9 needles and work in patt. with p.g.st. border.
1st row. For size 34: p.3, k.5; **for size 36**: k.1; **for size 38**: k.4; then **for all sizes**: * p.5, k.5; rep. from * to last 8 sts., p.8.
2nd row: p.
These 2 rows form patt. for left front. Continue in patt. working the side decs. in same positions as on right front but at opposite edge, until 61 (64, 67) sts. remain, then continue without shaping until work measures 24 in. from beg., ending with a wrong-side row. Change to yoke patt.
1st row: k.1 (2, 1), * p.1, k.1; rep. from * to last 8 sts., p.8.
2nd row: p.
Rep. these 2 rows once, thus ending at side. Complete as given for right front from ** to ** working all shapings at opposite edges.

SLEEVES (make 2 alike)
With No. 10 needles cast on 53 (57, 61) sts. and work in yoke patt. as given for Back for 2 in.
Change to No. 9 needles and continue in same patt. but inc. 1 st. at both ends of next row and every following 8th row until there are 85 (89, 93) sts. taking extra sts. into patt. Continue without shaping until work measures 18 in. from beg. Place marker loops of contrast wool at each end of last row, then work 22 (24, 26) rows straight. Cast off in patt. 4 sts. at beg. of next 16 rows. Cast off remaining 21 (25, 29) sts.

TO COMPLETE
Neck Border
First join shoulder seams. Slip sts. from left front border on to a No. 9 needle so that point is at inner edge, then with wrong side of work facing you pick up and p.20 (22, 24) sts. along left front neck, 33 sts. across back neck and 20 (22, 24) sts. along right front neck, then p. sts. from front border. Work 4 rows in g.st. across all sts., then make 15th buttonhole on next 2 rows. Change to No. 10 needles and work 7 more rows in p.g.st. Cast off.

To Make Up
Press main patt. sections lightly on wrong side with warm iron and damp cloth. Do not press borders, sleeves or yoke, but lightly press shoulder seams using point of iron. Sew in sleeves joining straight rows above markers to armhole casting-off and cast-off edges of sleeves to sides of armholes. Remove markers and press seams using point of iron, then join side sleeve seams and press in same way. Join side seams matching patt. and press. Sew on buttons.

TROUSERS RIGHT LEG
With No. 10 needles cast on 112 (118, 124) sts. and work 13 rows in p.g.st.
14th row: p.2 (5, 8), * p.f.b., p.8; rep. from * to last 2 (5, 8) sts., p.f.b., p.1 (4, 7): 125 (131, 137) sts.
Change to No. 9 needles and patt.
1st row. For size 34: p.5, * k.5, p.5; rep. from * to end. **For size 36**: k.3, * p.5, k.5; rep. from * to last 8 sts., p.5, k.3. **For size 38**: p.1, * k.5, p.5; rep. from * to last 6 sts., k.5, p.1.
2nd row (all sizes): p.
These 2 rows form patt. Work a further 20 rows straight, then dec. 1 st. at both ends of next row and every following 22nd row until 113 (119, 125) sts. remain. Continue without shaping until work measures 18 in. from beg. Now inc. 1 st. at both ends of next row and every following 8th row until there are 131 (137, 143)

sts., then continue without shaping until work measures 26½ in. from beg., ending with a wrong-side row. **
Inc. 1 st. at both ends of next row, then work 2 rows straight. Rep. last 3 rows 3 times more. Inc. 1 st. at both ends of next row, then work 5 rows straight: 141 (147, 153) sts. and you have ended with a wrong-side row.

*** Crutch Shaping
1st row: cast off 3, work to end.
2nd row: cast off 6, work to end.
3rd row: cast off 2, work to end.
4th row: cast off 5, work to end.
Cast off 2 sts. at beg. of next 2 rows and 1 st. at beg. of next 2 rows. Work 1 row straight, then cast off 1 st. at beg. of next 3 rows. Rep. last 4 rows once: 113 (119, 125) sts.
Continue as follows: work first and 2nd patt. rows straight, dec. 1 st. at both ends of 3rd row, work 4th row straight, dec. at end of 15th row, work 6th row straight, dec. at beg. of 7th and 8th rows, work 9th row straight and dec. at both ends of 10th row. Rep. last 10 rows again: 99 (105, 111) sts. Now dec. 1 st. at both ends of every following 6th row until 83 (89, 95) sts. remain, then continue without shaping until work measures 39½ in. from beg., ending with a wrong-side row.

Waist Shaping
Cast off 11 (14, 17) sts. at beg. of next row and 15 sts. at same edge on next 4 alternate rows. Work 1 row. Cast off remaining 12 (15, 18) sts.

LEFT LEG
Work as given for Right Leg as far as ** but ending with a right-side row. Work next 18 rows as for Right Leg, thus ending again with a right-side row. Complete as for Right Leg from *** to end noting that odd-numbered shaping rows are worked on wrong side and even-numbered rows on right side and waist shaping must start on a wrong-side row.

TO COMPLETE
Press patt. sections lightly on wrong side with warm iron and damp cloth. Backstitch inner leg seams from cast-on edge to beg. of crutch shaping. Press seams. Backstitch leg sections tog. along entire centre front and back seam matching patt. Press seams. Cut elastic to your waist size, overlap ends ½ in. to form a ring and sew securely. Pin elastic inside waist edge of trousers and hold in place with a row of herringbone sts.

DAUGHTER'S TROUSER SUIT
COAT LEFT FRONT
With No. 11 needles cast on 38 (42, 46) sts. and work 7 rows in st.st.
8th row: k. to mark hemline.
Change to No. 8 needles.
1st row: k. to end. Cast on 17 sts.: 55 (59, 63) sts.
2nd row: p.8, keep yarn forward and sl.1 purlwise, p. to end.
3rd row: k.
Rep. these last 2 rows twice more.
8th row: as 2nd row.
9th row: * m.1, k.2 tog.; rep. from * until 15 sts. rem., k.15.
10th row: as 2nd row.
11th row: k. until 17 sts. rem., m.1, k.2 tog., k.15.
Cont. to rep. these last 2 rows, dec. 1 st. at side edge on 13th row from hemline and on every foll. 12th (12th, 14th) row until you have 50 (53, 56) sts. Work straight to complete 10½ (12, 14½) in. from hemline, ending at side edge.
(Note. If necessary, adjust length here.)

Shape Raglan Armholes

Keeping slipped st. and eyelet edging always correct at centre edge, cast off 4 sts. at beg. of next row. Patt. one row.

Next row: k.2, m.1, sl.1 knitwise, k.2 tog., p.s.s.o., patt. to end.

Next row: p.8, with yarn forward, sl.1 purlwise, p. to end.

Rep. these last 2 rows until 31 (32, 33) sts. rem., ending at centre edge.

Shape Front Neck

Next row: cast off 9, patt. 11 (12, 13), and leave these 12 (13, 14) sts. on a spare needle; patt. 10. Dec. 1 st. at neck edge every wrong-side row, cont. to dec. by 1 st. for armhole shaping every right-side row until 1 st. rem. Fasten off. Now mark the positions for 3 equally-spaced buttons on this Front, allowing for a 4th buttonhole on 2nd or 3rd row of neckband.

RIGHT FRONT

Work as Left Front, reversing all shapings. Set patt. on 9th row from hemline as: (9th row) k.15, * k.2 tog., m.1; rep. from * to end.

11th row: k.15, k.2 tog., m.1, k. to end.

Cont. to match Left Front to beg. of armhole shaping, making buttonholes to correspond with button markers as follows:

Buttonhole row: k.4, wind yarn 3 times round needle, k.2 tog., k.6, wind yarn 3 times round needle, k.2 tog., k to end.

Drop the extra double loops on next row.

Shape Armhole

1st row (wrong side): cast off 4, patt. to end.

Next row: k.15, k.2 tog., m.1, k. until 5 sts. rem., k.3 tog., m.1, k.2.

Working armhole shaping in this fashion, cont. and complete to match Left Front.

BACK

With No. 11 needles cast on 84 (92, 100) sts. and work 7 rows in st.st.

8th row: k. to mark hemline.

Change to No. 8 needles and, beg. with a k. row, work 8 rows in st. st.

9th row: k.1, (m.1, k.2 tog.) until 1 st. rem. k.1. **

Starting with a p. row, cont. in st.st., dec. 1 st. at both ends of 13th row from hemline and of every foll. 12th (12th, 14th) row until you have 74 (80, 86) sts. Work straight until Back matches Fronts to beg. of armholes.

Shape Raglan Armholes

Cast off 4 sts. at beg. of next 2 rows.

Next row: k.2, m.1, sl.1 knitwise, k.2 tog., p.s.s.o., k. until 5 sts. rem., k.3 tog., m.1, k.2.

Next row: p.

Rep. these last 2 rows until 26 (28, 30) sts. rem. Leave sts. on a spare needle.

SLEEVES (make 2 alike)

With No. 11 needles cast on 44 (46, 48) sts. and work as for Back to **. Cont. on No. 8 needles and beg. with a p. row, proceed in st. st., inc. 1 st. at both ends of 12th row from hemline and of every foll. 7th row until you have 54 (58, 62) sts. Work straight to complete 7½ (9, 10½) in. (or length required) from hemline, ending after a p. row.

Top of Sleeve

Follow instructions for shaping armholes for Back, cont. to dec. until 8 sts. rem., ending after a p. row.

Next row: k.2, sl.1 knitwise, k.1, p.s.s.o., k.2 tog., k.2. Leave rem. 6 sts. on a spare needle.

TO COMPLETE

Sew raglan seams.

Neckband

With right side facing and No. 11 needles, start at top of Right Front and pick up sts. from spare needles round neck, and also 7 sts. from each side of neck: 76 (80, 84) sts.

P. 1 row. Making a 4th buttonhole in position required, cont as follows:

Next row: k.8, (m.1, k.2 tog.) until 8 sts. rem., k.8. Starting with a p. row, work 6 rows in st. st.

Next row: k. (to form a ridge row on right side). Starting with a k. row, and making another buttonhole to correspond with the one already worked in front of fabric, k. 5 rows. Cast off loosely.

To Make Up

Press lightly, using a cool iron. Sew side and sleeve seams. Turn in front facings and catch lightly in position. Turn up hems and sew. Turn in neckband and sew on inside. Neaten double buttonholes. Press all seams. Sew buttons to correspond with buttonholes.

TROUSERS FRONT

With No. 11 needles cast on 41 (43, 47) sts. and work 7 rows in st. st.

8th row: k. to mark hemline. Change to No. 8 needles.

1st row: k.

2nd row: p.20 (21, 23), keep yarn forward and sl.1 purlwise, p.20 (21, 23).

Rep these last 2 rows 3 times more.

9th row: k.1, * m.1, k.2 tog.; rep. from * to end.

10th row: p.

Keeping the slipped st. correct as in 2nd row on all p. rows, cont. in st.st., dec. 1 st. at both ends of 13th, 23rd and 33rd rows from hemline. Work straight on rem. 35 (37, 41) sts. to complete 10 (12, 14) in. (or length required) from hemline, ending after a p. row, and inc. 1 st. at inner leg edge on final row for 24 in. size only. This completes Right Leg.

Leave these 35 (38, 41) sts. on a spare needle and work another, similar piece for Left Leg.

To Join Legs and Work Crutch

1st row: k. sts. for Left Leg; cast on 10 sts.; k. sts. for Right Leg.

2nd and alt. rows: p., keeping slipped sts. correct.

3rd row: k.34 (37, 40), sl.1 knitwise, k.1, p.s.s.o., k.8, k.2 tog., k.34 (37, 40).

5th row: k.34 (37, 40), sl.1 knitwise, k.1, p.s.s.o., k.6, k.2 tog., k.34 (37, 40).

Cont. to dec. by 2 sts. in a similar way on every right-side row until 70 (76, 82) sts. rem. Work straight to complete 4 (4½, 5) in. from joining of legs, ending after a p. row. *(Note. If necessary adjust length here.)*

Shape for Waist

1st row: k.2 tog., k.24 (27, 30), k.2 tog., k.14, sl.1 knitwise, k.1, p.s.s.o., k.24 (27, 30), sl.1 knitwise, k.1, p.s.s.o.

Keeping slipped sts. correct and starting with a p. row, work another 11 rows in st.st.

Waistband

Change to No. 11 needles and work 1 in. in k.1, p.1 rib. Cast off in rib.

BACK

Work as Front until Back is one row shorter than Front to beg. of waistband: 66 (72, 78) sts.

Keeping slipped sts. correct, work as follows:

Next rows: patt. 60 (63, 66); turn, k.54; turn, patt. 48; turn, k.42; turn, patt. 36; turn, k.30; turn, patt. 24; turn, k.18; turn, patt. to end of row.

Change to No. 11 needles and work waistband to match Front.

TO COMPLETE

Press lightly, using a cool iron. Block hems and 'creases' in trousers. Sew side seams and inner leg seams. Turn up hems and catch in position. Press all seams. Make a herringbone casing inside waistband and thread elastic through.

Fair Isle Cap and Mitts

illustrated opposite, right

MATERIALS

Of Wendy Double Knit Nylonised — 3 oz. green, 2 oz. rust, 1 (2, 2) oz. cream. One pair each Nos. 9 and 11 knitting needles (USA sizes 5 and 2).

MEASUREMENTS

To fit a child of about 2 (4, 6) years; cap at brim 16 (17, 18) in.; mitt from wrist ribbing to fingertip 4 (4½, 5) in.

TENSION

6 sts. to 1 in. over st.st. on No. 9 needles.

ABBREVIATIONS

See page 22; m.1, make one st., by lifting yarn between sts. on row below and k. it t.b.l.; G., green; R., rust; C., cream.

CAP

With G. and No. 11 needles cast on 96 (102, 108) sts. and work 6 rows in k.1, p.1 rib, inc. 1 st. at end of final row.

Change to No. 9 needles and work colour patt. as follows:

1st row: k.1 G., * k.1 R., k.1 G.; rep. from * to end.

2nd row: p.1 G., * p.1 R., p.1 G; rep. from * to end.

3rd row: k. in R.

4th row: p.1 R., * p.2 R., p.1 C., p.3 R.; rep. from * to end.

5th row: k.1 R., * k.1 R., k.3 C., k.2 R.; rep. from * to end.

6th row: p.1 R., * p.1 R., p.3 C., p.2 R.; rep. from * to end.

7th row: k.1 R., * k.2 R., k.1 C., k.3 R.; rep. from * to end.

8th row: p. in R.

This completes one rep. of the 8-row patt.

Work patt. once more, using R. for G. and C. for R., and introducing G. on 4th row.

Work patt. once more, using C. for G. and G. for R., introducing R. on 4th row and working 8th row as follows: in G., p.1, (p.2 tog., p.14 (15, 16)) 6 times: 91 (97, 103) sts.

Rep. 8-row patt. exactly as before, working G. diamonds on R. ground and working 8th patt. row as follows: in R., p.1, (p.2 tog., p.13 (14, 15)) 6 times: 85 (91, 97) sts.

Work 8-row patt. as before, working R. diamonds on C. ground and dec. by 6 sts. in a similar way on 3rd and 8th rows: 73 (79, 85) sts.

Work 8-row patt. as before, working C. diamonds on G. ground and dec. by 6 sts. as before on 3rd and 8th rows: 61 (67, 73) sts. Change to No. 11 needles.

Working in G., k. 1 row, p. 1 row.

Next row: k.1, (k.2 tog., k.8 (9, 10)) 6 times. Dec. by 6 sts. every right-side row until 25 sts. rem., ending after a p. row.

Next row: k.1, * k.2 tog.; rep. from * to end. Thread rem. sts. on to double yarn, pull tight and knot.

MITTS (make 2 alike)

With G. and No. 11 needles cast on 36 (40, 44) sts. and work 2 in. in k.1, p.1 rib, inc. 1 st. at end of final row. Cont. on No. 11 needles, k. 1 row, p. 1 row.

Now work colour patt. as follows:

1st row: k.1 G., * k.1 R., k.1 G.; rep. from * to end.

2nd row: p.1 G., * p.1 R., p.1 G.; rep. from * to end.

3rd row: with R., k.18 (20, 22), m.1 (see Abbreviations), k.1, m.1, k.18 (20, 22).

4th row: p.6 (2, 4) R., (p.1 C., p.5 R.) 2 (3, 3) times, p.1 R., p.1 C., p.1 R., (p.5 R., p.1 C.) 2 (3, 3) times, p.6 (2, 4).

5th row: k.5 (1, 3) R., (k.3 C., k.3 R.) 2 (3, 3) times, with R., k.1, m.1, k.2 C., with R., m.1, k.1, (k.3 R., k.3 C.) 2 (3, 3) times, k.5 (1, 3) R.

6th row: p.5 (1, 3) R., (p.3 C., p.3 R.) 2 (3, 3) times, p.2 R., p.3 C., p.2 R., (p.3 R., p.3 C.) 2 (3, 3) times, p.5 (1, 3) R.

7th row: k.6 (2, 4) R., (k.1 C., k.5 R.) 2 (3, 3) times, with R., k.1, m.1, k.1, k.1 C., with R., k.1, m.1, k.1, (k.5 R., k.1 C.) 2 (3, 3) times, k.6 (2, 4) R.

8th row: p. in R.: 43 (47, 51) sts.

9th row: (k.1 R., k.1 C.) 9 (10, 11) times, m.1 R., k.1 C., (k.1 R., k.1 C.) 3 times, m.1 R., (k.1 C., k.1 R.) 9 (10, 11) times.

10th row: p.1 R., * p.1 C., p.1 R.; rep. from * to end.

Next row: with C. k.27 (29, 31); turn.

Next row: p.9, cast on 2; turn.

Work 2 (2½, 3) in. in st.st. on these sts.

Thread sts. on to a length of yarn, pull tight and knot on inside.

Return to sts. still on needle, and with right side facing, join in C., k. 18 (20, 22) sts. on left-hand needle; turn.

Next row: p.6 (2, 4) C., (p.1 G., p.5 C.) 2 (3, 3) times, pick up and p. 1 st. from base of thumb in G., patt. rem. sts. as (p.5 C., p.1 G.) 2 (3, 3) times, p.6 (2, 4) C.

Complete the G. diamonds on the C. ground and cont. in patt. on sts. as set, matching colour sequence with colour sequence on cap, until work measures 4 (4½, 5) in. (or length required) from top of wrist ribbing. Thread rem. sts. on to double yarn, pull tight and knot on inside.

TO COMPLETE

Press st.st. sections well. Sew seam at back of head of cap. Sew seam round hand of mitt, and sew thumb seam. Press seams. Finish cap with a pompon in the three colours together.

Two-colour cap and mitts (see page 70) and Fair
Isle cap and mitts (see opposite).

Two-colour cap and mitts

illustrated on previous page

MATERIALS
2 oz. Wendy Double Knit Nylonised in main shade, 1 (2, 2) oz. in a contrasting shade. One pair each Nos. 7 and 9 knitting needles (USA sizes 7 and 5).

MEASUREMENTS
To fit a child of about 2 (4, 6) years; cap at brim (slightly stretched) 16 (17, 18) in.; mitt from top of wrist ribbing to fingertip 4 (4½, 5) in.

TENSION
5 sts. and 10 rows to 1 in. on No. 7 needles over the colour patt.

ABBREVIATIONS
See page 22; m.1, make one st., by lifting yarn between sts. on row below and work it in patt. t.b.l.; M., main shade; C., contrasting shade.

CAP
With M. and No. 9 needles cast on 88 (96, 104) sts. and work 8 rows in k.1, p.1 rib, inc. 1 st. at end of final row. Change to No. 7 needles and C. and work colour patt. as follows:
1st row: k.
2nd row: p.
Change to M.
3rd row: k.1, * sl.1 purlwise, k.1; rep. from * to end.
4th row: k.1, * y.fwd., sl.1 purlwise, y.b., k.1; rep. from * to end.
These 4 rows form patt. Cont. in patt. until work measures 5 (5½, 6) in. approx. from cast-on edge, ending after a 2nd patt. row.
Change to No. 9 needles and C.

Crown
1st row: k.1, (k.2 tog., k.7 (8, 9), sl.1 knitwise, k.1, p.s.s.o.) 8 times.
2nd and alt. rows: p.
3rd row: k.1, (k.2 tog., k.5 (6, 7), sl. 1 knitwise, k.1, p.s.s.o.) 8 times: 57 (65, 73) sts.
Cont. to dec. by 16 sts. in a similar way every right-side row until 25 (17, 25) sts. rem., ending after a p. row.
1st and 3rd sizes only. Next row: k.1, * k.2 tog.; rep. from * to end.
All sizes. Thread rem. sts. on to double yarn, pull tight and knot in inside.

MITTS (make 2 alike)
With M. and No. 9 needles cast on 34 (38, 42) sts. and work 2 in. in k.1, p.1 rib, inc. 1 st. at end of final row. Change to No. 9 needles and cont. in patt. as given for Cap for 6 rows.

Shape for Thumb
1st row: k.16 (18, 20), k. twice in next st., sl. 1 st. in patt., k. twice in next st., patt. 16 (18, 20).
2nd row: patt. 16 (18, 20), k.2, patt.1, k.2, patt. 16 (18, 20).
3rd row: patt. 17 (19, 21), m.1 (see Abbreviations), k.3, m.1, patt. 17 (19, 21).
4th row: patt.
5th row: patt. 16 (18, 20), k. twice in next st., patt. 5, k. twice in next st., patt. 16 (18, 20).
Cont. to inc. in a similar way until you have 43 (47, 51) sts., ending after a wrong-side row.
Next row: patt. 26 (28, 30), cast on 1 st.; turn.
Next row: patt. 10, cast on 1 st.; turn.
Patt. 2¼ (2½, 2¾) in. on these 11 sts. Thread sts. on to double yarn, pull tight and knot.

Hand
Return to sts. still on needle and with right side facing, join in yarn to keep patt. correct and patt. the 17 (19, 21) sts. on left-hand needle; turn.
Next row: patt. 17 (19, 21), pick up and patt. 1 st. from base of thumb, patt. rem. 17 (19, 21) sts.
Cont. in patt. on these 35 (39, 43) sts. until work measures 4 (4½, 5) in. (or length required) from top of wrist ribbing. Thread sts. on to double yarn, pull tight and knot.

TO COMPLETE
Do not press. Sew seam at back of head of cap. Sew seam round hand of mitt, and thumb seam.
Finish cap with a pompon in M. on top.

Big and little sister tunics

illustrated in colour on page 53

MATERIALS
3 (4, 4, 5) balls (25 gr. each) Mahony's Blarney Berella Baby yarn in white, 2 (2, 3, 3) balls in green. One pair each Nos. 10 and 11 knitting needles (USA sizes 3 and 2).

MEASUREMENTS
To fit chest size 20 (22, 24, 26) in.; length of tunic 17 (19, 21, 23) in.

TENSION
7 sts. and 14 rows to 1 in. over patt. on No. 10 needles.

ABBREVIATIONS
See page 22; W., white; G., green.

BACK
With No. 11 needles and W. cast on 91 (99, 111, 123) sts. and work in rib.
1st row (right side): k.2, * p.1, k.1; rep. from * to last st., k.1.
2nd row: k.1, * p.1, k.1; rep. from * to end.
Rep. these 2 rows 4 times more, then first row again. Change to No. 10 needles and k.1 row. Join on G. and work in patt. as follows.
1st row: with G. k.3, * sl.1 purlwise keeping y.b., k.3; rep. from * to end.
2nd row: with G. k.3, * y.fwd., sl.1 purlwise, y.b., k.3; rep. from * to end.
3rd and 4th rows: k. in W.
5th row: with G. k.1, * sl.1 purlwise keeping y.b., k.3; rep. from * to last 2 sts., sl.1 purlwise, k.1.
6th row: with G. k.1, * y.fwd., sl.1 purlwise, y.b., k.3; rep. from * to last 2 sts., y.fwd., sl.1 purlwise, y.b., k.1.
7th and 8th rows: k. in W.

These 8 rows form one patt. Continue until 2nd patt. is completed, then dec. 1 st. at both ends of next row and every foll. 16th row until 81 (89, 97, 107) sts. remain, then dec. 1 st. at both ends of every foll. 20th row until 75 (83, 91, 99) sts. remain, taking care to keep patt. correct. Continue without shaping until work measures 12 (13½, 15½, 17) in. from beg., ending with a 2nd or 6th patt. row. **

Armhole Shaping
Cast off 4 (5, 4, 5) sts. at beg. of next 2 rows and 2 sts. at beg. of next 2 (2, 6, 6) rows. Now dec. 1 st. at both ends of next 2 alternate rows after which dec. 1 st. at both ends of every following 4th row 2 (3, 2, 3) times: 55 (59, 63, 67) sts.
Continue without shaping until work measures 16 (18, 20, 22) in. from beg., ending with a 2nd or 6th patt. row.

Neck and Shoulder Shaping
Next row: with W. k.23 (25, 26, 28) and leave these sts. on a spare needle for right back, continue along row, cast off 9 (9, 11, 11) sts., k. to end.
Continue on the 23 (25, 26, 28) sts. now remaining on needle for left back and work 1 row straight. *** Cast off 2 sts. at beg. of next row and next 2 (2, 3, 3) alternate rows and 1 st. at same edge on next 4 (4, 3, 3) alternate rows. You have thus ended at side edge with 13 (15, 15, 17) sts. remaining. Keeping neck edge straight cast off for shoulder 6 (8, 8, 10) sts. at beg. of next row, work 1 row, then cast off remaining 7 sts. ***
With wrong side facing rejoin yarn to inner edge of right back sts. Complete to match left back from *** to ***.

FRONT
Work as for Back to ** making sure there are the same number of patts.

Armhole and Neck Shaping
Cast off 4 (5, 4, 5) sts. at beg. of next 2 rows and 2 sts. at beg. of next 2 (2, 6, 6) rows: 63 (69, 71, 77) sts. remain and you have ended with a 2nd or 6th patt. row.
Next row: with W. k.28 (30, 31, 33) and leave these sts. on a spare needle for left front, continue along row, cast off 7 (9, 9, 11), k. to end.
Continue on the 28 (30, 31, 33) sts. now remaining on needle for right front and work 1 row straight.
**** Cast off 2 sts. at beg. of next row, then dec. 1 st. at armhole edge on following row.
Rep. last 2 rows once. Dec. 1 st. at neck edge on next row, work 1 row straight, dec. at neck edge on next row, then dec. at armhole edge on following row. Rep. last 4 rows once.
For size 20 only: keep armhole edge straight but dec. 1 st. at neck edge on every following 4th row 3 times.
For size 22 only: work 3 rows straight then dec. at both ends of next row, then work 3 rows straight and dec. at neck edge on following row.
For size 24 only: dec. 1 st. at neck edge on every following 4th row 4 times.
For size 26 only: dec. 1 st. at both ends of following 4th row, then dec. at neck edge on every 4th row twice more.
For all sizes: continue on remaining 13 (15, 15, 17) sts. until work measures 17 (19, 21, 23) in. from beg., ending at side.

Shoulder Shaping
Cast off 6 (8, 8, 10) sts. at beg. of next row, work 1 row, then cast off remaining 7 sts. **** With wrong side facing rejoin yarn to inner edge of left front sts. Complete as given for right front from **** to ****.

ARMHOLE BORDERS (make 2 alike)
With No. 11 needles and W. cast on 107 (115, 119, 127) sts. and work 11 rows in rib as on welt. Cast off loosely ribwise.

NECK BORDERS
For front neck work one piece as given for armhole border of same size. For back neck cast on 47 (47, 53, 53) sts. using No. 11 needles and W. Work as for other borders.

TO COMPLETE
Press patt. sections very lightly on wrong side with cool iron; do not use a damp cloth. Backstitch shoulder and side seams carefully matching patt. along sides. Press seams. Join ends of armhole borders. With right side to wrong side of tunic and seam level with side seam, sew cast-on edge of borders to armhole edges with a flat join. Fold border over on to right side so that cast-off edge just covers previous seam. Hold in place by taking a small st. into each p. rib below cast-off edge. Join ends of front neck border to back neck border. Placing seams level with shoulder seams sew on as for armhole borders.

Father and son jackets
illustrated on page 72

MATERIALS
18 (20, 22, 24, 26, 28) balls (¾ oz. each) Hayfield Courtier Double Knitting. One pair each Nos. 10 and 8 knitting needles (USA sizes 3 and 6). 7 (7, 8, 8, 9, 9) buttons ¾ in. in diameter.

MEASUREMENTS
To fit chest size 32 (34, 36, 38, 40, 42) in.; length 24 (26, 28, 29½, 30, 30) in.; sleeve seam 17 (17½, 17½, 18, 18½, 19) in.

TENSION
5½ sts. and 7 rows to 1 in. with No. 8 needles over st.st.

ABBREVIATIONS
See page 22.

BACK
With No. 10 needles cast on 104 (112, 116, 124, 132, 138) sts.
1st row: k.3 (3, 1, 1, 1, 4), p.2, * k.6, p.2; rep. from * to last 3 (3, 1, 1, 1, 4) sts., k. to end.
2nd row: p.3 (3, 1, 1, 1, 4), k.2, * p.6, k.2; rep. from * to last 3 (3, 1, 1, 1, 4) sts., p. to end.
Rep. these 2 rows for 1½ in.
Change to No. 8 needles.
1st row: k.3 (3, 1, 1, 1, 4), p.2, * k.6, p.2; rep. from * to last 3 (3, 1, 1, 1, 4) sts., k. to end.

2nd row: p.

The last 2 rows form the patt. Cont. in patt. Cont. straight until work measures 16 (17, 18, 18, 19, 19) in. ending with a wrong-side row.

Shape Armholes

Cast off 3 (3, 3, 4, 5, 5) sts. at beg. of next 2 rows. Keeping rib patt. correct. dec. 1 st. at each end of the next and every foll. alt. row until 88 (94, 98, 104, 108, 114) sts. remain. Cont. straight until work measures 23 (25, 27, 28½, 29, 29) in.; end with wrong-side row.

Shape Shoulders

Cast off 9 (9, 9, 10, 10, 11) sts. at beg. of next 4 rows, then 8 (9, 10, 10, 11, 11) sts. at beg. of next 2 rows. Cast off rem. 36 (40, 42, 44, 46, 48) sts.

POCKET LININGS (make 2 alike)

With No. 8 needles cast on 24 (24, 28, 28, 30, 30) sts. and work in st.st. for 4 in., ending with a wrong-side row. Leave sts. on a st. holder.

LEFT FRONT

With No. 10 needles cast on 48 (52, 54, 58, 62, 65) sts.
1st row: k.3 (3, 1, 1, 1, 4), p.2, * k.6, p.2; rep. from * to last 3 (7, 3, 7, 3, 3) sts., k. to end.
2nd row: p.3 (7, 3, 7, 3, 3), * k.2, p.6; rep. from * to last 5 (5, 3, 3, 3, 6) sts., k.2, p. to end.
Rep. these 2 rows for 1½ in.
Change to No. 8 needles.
1st row: k.3 (3, 1, 1, 1, 4), p.2, * k.6, p.2; rep. from * to last 3 (7, 3, 7, 3, 3) sts., k. to end.
2nd row: p.
Cont. in patt. as now set. Cont. until work measures 5½ in. ending with a wrong-side row.

Place Pocket

Next row: patt. 14 (18, 17, 21, 22, 25), slip next 24 (24, 28, 28, 30, 30) sts. on to a st. holder, with right side facing, patt. across the sts. of one Pocket Lining, patt. to end.
Cont. now on all sts. until Front measures same as Back to armhole, ending with a wrong-side row.

Shape Armhole and Front Slope

Next row: cast off 3 (3, 3, 4, 5, 5) sts., patt. to last 2 sts., k.2 tog. Dec. 1 st. at front edge on every foll. 4th row until 13 decs. in all have been made at this edge, then on every foll. 3rd row until 14 (16, 17, 18, 19, 20) sts. in all have been dec. at this edge, and at the same time dec. 1 st. at armhole edge on the next 5 (6, 6, 6, 7, 7) alt. rows. Cont. straight until Front measures same as Back to shoulder, ending with a wrong-side row.

Shape Shoulder

Cast off 9 (9, 9, 10, 10, 11) sts. at the beg. of the next and foll. alt. row. Work 1 row, then cast off the rem. 8 (9, 10, 10, 11, 11) sts.

RIGHT FRONT

Work as Left Front, reversing all shapings and position of pocket.

SLEEVES (make 2 alike)

With No. 10 needles cast on 50 (50, 58, 58, 66, 66) sts.
1st row: p.2, * k.6, p.2; rep. from * to end.
2nd row: k.2, * p.6, k.2; rep. from * to end.
Rep. these 2 rows for 3 in.
Change to No. 8 needles.
1st row: p.2, * k.6, p.2; rep. from * to end.
2nd row: p.
Cont. in patt. as now set inc. 1 st. at each end of 7th and every foll. 6th row until there are 74 (80, 86, 92, 96, 96) sts. Cont. straight until Sleeve measures 17 (17½, 17½, 18, 18½, 19) in., ending with a wrong-side row.

Shape Top

Cast off 3 (3, 3, 4, 5, 5) sts. at beg. of the next 2 rows. Dec. 1 st. at each end of the next and every alt. row until 42 (44, 42, 40, 44, 44) sts. remain, then 1 st. at each end of every row until 20 (22, 24, 26, 26, 26) sts. remain. Cast off.

BUTTONBAND

With No. 10 needles cast on 13 sts.
1st row: k.2, * p.1, k.1; rep. from * to last st., k.1.
2nd row: * k.1, p.1; rep. from * to last st., k.1.
Rep. these 2 rows until Band will fit up front edge of Right Front and round to centre back neck when slightly stretched. Cast off.
Mark positions for 7 (7, 8, 8, 9, 9) buttons on this Band, the first ½ in. from bottom, the last just before front slope, and others evenly spaced between.

BUTTONHOLE BAND

Work as Buttonband making buttonholes to correspond with markers as follows:
1st buttonhole row (right side): k.2, p.1, k.1, p.1, cast off 3 sts., work to end.
On the next row, cast on 3 sts. above those cast off. Cont. until band will fit up Left Front and round to centre back neck when slightly stretched. Cast off.

TO COMPLETE

Press all parts with a cool iron over a dry cloth. Join shoulder seams. Set in sleeves, then join side and sleeve seams. Sew on bands and join at back of neck. Sew buttons on to Right Front to match buttonholes.

Pocket Tops

With right side facing and No. 8 needles pick up sts. of one pocket top. Work 8 rows in k.1, p.1 rib, inc. 1 st. at each end of the first row. Cast off in rib.
Work other pocket top in same way.
Sew down pocket linings on inside, then sew down the sides of pocket tops neatly on right side.

Blue and cream cape set

illustrated in colour on pages 56 and 57

MATERIALS

For tunic: 10 (11, 12) balls (50 gr. each) Mahony's Blarney Bainin (USA Blarneyspun). **For cape**: 14 (15, 16) balls (50 gr. each) Mahony's Blarney Bainin (USA Blarneyspun). **For both**: one pair each Nos. 7, 9 and 10 knitting needles (USA sizes 7, 5 and 3). One cable needle. Three buttons ¾ in. in diameter. 1 yard facing ribbon, 1 in. wide.

MEASUREMENTS

To fit chest size 26 (28, 30) in.; length of tunic 23 (24½, 26) in.; length of cape 24½ (26, 27½) in.

TENSION

5 sts. and 6½ rows to 1 in. over rice st. with No. 7 needles.

ABBREVIATIONS

See page 22; k.f.b. (or p.f.b.), k. (or p.) into front and back of next st.; tw.r., twist right: slip next 2 sts. on to cable needle and leave at back of work, k.1, then k.2 from cable needle; tw.l., twist left: slip next st. on to cable needle and leave at front of work, k.2, then k.1 from cable needle.

TUNIC
BACK

With No. 10 needles cast on 85 (93, 101) sts.
1st rib row: k.2, * p.1, k.1; rep. from * to last st., k.1.
2nd rib row: k.1, * p.1, k.1; rep. from * to end. Rep. these 2 rows 3 times.
Inc. row (right side): k.f.b., rib 12 (14, 16), * k.1, (k.f.b., k.1) twice, p.f.b., (k.f.b., k.2) 4 times, k.f.b., p.f.b., (k.1, k.f.b.) twice, k.1 *, rib 9 (13, 17); rep. from * to *, rib 12 (14, 16), k.f.b.: 109 (117, 125) sts. Change to No. 7 needles.
Foundation row: k.14 (16, 18), * p.7, k.2, p.18, k.2, p.7 *, k.9 (13, 17); rep. from * to *, k.14 (16, 18). Now work in patt.
1st patt. row: (k.1 t.b.l., p.1) 7 (8, 9) times, * k.7, p.2, (tw.r., tw.l.) 3 times, p.2, k.7 *, p.1, (k.1 t.b.l., p.1) 4 (6, 8) times; rep. from * to *, (p.1, k.1 t.b.l.) 7 (8, 9) times.
2nd patt. row: as foundation row.
These 2 rows form rice st. patt. over 14 (16, 18) sts. at each side and 9 (13, 17) sts. in centre. Cont. working in rice st. over these sts.
3rd patt. row: rice st. 14 (16, 18), * tw.r., k.1, tw.l., p.2, (tw.l., tw.r.,) 3 times, p.2, tw.r., k.1, tw.l. *, rice st. 9 (13, 17); rep. from * to *, rice st. 14 (16, 18).
4th patt. row: as foundation row.
These 4 rows form patt. over rem. sts. Cont. in patt. Work 4 more rows straight then dec. 1 st. at each end of next row and every foll. 8th row until 97 (103, 109) sts. remain, then dec. 1 st. at each end of every foll. 12th row until 91 (97, 103) sts. remain: 5 (6, 7) sts. in rice st. at each side.
Cont. straight until work measures 16½ (17½, 18½) in.

Shape Armholes

Cast off 4 sts. at beg. of next 2 rows, 2 sts. at beg. of next 4 rows and 1 st. at beg. of next 10 (12, 14) rows: 65 (69, 73) sts.
Cont. straight in patt. with 1 st. at each end in garter st. until work measures 21½ (23, 24½) in., ending with a wrong-side row.

Shape Neck and Shoulders

1st row: patt. 29 (30, 31) and leave these sts. on a st. holder for right back, cast off 7 (9, 11) sts., patt. to end. Cont. on the last set of 29 (30, 31) sts. for left back and

work 1 row straight.
** Cast off 2 (3, 4) sts. at beg. of next row, 2 sts. at same edge on next 3 alt. rows and 1 st. at same edge on next alt. row.
Keeping neck edge straight cast off 9 sts. for shoulder shaping at beg. of next row, work 1 row, then cast off rem. 11 sts. **
With wrong side facing rejoin yarn to inner edge of right back sts. Complete to match left back from ** to **.

FRONT
Work as Back until the first 10 rows of armhole shaping have been worked: 71 (77, 83) sts.

Shape Neck
1st row: cast off 1, patt. until there are 28 (31, 34) sts. on right-hand needle, leave these sts. on a st. holder for left front, cast off 13, patt. to end.
Cont. on the last set of 29 (32, 35) sts. for right front.
2nd row: cast off 1, patt. back to neck edge.
*** Cast off 2 sts. at beg. of next row and 1 st. at armhole edge on foll. row. Rep. last 2 rows 1 (2, 3) times. Cast off 2 sts. at beg. of foll. row, then cont. in patt. on rem. 20 sts. working 1 st. at each end in garter st. until work measures same as Back to beg. of shoulder shaping, ending at side edge.
Cast off 9 sts. at beg. of next row, work 1 row, then cast off rem. 11 sts. ***
With wrong side facing rejoin yarn to inner edge of left front sts. Complete as for right front from *** to ***.

ARMHOLE BORDERS (make 2 alike)
With No. 9 needles cast on 89 (95, 101) sts. and work 4 rows in rib as for welt. Change to No. 10 needles and work 4 more rows. Cast off ribwise.

NECK BORDERS
Front Border
With No. 9 needles cast on 81 (87, 93) sts. and work as for armhole border.

Back Border
With No. 9 needles cast on 51 (53, 55) sts. and work as for armhole border.

TO COMPLETE
Do not press. Join shoulder and side seams using back st. Press seams on wrong side with warm iron and damp cloth. Join ends of armhole borders. With right sides tog. and join level with side seam, back st. cast-on edge of armhole borders to armholes stretching them to fit. Join front and back neck borders at ends. Placing seams at shoulders sew on as for armhole borders. Press border seams with point of iron so as not to flatten rib.

CAPE
BACK
With No. 9 needles cast on 103 (111, 119) sts. Work 8 rows in rib as for Tunic Back but reverse rib by beg. with a 2nd row and ending with a first row.
Inc. row (right side): rib 26 (30, 34), work from * to * of same row of Tunic Back, p.f.b., work from * to * again, rib 26 (30, 34): 126 (134, 142) sts.
Change to No. 7 needles.
Foundation row: k.26 (30, 34), * p.7, k.2, p.18, k.2, p.7 *, k.2; rep. from * to *, k.26 (30, 34).
Now work in patt.
1st patt. row: (k.1 t.b.l., p.1) 13 (15, 17) times, work from * to * of first patt. row of Tunic Back, p.2, work from * to * again, (p.1, k.1 t.b.l.) 13 (15, 17) times.
Cont. in patt. as now set working the 2 patt. panels with 26 (30, 34) sts. in rice st. at each side until the 6th (7th, 8th) patt. is completed. Dec. 1 st. at each end of next row,

then work 11 rows straight. Rep. last 12 rows twice. Dec. 1 st. at each end of next row and every foll. 8th row until 112 (120, 128) sts. remain. Work 7 rows after last dec. row: 23rd (24th, 25th) patt. completed. Now dec. 1 st. at each end of next row and every first patt. row until 100 (106, 112) sts. remain. Work 3 rows straight. Now dec. 1 st. at each end of next row and every right-side row until 86 (90, 94) sts. remain. Work 1 row straight.

Shape Shoulders
Cast off 2 sts. at beg. of next 12 rows, 3 sts. at beg. of next 4 rows, 4 (5, 6) sts. at beg. of next 2 rows and 7 sts. at beg. of next 2 rows. Cast off 28 (30, 32) sts.

RIGHT FRONT
With No. 9 needles cast on 60 (64, 68) sts.
1st rib row: k.2, * p.1, k.1; rep. from * to end. Rep. this row 7 times.
Inc. row (right side): rib 8 and slip these sts. on to a safety pin for border, p.f.b., work from * to * of the inc. row of Tunic Back, rib 26 (30, 34): 64 (68, 72) sts. Change to No 7 needles.
Foundation row: k.26 (30, 34), work from * to * of same row of Back, k.2.
1st patt. row: p.2, work from * to * of first patt. of Tunic Back, (p.1, k.1 t.b.l.) 13 (15, 17) times. Cont. in patt. as now set until the 6th (7th, 8th) patt. has been completed. Dec. 1 st. at end of next row, then work 11 rows straight. Dec. 1 st. at end of next row, work 7 rows straight.

Divide for Slit
1st row of next patt.: p.2, patt. 36, k.1; turn.
Cont. on these 39 sts. for front section working in patt. with the st. next to opening in garter st. until the first row of the 23rd (24th, 25th) patt. has been worked, thus ending at opening edge. Break yarn.
With right side facing rejoin yarn to rem. 23 (27, 31) sts. at opening, rice st. to end. Work 3 rows straight. Dec. 1 st. at side edge on next row then work 11 rows straight. Dec. 1 st. at side edge on next row and every foll. 8th row until 18 (22, 26) sts. remain. Work 4 rows straight, thus having worked same number of rows as on front section, and ending at side edge.
2nd row of patt.: k.18 (22, 26), patt. across 39 sts. of main part pulling yarn tightly across join.
Work 2 rows straight, thus completing 23rd (24th, 25th) patt.
** Cont. across all sts., dec. 1 st. at side edge of next row and every first patt. row until 51 (54, 57) sts. remain. Work 3 rows straight. Dec. 1 st. at side edge on next row and every right-side row until 44 (46, 48) sts. remain. **
Work 2 rows straight, thus ending at side edge.

Shape Shoulder and Neck
Cast off 2 sts. at beg. of next row and next 3 alt. rows. Now cast off 5 (6, 7) sts. for neck shaping at beg. of next row. Cast off 2 sts. at beg. of next 4 rows. Now cast off 3 sts. for shoulder shaping at beg. of next row and 2 sts. at neck edge on foll. row. Rep. last 2 rows once. Cast off 4 (5, 6) sts. at beg. of next row and 2 sts. at neck edge on foll. row. Cast off rem. 7 sts.

LEFT FRONT
With No. 9 needles cast on 60 (64, 68) sts.
1st rib row: * k.1, p.1; rep. from * to last 2 sts., k.2. Rep. this row 7 times.
Inc. row: rib 26 (30, 34), work from * to * of the inc. row of Tunic Back, p.f.b.; turn and slip rem. 8 sts. on to a safety pin for front border.
Change to No. 7 needles.
Foundation row: k.2, work from * to * of same row of

Back, k.26 (30, 34).

1st patt. row: (k.1 t.b.l., p.1) 13 (15, 17) times, work from * to * of first patt. row, p.2.
Cont. in patt. as now set until the 6th (7th, 8th) patt. is completed. Dec. 1 st. at beg. of next row, then work 11 rows straight. Dec. 1 st. at beg. of next row, then work 7 rows.

Divide for Slit

1st row: rice st. 23 (27, 31); turn. Cont. on these sts. Work 3 rows straight, then dec. 1 st. at beg. of next row, work 11 rows straight. Dec. 1 st. at beg. of next row and every foll. 8th row until 18 (22, 26) sts. remain. Work 4 rows straight, thus ending at opening edge. Break yarn. With right side facing rejoin yarn to 39 sts. of front side of opening.
Next row: k.1, patt. 36, p.2.
Cont. in patt. with the st. next to opening in garter st. until the first row of the 23rd (24th, 25th) patt. has been worked.
2nd row: k.2, patt. 36, k.1, then k.18 (22, 26) sts. of side section.
Working shapings at opposite edge cont. as for Right Front from ** to **. Work 1 row straight thus ending at side edge. Work shoulder and neck shaping as for Right Front.

TO COMPLETE
Borders
Slip sts. of Left Front border on to a No. 9 needle with point at inner edge, cast on 1, k. this st. and next st., (p.1., k.1) 3 times, k.1.
Beg. with a 2nd rib row of Tunic Back cont. in rib on these 9 sts. until strip measures 22 (23½, 25) in., ending with a 2nd rib row.
Break yarn and leave sts. on a safety pin.
Slip sts. of Right Front border on to a No. 9 needle with point at inner edge, join yarn, cast on 1, k. this st., (p.1, k. 1) 4 times. Cont. in rib beg. with a first rib row of Tunic Back until strip measures 16½ (18, 19½) in. from beg., ending with a 2nd rib row.
Next (buttonhole) row: rib 3, cast off 3, rib to end.
On next row cast on 3 sts. over buttonhole.
Work 2nd buttonhole when work measures 19½ (21, 22½) in. Cont. until strip measures same as Left Front border, ending with a 2nd row. Do not break yarn. Back st. borders to front edges stretching them slightly to fit as you work.

Neckband
First back st. side and shoulder seams, leaving neck edges open. Return to sts. of Right Front border, rib 9, then on to same needle pick up and k.19 (20, 21) sts. round front neck, 23 (25, 27) sts. across back neck and 19 (20, 21) sts. round Left Front neck, then rib sts. of Left Front border.
Work 1 row in rib across all sts.
3rd row: rib 7, k.2 tog. t.b.l., rib to last 9 sts., k.2 tog., rib 7.
4th row: rib 7, p.2, rib to last 9 sts., p.2, rib 7.
5th and 6th rows: as 3rd and 4th rows but making buttonhole in same way as before.
Rep. 3rd and 4th rows once, then 3rd row again. Cast off ribwise.

To Make Up
Press shoulder and side seams and border seams lightly on wrong side with warm iron and damp cloth; use point of iron along borders so as not to flatten rib. Lightly press ribbing at lower edge so that it does not pull in. Face both sides of front slits with ribbon. Sew buttons on to Left Front to match buttonholes.
Press again lightly.

Red cape set
illustrated in colour on pages 56 and 57

MATERIALS
14 (16, 17, 18) balls (50 gr. each) Wendy Kinvara. One pair each Nos. 9 and 7 knitting needles (USA sizes 5 and 7). One cable needle. ¾ yard elastic, 1 in. wide. Small piece cardboard.

MEASUREMENTS
To fit chest size 26 (28, 30, 32) in.; length 20 (22, 24, 26) in.; trousers inside leg measurement 16 (17, 19, 21) in.; length at side 23 (25, 28, 30) in.

TENSION
4½ sts. and 6 rows to 1 in. with No. 7 needles.

ABBREVIATIONS
See page 22; c.6, cable 6: slip next 3 sts. on to cable needle and leave at back of work, k. next 3 sts. then k. the sts. from the cable needle.

CAPE
BACK
With No. 9 needles cast on 46 (50, 56, 62) sts.
Work 8 rows in k.1, p.1 rib.
Change to No. 7 needles and work in st.st.
Continue straight until work measures 19 (21, 23, 25) in.

Shape Shoulders
Cast off 7 (7, 8, 10) sts. at beg. of next 4 rows. Slip rem. sts. on to a st. holder.

FRONT
With No. 9 needles cast on 57 (57, 66, 75) sts.
Work 8 rows in k.1, p.1 rib.
Change to No. 7 needles and cont. in patt.
1st row: p.3, * k.6, p.3; rep. from * to end.
2nd row: k.3, * p.6, k.3; rep. from * to end.
3rd row: p.3, * c.6, p.3; rep. from * to end.
4th row: as 2nd row.
5th to 8th rows: rep. first and 2nd rows twice. These 8 rows form patt. Cont. straight in patt. until work measures 19 (21, 23, 25) in., ending with a

right-side row.

Next row: (p.1, p.2 tog.) 5 (4, 4, 6) times, patt. to last 15 (12, 12, 18) sts., (p.2 tog., p.1) 5 (4, 4, 6) times.

Shape Shoulder
Next 3 rows: patt. 14 (14, 16, 20) sts.; turn; patt. 7 (7, 8, 10) sts.; turn; patt. 7 (7, 8, 10) sts.; turn.
Cast off these 14 (14, 16, 20) sts.
Leave centre 19 (21, 26, 23) sts. on st. holder, then work on rem. sts. to match first shoulder.

SIDE PANELS (make 2 alike)
With No. 9 needles cast on 56 (64, 72, 76) sts.
Work 8 rows in k.1, p.1 rib.
Change to No. 7 needles and cont. in st.st. Dec. 1 st. at each end of next and every foll. 6th row until 20 (22, 24, 26) sts. remain. Cont. straight until work measures 19 (21, 23, 25) in. Mark this row with a coloured thread.
Cont. straight until Side Panel from marked row matches cast-off sts. of Back shoulders. Slip these 20 (22, 24, 26) sts. on to a st. holder.

TO COMPLETE
Armflaps
With No. 9 needles pick up and k. 40 sts. along front side edges of one Panel, beg. approx. 6 in. from ribbing. Work in k.1, p.1 rib for 10 rows. Cast off in rib. Work other armflap in same way.

Neckband
With No. 9 needles, k. across sts. on st. holder at back neck, k.2 tog. across one Side Panel sts., pick up and k. 3 sts. down side of front neck, k. across centre sts., pick up and k.3 sts. up other side of front neck, k.2 tog. across 2nd Side Panel. Work 34 (34, 36, 36) rows in k.1, p.1 rib. Cast off in rib.

To Make Up
Press lightly on wrong side. Join side seams, leaving armflaps open. Sew sides of armflaps down on right side.

TROUSERS
LEFT LEG
With No. 9 needles cast on 46 (50, 56, 62) sts. Work in k.1, p.1 rib.
Change to No. 7 needles and cont. in patt.
1st row: k.17 (19, 22, 25), p.3, k.6, p.3, k. to end.
2nd row: p.17 (19, 22, 25), k.3, p.6, k.3, p. to end.
3rd row: k.17 (19, 22, 25), p.3, c.6, p.3, k. to end.
4th row: as 2nd row.
5th to 8th rows: rep. first and 2nd rows twice.
Cont. to work this 8-row patt.
Cont. straight until work measures 8 (8, 9, 9) in. Keeping patt. correct, inc. 1 st. at each end of next and every foll. 6th row until there are 56 (62, 68, 74) sts.
Cont. straight on these sts. until work measures 16 (17, 19, 21) in. (or length required to crutch). Inc. 1 st. at each end of every alt. row until there are 64 (70, 76, 80) sts.
Work 10 rows straight.
Dec. 1 st. at each end of next and every foll. 4th row until 50 (56, 62, 68) sts. remain.
Cont. straight until work measures 22 (24, 27, 29) in. (or length required to waist) ending with a wrong-side row.

Shape Back
Next 6 rows: patt. 32 sts.; turn; patt. back; turn; patt. 24 sts.; turn; patt. back; turn; patt. 16 sts.; turn; patt. back.

Waistband
With No. 9 needles work across all sts. in k.1, p.1 rib for 1 in. Cast off in rib.

RIGHT LEG
Work as Left Leg, but end with a right-side row before shaping back.

TO COMPLETE
Press lightly on wrong side. Join inside leg seams, then join back and front seams. Cut elastic to waist measurement and join ends. Place inside waist ribbing and work herringbone st. over it.

CAP
Main Piece
With No. 9 needles cast on 84 (92, 92, 92) sts.
Work 18 rows in k.1, p.1 rib.
Next (hem) row: k.1 st. tog. with 1 cast-on st. all along row.
Change to No. 7 needles and cont. in st.st., beg. with a p. row. Cont. straight until work measures 2½ (3, 3, 3) in., ending with a p. row.
Next row: k.2 (1, 1, 1), * k.2 tog., k.8; rep. from * to last 2 (1, 1, 1) sts., k.2 (1, 1, 1).
Work 3 rows straight.
Next row: k.2 (1, 1, 1), * k.2 tog., k.7; rep. from * to last 2 (1, 1, 1) sts., k.2 (1, 1, 1).
Work 3 rows straight.
Cont. in this way, working 1 st. fewer between decs. on each dec. row until 36 (38, 38, 38) sts. remain. Draw yarn through these sts., pull up tightly and fasten.

Peak
With No. 9 needles pick up the centre 36 (40, 40, 40) sts. on outer edge. Work 2 rows in st.st.
Next row: k.2 tog., k. to last 2 sts., k.2 tog.
Work 1 row.
Cont. to dec. at each end of every alt. row until 24 (28, 28, 28) sts. remain.
Work 1 row. Inc. 1 st. at each end of next and every foll. alt. row until there are 36 (40, 40, 40) sts. Work 1 row. Cast off.

TO COMPLETE
Press lightly on wrong side. St. back seam. Cut cardboard to fit peak, fold peak, insert cardboard and st. peak. Make pompon and stitch in place in centre of cap.

His and hers classic sweaters
in eleven sizes, including children's, and with a choice of three neckline styles

MATERIALS
For V-necked sweater: 7 (9, 11, 12, 13, 14, 15, 17, 19, 21, 24) balls (1 oz. each) Emu Scotch 4-ply. One pair each Nos. 11 and 9 knitting needles (USA sizes 2 and 5). **For round-necked sweater** (not illustrated): 7 (9, 11, 12, 13, 14, 15, 17, 19, 21, 24) balls (1 oz. each) Emu Scotch 4-ply. One pair each Nos. 11 and 9 knitting needles (USA sizes 2 and 5). One set of four No. 11 needles (USA size 2) with points at both ends. **For polo-necked sweater:** 8 (10, 12, 13, 14, 16, 17, 19, 21, 23, 26) balls (1 oz. each) Emu Scotch 4-ply. One pair each Nos. 11 and 9 knitting needles (USA sizes 2 and 5). One set of four No. 11 needles (USA size 2) with points at both ends.

MEASUREMENTS
To fit chest or bust size 24 (26, 28, 30, 32, 34, 36, 38, 40, 42, 44) in.; length 15 (16, 17, 19, 20, 21, 22½, 24, 25, 27, 27½) in.; sleeve seam 10½ (11, 12, 14, 15, 15½, 16½, 17, 18, 19, 19½) in.

TENSION
7 sts. to 1 in. over patt. with No. 9 needles.

ABBREVIATIONS
See page 22.

ALL SWEATERS
BACK
With No. 11 needles cast on 92 (100, 108, 112, 118, 124, 128, 136, 144, 156, 162) sts. Work 9 (9, 13, 13, 15, 15, 15, 17, 17, 17, 19) rows in k.1, p.1 rib, inc. 1 st. at beg. of last row.

Change to No. 9 needles and patt.

1st patt. row (wrong side): k.1, * y.f., sl.1 purlwise, keep y.f., k.1; rep. from * to end.

2nd patt. row: * k.1, k.2 tog. t.b.l.; rep. from * to last st., k.1.

These 2 rows form the patt. and are rep. throughout. Work straight until Back measures 9½ (10, 10½, 12, 13, 14, 15, 16, 17, 18, 18) in. ending with a wrong-side row.

Shape Armholes
When casting off on right side remember to k.2 tog. t.b.l. on alt. sts. as in 2nd patt. row. ** Cast off 4 (4, 6, 6, 6, 6, 6, 6, 6, 6, 6) sts. at beg. of next 2 rows. Cast off 2 (2, 2, 2, 2, 2, 2, 2, 2, 3, 3) sts. at beg. of next 2 (2, 2, 2, 2, 2, 2, 2, 2, 4, 4) rows. **

Dec. 1 st. at each end of next row and every alt. row until 69 (75, 79, 83, 89, 93, 97, 105, 109, 113, 117) sts. remain. ***

Cont. straight until work measures 15¼ (16¼, 17¼, 19¼, 20¼, 21¼, 22¾, 24¼, 25¼, 27¼, 27¾) in., ending with a wrong-side row.

Shape Shoulders
Cast off 6 (6, 6, 7, 7, 7, 8, 8, 8, 8, 9) sts. at beg. of next 4 rows. Cast off 6 (7, 7, 7, 7, 7, 7, 8, 8, 10, 10) sts. at beg. of next 2 rows. Leave rem. 33 (37, 41, 41, 47, 51, 51, 57, 61, 61, 61) sts. on a st. holder.

V-NECKED SWEATER
FRONT
Work as Back to ***. Work 1 row straight.

Shape Neck
Next row: patt. 34 (37, 39, 41, 44, 46, 48, 52, 54, 56, 58) sts.; turn and work on these sts. only.

Dec. 1 st. at beg. of next row and every foll. 4th row until 18 (19, 19, 21, 21, 21, 23, 24, 24, 26, 28) sts. remain. Work straight until armhole measures same as Back, ending with a wrong-side row.

Shape Shoulder
Cast off 6 (6, 6, 7, 7, 7, 8, 8, 8, 8, 9) sts. at beg. of next row and foll. alt. row. Cast off 6 (7, 7, 7, 7, 7, 7, 8, 8, 10, 10) sts. at beg. of next alt. row.

Rejoin yarn to rem. sts., dec. 1 st. at beg. of next row and every foll. 4th row and complete to match first side of neck.

ROUND AND POLO-NECKED SWEATERS
FRONT
Work as Back to ***. Cont. straight until armhole measures 3½ (3¾, 4¼, 4¼, 4¼, 5, 5, 5½, 5¾, 6, 6¼) in., ending with a wrong-side row.

Shape Neck
Next row: patt. 30 (33, 35, 36, 39, 40, 42, 45, 47, 49, 51) sts.; turn and work on these sts. only.

Cast off 3 sts. at beg. of next row and foll. alt. row. Cast off 2 (2, 2, 3, 2, 3, 3, 3, 3, 3, 3) sts. at beg. of next alt. row. Cast off 2 sts. at beg. of every alt. row (neck edge) until 18 (19, 19, 21, 21, 21, 23, 24, 24, 26, 28) sts.

remain. Work straight until the armhole is same length as Back, ending with a wrong-side row.

Shape Shoulder
Work as given for V-necked Sweater. Rejoin yarn to rem. sts., cast off 9 (9, 9, 11, 11, 13, 13, 15, 15, 15, 15) sts., patt. to end.

Work 1 row back to neck edge. Complete to match first side of neck, reversing shapings.

ALL SWEATERS
SLEEVES (make 2 alike)
With No. 11 needles cast on 48 (50, 52, 60, 62, 64, 68, 70, 72, 76, 78) sts., and work the same number of rib rows as given for Back, inc. 1 st. at end of last row. Change to No. 9 needles and patt., inc. 1 st. at each end of 7th and every foll. 8th row until there are 73 (77, 81, 97, 99, 101, 109, 113, 115, 121, 125) sts.

Work straight until Sleeve measures 10½ (11, 12, 14, 15, 15½, 16½, 17, 18, 19, 19½) in., ending with a wrong-side row.

Shape Top
Work from ** to ** as given for Back. Now dec. 1 st. at each end of alt. rows until 29 (31, 33, 35, 35, 37, 39, 41, 41, 43, 43) sts. remain. Work 1 row. Cast off 3 sts. at beg. of next 6 (6, 6, 6, 6, 6, 8, 8, 8, 8, 8) rows. Cast off rem. sts.

ROUND-NECKED SWEATER NECKBAND
Join shoulder seams. With right side facing and first No. 11 needle with points at both ends, beg. at left shoulder and pick up and k.26 (28, 30, 32, 34, 38, 42, 46, 48, 50, 50) sts. round side of front neck, k. across centre cast-off sts., with 2nd needle pick up and k.26 (28, 30, 32, 34, 38, 42, 46, 48, 50, 50) sts. round front neck to right shoulder, with 3rd needle patt. sts. from Back on st. holder: 94 (102, 110, 116, 126, 140, 148, 164, 172, 176, 176) sts.

Work in rounds of k.1, p.1 rib for 1 (1¼, 1¼, 1½, 1½, 1½, 1½, 1¾, 1¾, 2, 2) in.

Cast off in rib.

POLO-NECKED SWEATER NECKBAND
Work as for Round-necked Sweater but work rib for 5 (5, 5, 5½, 5½, 5½, 5½, 6, 6, 6¼, 6½) in.

V-NECKED SWEATER NECKBAND
Join right shoulder seam. With No. 11 needles beg. at left shoulder and pick up and k. 50 (56, 60, 68, 74, 78, 84, 86, 88, 92, 96) sts. down to centre of 'V', pick up and k.1, pick up and k. 50 (56, 60, 68, 74, 78, 84, 86, 88, 92, 96) sts. up to right shoulder, k. sts. from Back on st. holder. Work 1 row in k.1, p.1 rib.

Next row: rib 48 (54, 58, 66, 72, 76, 82, 84, 86, 90, 94) sts., p.2 tog., p.1, p.2 tog., rib to end.

Next row: rib to 2 sts. before centre st., p.2 tog., k.1, p.2 tog., rib to end.

Cont. to dec. in this way each side of centre st. every row until band measures 1 in., ending with a wrong-side row.

Cast off in rib. Join rem. shoulder seam.

TO COMPLETE (all sweaters)
Sew in sleeves. Press all work on wrong side using a warm iron and damp cloth. Sew up side and sleeve seams. Press seams.

Chapter six
JUST FOR FUN

Zip-up sleeveless jacket in casual style (see page 80).

Zip-up sleeveless jacket

illustrated on previous page

MATERIALS

6 (7, 7) balls (50 gr. each) Madame Pinguoin Double Knitting. One pair each Nos. 8 and 10 knitting needles (USA sizes 6 and 3). A medium size crochet hook. A 22-in. open-ended zip fastener.

MEASUREMENTS

To fit bust size 33/34 (36/37, 38/39) in.; length 23 (23½, 23½) in.

TENSION

2 patterns (14 sts.) to approx. 2¼ in.

ABBREVIATIONS

See page 22; tw. 2r., twist 2 right (k. next 2 sts. together but do not slip off needle, k. into first st. again, then slip both sts. off needle); tw. 2l., twist 2 left (k. into back of second st. on left-hand needle, then k. into front of first st., then slip both sts. off needle).

BACK

With No. 10 needles cast on 113 (120, 127) sts. Work 1½ in. in k.1 t.b.l., p.1 rib.
(1st and 3rd sizes only: beg. alternate rows p.1.)
Change to No. 8 needles and patt. as follows:
1st row: p.3, * k.2, p.5; rep. from * to last 5 sts., k.2, p.3.
2nd row: k.3, * p.2, k.5; rep. from * to last 5 sts., p.2, k.3. Rep. last 2 rows once more.
5th row: p.2, * tw. 2r., tw. 2l., p.3; rep. from * ending last rep. with p.2.
6th row: k.2, * p.4, k.3; rep. from * ending last rep. with k.2.
7th row: p.1, * tw. 2r., k.2, tw. 2l., p.1; rep. from * to end.
8th row: k.1, * p.6, k.1; rep. from * to end.
These 8 rows form patt. Continue in patt. until back measures 15 in.

Shape Armholes

Keeping patt. correct, cast off 6 sts. at beg. of next 2 rows, then dec. 1 st. at both ends of every row until 85 (92, 99) sts. remain. Continue straight until armhole measures 8 (8½, 8½) in.

Shape Shoulders

Cast off 7 (8, 9) sts. at beg. of next 4 rows and 8 (9, 8) sts. at beg. of following 2 rows. Slip remaining 41 (42, 47) sts. on to a spare needle.

LEFT FRONT

With No. 10 needles cast on 57 (64, 64) sts. Work 1½ in. in k.1 t.b.l., p.1 rib **(for first size only: beg. alternate rows p.1)**.
Change to No. 8 needles and patt. Work straight until work measures 15 in., ending with a wrong-side row.

Shape Armhole

Cast off 6 sts. at beg. of next row, then dec. 1 st. at armhole edge on every row until 43 (50, 50) sts. remain. Continue straight until armhole measures 6 in., ending at front edge.

Shape Neck

Cast off 5 sts. at beg. of next row, then dec. 1 st. at neck edge on every row until 22 (25, 26) sts. remain. Continue straight until armhole measures 8 (8½, 8½) in., ending at armhole edge.

Shape Shoulder

Cast off 7 (8, 9) sts. at beg. of next and following alternate row. Work one row. Cast off remaining 8 (9, 8) sts.

RIGHT FRONT

Work as for Left Front, reversing shapings.

TO COMPLETE

Join shoulder seams.

Arm Borders (make 2 alike)

With No. 10 needles pick up and k. 124 (130, 130) sts. along armhole edge. Work 7 rows in k.1 t.b.l., p.1 rib. Cast off in rib.

Neck Border

With No. 10 needles pick up and k.30 (34, 34) sts. up right side of neck, k. across sts. from back and pick up and k.30 (34, 34) sts. down left side of neck. Work 2 in. in k.1 t.b.l., p.1 rib, beg. alternate rows p.1. Cast off.

To Make Up

Join side seams. Using crochet hook, work 2 rows of double crochet along front edges, including side edge of neck border. Sew in zip to centre front edges. Fold neck border in half and sl.st. to wrong side. Press seams lightly.

Ladybird jacket

illustrated opposite

MATERIALS

9 (10, 11) oz. Robin Vogue Double Knitting in main shade (grey), 1 ball each in red and black, plus an oddment of yellow. One pair each Nos. 8 and 10 knitting needles (USA sizes 6 and 3). One crochet hook International Standard Size 3.00.

MEASUREMENTS

To fit bust size 32 (34, 36) in.; length 19 (19½, 20) in.; sleeve seam 3½ in.

TENSION

6 sts. and 8 rows to 1 in. over st.st. on No. 8 needles.

ABBREVIATIONS

See page 22; M., main shade; R., red; B., black; Y., yellow.

BACK

With No. 10 needles and M. cast on 89 (95, 101) sts. and work 26 rows in k.1, p.1 rib.
Change to No. 8 needles and work in st.st., inc. 1 st. at each end of the 9th and every following 10th row to 99 (105, 111) sts. Continue without further shaping until work measures 12½ in. from beg. ending with a wrong-side row.

Shape Armholes

Cast off 2 (3, 4) sts. at beg. of each of next 2 rows. Dec. 1 st. at each end of next 5 rows, then the next 5 alternate rows: 75 (79, 83) sts.

Continue without further shaping until work measures 19 (19½, 20) in. from beg. ending with a wrong-side row.

Shape Shoulders

Cast off 8 (9, 9) sts. at beg. of next 4 rows, then 9 (8, 9) sts. at beg. of next 2 rows. Cast off.

LEFT FRONT

With No. 10 needles and M. cast on 46 (48, 52) sts. and work 26 rows in k.1, p.1 rib.

1st and 3rd sizes only: dec. 1 st. at end of last row.
All sizes. Change to No. 8 needles and st.st. inc. 1 st. at beg. of 9th and every following 10th row to 50 (53, 56) sts. Continue without further shaping until work measures same as back to armhole shaping, ending with a wrong-side row.

Shape Armhole and Commence Motif

Note. 18-in. lengths of B. yarn can be used for each spot and 2 separate balls of M. for each side of Motif to avoid carrying all yarns right across back of work.

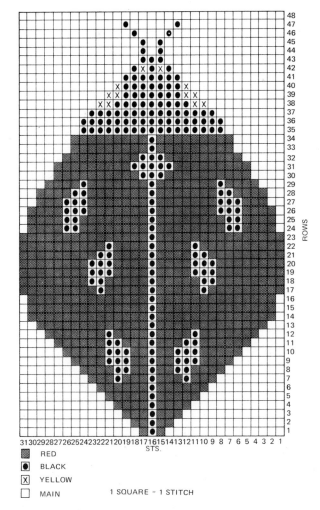

		48
		47
		46
		45
		44

ROWS

31 30 29 28 27 26 25 24 23 22 21 20 19 18 17 16 15 14 13 12 11 10 9 8 7 6 5 4 3 2 1
STS.

RED

BLACK

YELLOW

MAIN

1 SQUARE = 1 STITCH

1st row: cast off 2 (3, 4) sts., k.27 (28, 29) M., 1 R., 1 M., 1 R., 18 (19, 20) M.
2nd row: p.17 (18, 19) M., 2 R., 1 B., 2 R., 26 (27, 28) M.
Keeping the Motif correct beg. on 3rd row of chart but at the same time dec. 1 st. at armhole edge on next 5 rows, then the 5 following alternate rows: 38 (40, 42) sts. Continue without further shaping until the 35th row from chart has been worked.

Shape Neck
1st row: cast off 2 sts., patt. to end.
Dec. 1 st. at neck edge on every row until 25 (26, 27) sts. remain, ending on wrong side. Continue until work measures same as Back to shoulder shaping, ending on wrong side.

Shape Shoulder
Cast off 8 (9, 9) sts. at beg. of next and following alternate row. Patt. one row then cast off.

RIGHT FRONT
Work to correspond with Left Front making inc. at end of row unstead of beg. until work measures same as Left Front to armhole shaping, ending on wrong side.
Next row: k.18 (19, 20) M., 1 R., 1 M., 1 R., 29 (31, 33) M.

Shape Armhole
Next row: cast off 2 (3, 4) sts., p.26 (27, 28) M., 2 R., 1 B., 2 R., 17 (18, 19) M.

Complete to correspond with Left Front reversing all shapings.

SLEEVES (make 2 alike)
With No. 10 needles and M. cast on 58 (60, 62) sts. and work 8 rows in k.1, p.1 rib.
Change to No. 8 needles and work in st.st. until work measures 3½ in. from beg., ending on wrong side.

Shape Top
1st row: k.27, cast off 4 (6, 8) sts., k. to end. Dec. 1 st. at inside edge on each of the next 5 rows, then on every alternate row to 8 sts. Leave these sts. on a spare needle. With wrong side facing rejoin yarn to sts. left for other side, patt. to end. Dec. 1 st. at inside edge on each of the next 5 rows then every alternate row to 8 sts.
Next row: p.8, cast on 6 (8, 10) sts. taking care not to twist work, p. across 8 sts. left on needle.
Next row: k.2 tog., k. to last 2 sts., k.2 tog. Patt. one row. Cast off 3 sts. at beg. of next 4 rows. Cast off.

TO COMPLETE
Press each piece carefully using a warm iron over a damp cloth.
Join shoulder and side seams. Set in sleeves placing centre of cast-on sts. at sleeve top to shoulder seam.

Sleeve Vent Edging
With crochet hook and M., and with right side facing beg. at lower edge and work one row d.c. evenly around vent.
Next row: 1 d.c. in each of first 3 d.c., 1 ch., miss 1 d.c.: a lace hole made. Continue in d.c. making 4 more lace holes at 1¼-in. intervals to sleeve top, miss 1 d.c. at each corner of vent then work down other side to correspond. Work one more row d.c. all round working 1 d.c. in ch. spaces of previous row.

Front Borders
With crochet hook and M. work one row d.c. evenly all round front edges, work up front edge making 11 lace holes as given for sleeves evenly spaced, the first lace hole to be 3 sts. up from lower edge and the last 3 sts. from neck edge. Break off yarn, rejoin at neck edge of other side and work to correspond with first side. Fasten off.
With right side facing and R., beg. at lower edge and work 1 d.c. in first st., 1 tr. in next st. Continue in this manner all round front and neck edge. Break off R.
With right side facing and B., work 1 tr. in each d.c., 1 d.c. in each tr., all round. Break off B.

To Make Up
Press all seams and borders carefully. Using yarn double and B. make 2 crochet chains each 26 in. long. Thread one cord through holes in each sleeve to fasten at lower edge of sleeve. Make another chain 52 in. long and thread through holes up front of jacket.

Striped jumper and knickerbockers
illustrated in colour on page 60

MATERIALS
For jumper: 2 oz. Hayfield Gaylon Double Knitting in each of blue, white, kingfisher, emerald, green, gold, amber, yellow and orange, and 1 oz. each in bouquet and carnation. One pair each Nos. 9, 10, 11 and 12 knitting needles (USA sizes 5, 3, 2 and 1). **For knickerbockers:** 16 (17, 18) oz. Robin Vogue Double Knitting. One pair each Nos. 8 and 10 knitting needles (USA sizes 6 and 3). A waist length of elastic, 1 in. wide.

82

MEASUREMENTS
Jumper: to fit bust size 34/36 (38/40) in.; length 23 (25) in.; sleeve seam 16½ (17½) in. **Knickerbockers:** to fit hip size 36 (38, 40) in.; length at side 31 in.

TENSION
5½ sts. and 7½ rows to 1 in. with No. 9 needles; 6 sts. and 8 rows to 1 in. over st.st. on No. 8 needles.

ABBREVIATIONS
See page 22; A., blue; B., white; C., kingfisher; D., emerald; E., green; F., gold; G., amber; H., yellow; J., orange; K., bouquet; L., carnation.

JUMPER
BACK
With No. 11 needles and A., cast on 98 (116) sts. and, beg. with a k. row, work in st.st. for 5 rows.
Next row (hem ridge): k.
Change to No. 9 needles and, beg. with a k. row, work in st.st. in the foll. colour patt.:
Work 17 (18) rows each in A., B., C., D., E., F., G., H., J., K., L. Work straight until Back measures 15 (16) in. from hem ridge, ending with a p. row.

Shape Raglan
Cast off 2 sts. at beg. of next 2 rows. Work 2 rows straight. Dec. 1 st. at each end of next and every foll. k. row until 34 (38) sts. remain. Leave on a spare needle.

FRONT
Work as for Back until 46 (52) sts. remain when shaping raglan, ending with a k. row.

Shape Neck
Next row: p.16 (18), turn.
Dec. 1 st. at neck edge on every row and at the same time cont. raglan shaping as before until 6 sts. remain.
Next row: p. 2.
Next row: k.2 tog. Fasten off.
Place centre 14 (16) sts. on spare needle. Rejoin yarn to rem. 16 (18) sts. and work to match first side of neck.

SLEEVES (make 2 alike)
With No. 12 needles and L., cast on 48 (52) sts. and, beg. with a k. row, work 3 rows in st.st. K. 1 row for hem ridge.
Change to No. 11 needles and, beg. with a k. row, work 10 rows in st.st.
Change to No. 10 needles and work 4 (2) rows in st.st. Join A., and work 9 (10) rows in st.st.
Change to No. 9 needles and work 8 rows in st.st. Join B.
For size 34 only. Work 1 row.
For both sizes. Continue in st.st. in colour patt. given for Back, inc. 1 st. at each end of next and every foll. 8th row until there are 68 (78) sts. Continue until stripes match Back at beginning of armhole.

Shape Raglan
Work as given for Back until 6 sts. remain. Leave on safety pin.

TO COMPLETE
Press all pieces. Join front raglan seams and left back raglan seams. Press seams.

Neckband
With right side facing, No. 11 needles and L., k. 34 (38) sts. from back neck, k. 6 sts. from left shoulder, pick up and k. 17 sts. round left front neck, k. 14 (16) sts. from front neck, pick up and k. 17 sts. round neck, k. 6 sts.

from right shoulder: 94 (100) sts.
Beginning with a p. row, work 3 rows in st.st. Change to No. 12 needles and, beginning with a k. row, work 3 rows in st.st. K. 1 row for hem ridge. Beginning with a k. row, work 3 rows in st.st. Change to No. 11 needles, and, beginning with a p. row, work 3 rows in st.st. Cast off loosely.

To Make Up
Join raglan seam and neckband seam and press. Join side and sleeve seams and press. Turn under neckband, cuffs and hem and slip st. in place. Press.

KNICKERBOCKERS
RIGHT FRONT LEG
With No. 10 needles cast on 54 (58, 62) sts. and work 1 in. in k.1, p.1 rib.
Change to No. 8 needles and st.st. Work straight to 14 in. from beg., ending on a p. row. *
Inc. 1 st. at the beg. of the next and every following 4th row to 66 (70, 74) sts., ending on a p. row.

Shape Crutch
** Cast off 3 sts. at the beg. of the next and 2 following alternate rows, then dec. 1 st. at the same edge on every right-side row to 54 (58, 62) sts., then every 4th row to 48 (52, 56) sts.
Work straight to 30 in. from beg., ending on a p. row. Change to No. 10 needles and work 1 in. k.1, p.1 rib. Cast off in rib.

LEFT FRONT LEG
Work as Right Front Leg to *.
Inc. 1 st. at the end of the next and every following 4th row to 66 (70, 74) sts., ending on a k. row.

Shape Crutch
Now work from ** to end.

RIGHT BACK LEG
Work as Left Front Leg to 30 in. from beg., ending on a p. row. **Next row:** k.

Shape Back
Next row: p.47 (50, 53), turn, sl.1, k. to end.
Next row: p.38 (40, 42), turn, sl.1, k. to end.
Next row: p.29 (30, 31), turn, sl.1, k. to end.
Next row: p.20 (20, 20), turn, sl.1, k. to end.
Next row: p.10 (10, 10), turn, sl. 1, k. to end.
Next row: p.
Change to No. 10 needles and work 1 in. k.1, p.1 rib, cast off in rib.

LEFT BACK LEG
Work as Right Front Leg to 30 in. from beg., ending on a p. row.

Shape Back
Next row: k.47 (50, 53), turn, sl.1, p. to end.
Next row: k.38 (40, 42), turn, sl.1, p. to end.
Next row: k.29 (30, 31), turn, sl.1, p. to end.
Next row: k.20 (20, 20), turn, sl.1, p. to end.
Next row: k.10 (10, 10), turn, sl.1, p. to end.
Work 2 rows st.st. Change to No. 10 needles and work 1 in. k.1, p.1 rib, cast off in rib.

TO COMPLETE
Press work lightly on wrong side using a warm iron over a damp cloth. Join crutch, leg and side seams, press seams. Join elastic to form a ring and sew inside waist ribbing using a herringbone casing stitch. Crochet or twist 2 cords and thread through ribbing at lower edges of knickerbockers.

Striped halter top

MATERIALS
Of Hayfield Beaulon 4-ply — 1 oz. each in each of three contrasting shades. One pair each Nos. 10 and 12 knitting needles (USA sizes 3 and 1). One crochet hook International Standard Size 2.50.

MEASUREMENTS
To fit bust size 30 (32, 34, 36) in.

TENSION
7 sts. and 9 rows to 1 in. over st.st. on No. 10 needles.

ABBREVIATIONS
See page 22; A, first colour; B, second colour; C, third colour.

THE COLOUR PATTERN
Work in st.st. in the following colour sequence: 2 rows A, 10 rows B, 2 rows A, 10 rows C.
When working in rib, work in colour sequence as above, but always k. the first row of colour change.

FRONT
With No. 12 needles, and A, cast on 80 (88, 94, 100) sts. and work in k.1, p.1 rib for 4 rows.

Change to No. 10 needles and st. st. and work in colour pattern. Inc. 1 st. at each end of first and every following 6th row until you have 104 (112, 118, 124) sts. Work straight until 3 complete patts. have been worked.

Shape Top
Keeping colour patt. correct, k.2 tog. at beg. of next row, k. across 43 (45, 47, 48) sts., cast off centre 14 (18, 20, 24) sts. and work to last 2 sts., k.2 tog.
Work on this set of sts. only. Cont. in patt., dec. 1 st. at neck edge of next 10 rows, and at the same time dec. 1 st. at side edge on every alt. row. Cont. with side decs., keeping neck edge straight, until 10 sts. remain.
Work straight on these sts. for 5 in., or length required (longer if a lower neck is required; shorter if a higher neck is required).
Cast off.
Rejoin yarn to sts. at other side and work to match first side, reversing shapings.

BACK
With No. 12 needles and A, cast on 76 (84, 92, 96) sts. and work in k.1, p.1 rib for 4 rows. Change to No. 10 needles and cont. in rib., beg. colour patt.
Inc. 1 st. at side edges of next and every 6th row for 12 incs. in all on each side.
When 12 rows of patt. have been worked, cast off centre 12 (20, 28, 32) sts. and on the first set of sts. dec. 1 st. at centre edge on next 30 rows, then on every alt. row until all sts. have been dec.
(Note. Side edge should measure as side of front to decreasings.)
Fasten off.
Rejoin yarn to rem. sts. and finish to match first side.

TO COMPLETE
Press. Join side and back neck seams. With crochet hook and A, work 2 rows of d.c. round neck and back edges. Fasten off. Press.

Pretty for a teenager—full-sleeved jumper with matching tank top (see page 86).

Jumper and tank top

jumper and tank top are illustrated in colour on previous page, tank top worn over a shirt is shown opposite

MATERIALS
For jumper: 6 (6, 7, 7, 8, 8) balls (20 gr. each) Twilleys Mohair. One pair each Nos. 10 and 11 knitting needles (USA sizes 3 and 2). One crochet hook International Standard Size 3.00. Shirring elastic. 3 small buttons.
For tank top: 3 (3, 4, 4, 5, 5) balls (20 gr. each) Twilleys Mohair in each of two toning shades. One pair each No. 8 and No. 9 knitting needles (USA sizes 6 and 5).

MEASUREMENTS
To fit bust size 32 (34, 36, 38, 40, 42) in.; length of jumper 19 (19½, 20, 20½, 21, 21½) in.; length of jumper sleeve seam 19 in.; length of tank top 17½ (18, 18½, 19, 19½, 20) in.; length of tank top sleeve seam 6 in.

TENSION
Jumper: 5 sts. and 9 rows to 1 in. over st.st. with No. 10 needles. **Tank top:** 6 sts. and 8 rows to 1 in. over unstretched rib with No. 8 needles.

ABBREVIATIONS
See page 22.

JUMPER FRONT
With No. 11 needles and using yarn double cast on 80 (86, 90, 96, 100, 106) sts. Break off 1 strand and cont. with single yarn.
Work 4 in. in k.1, p.1 rib. Change to No. 10 needles. Cont. in st.st. Work straight until front measures 12 (12½, 12½, 13, 13, 13½) in. from beg.

Shape Armholes
Cast off 3 (4, 4, 5, 5, 6) sts. at beg. of next 2 rows then dec. 1 st. at each end of next 6 rows: 62 (66, 70, 74, 78, 82) sts. Cont. straight until work measures 17½ (18, 18½, 19, 19½, 20) in. from beg., ending with a p. row.

Shape Neck
Next row: k.22 (24, 26, 28, 30, 32), k.2 tog.; turn.
Work on these sts. only. Dec. 1 st. at neck edge on next 7 rows: 16 (18, 20, 22, 24, 26) sts. Work 6 rows straight.

Shape Shoulder
Using yarn double cast off 8 (9, 10, 11, 12, 13) sts. very loosely at beg. of next and foll. alt. row.
Place centre 14 sts. on a st. holder. Complete other side of neck to match first, reversing shapings.

BACK
Work as Front until Back measures 16 (16½, 17, 17½, 18, 18½) in. from beg. ending with a p. row.

Divide for Opening
Next row: k.31 (33, 35, 37, 39, 41); turn.
Work straight on these sts. only until work measures 19 (19½, 20, 20½, 21, 21½) in. from beg., ending at armhole edge.

Shape Shoulder
Using yarn double cast off 8 (9, 10, 11, 12, 13) sts. very loosely at beg. of next and foll. alt. row. Work 1 row. Leave rem. 15 sts. on st. holder. Complete other side of opening to match first, reversing shapings.

SLEEVES (make 2 alike)
With No. 11 needles and using yarn double cast on 40 (40, 44, 44, 48, 48) sts. Break off 1 strand and cont.

with single yarn. Work 1½ in. in k.1, p.1 rib.
Next row: k. twice into each st. to end.
Next row: * p. twice into next st., p.1; rep. from * to end: 120 (120, 132, 132, 144, 144) sts.
Change to No. 10 needles. Cont. in st.st., beg. with a k. row. Work straight until Sleeve measures 13 in. from beg., ending with a p. row.
Next row: * k.2 tog.; rep. from * to end: 60 (60, 66, 66, 72, 72) sts.
Now work in k.1, p.1 rib until work measures 19 in. from beg.

Shape Top
Cont. in rib, cast off 4 sts. at beg. of next 2 rows then dec. 1 st. at each end of every alt. row until 20 (20, 20, 20, 20, 20) sts. remain. Dec. 1 st. at each end of next 6 rows.
Cast off.

TO COMPLETE
Collar
Join shoulders. With No. 11 needles and using yarn double k. sts. from left side of back neck, pick up and k. 18 sts. down left side of front neck, k. sts. from st. holder, pick up and k. 18 sts. up right side of front neck then k. sts. from right side of back neck: 80 sts. Break off 1 strand and cont. with single yarn.
Work 7 rows in k.1, p.1 rib.
Next row: rib 40; turn.
Work on these sts. only for first half of collar.
Next row: rib 2, * work k.1, p.1 and k.1 all into next st., rib 3; rep. from * ending last rep. rib 1: 60 sts.
Work 4 in. in k.1, p.1 rib on these sts. Dec. 1 st. at each end of next 6 rows.
Cast off loosely ribwise.
Rejoin yarn to rem. 40 sts. and complete 2nd half of collar to match first, reversing shapings.

To Make Up
Press lightly, omitting ribbing. Join side and sleeve seams. Set in Sleeves. With crochet hook and using yarn double work 2 rows of d.c. around collar edges and back opening edges, working loosely around collar and making 3 evenly-spaced buttonhole loops on right side of back opening on 2nd row by working 3 ch., miss 3 d.c. for each. Press collar and press all seams. Sew buttons on to left side of back opening. Thread shirring elastic through wrong side of wrist ribbing.

TANK TOP
Note. Use one strand of each shade together throughout.

BACK AND FRONT (make 2 pieces alike)
With No. 9 needles cast on 81 (87, 93, 99, 105, 111) sts.
Work 5 in. in k.1, p.1 rib, beg. 2nd and alt. rows p.1. Change to No. 8 needles and cont. in rib. Work straight until work measures 10 (10½, 10½, 11, 11, 11½) in. from beg.

Shape Armholes
Still working in rib, cast off 2 sts. at beg. of next 2 rows then dec. 1 st. at each end of next 6 rows: 65 (71, 77, 83, 89, 95) sts. Cont. straight in rib until work measures 13½ (14, 14½, 15, 15½, 16) in. from beg., ending with a 2nd row.

Shape Neck
Next row: rib 13 (15, 17, 19, 21, 23), cast off 39 (41, 43, 45, 47, 49) loosely ribwise, rib to end.
Work on last set of sts. only.
Next row: rib to last 2 sts., k.2.
Next row: k.2, rib to end.
Rep. last 2 rows for 4 in., ending at armhole edge.

Shape Shoulder
Cast off 7 sts. loosely at beg. of next row. Work 1 row.
Cast off rem. sts. loosely.
Rejoin yarn to inner edge of rem. sts.
Next row: k.2, rib to end.
Next row: rib to last 2 sts., k.2.
Working in this way, complete to match first side of neck.

SLEEVES (make 2 alike)
With No. 9 needles cast on 73 (73, 79, 79, 85, 85) sts.
Work 2 in. in k.1, p.1 rib, beg. 2nd and alt. rows p.1.

Change to No. 8 needles and work 4 in. more in rib.

Shape Top
Cont. in rib, cast off 2 sts. at beg. of next 2 rows then
dec. 1 st. at each end of every alt. row until 43 (43, 45,
45, 47, 47) sts. remain. Dec. 1 st. at each end of next
10 rows. Cast off.

TO COMPLETE
Do not press. Join shoulder, side and sleeve seams. Set in
sleeves. Press seams lightly.

Lime green and white sweater is worked in an unusual rib pattern (see page 100).

FRONT

Work as given for Back as far as **. Continue without shaping until work measures 22 (22¼, 22½) in. from beg., ending with a p. row. Divide for front opening as follows:

Next row: k.50 (53, 56), and leave these sts. on a spare needle for left front, continue along row, cast off 7, k. to end.

Continue on the 50 (53, 56) sts. now remaining on needle for right front. Work 8 (6, 4) rows straight, thus ending at side edge.

Armhole Shaping

Cast off 2 (3, 4) sts. at beg. of next row, then cast off 4 sts. at same edge on next 3 alternate rows. Continue on remaining 36 (38, 40) sts. until work measures 28 (28¼, 28½) in. from beg., ending at the opening.

Neck and Shoulder Shaping

*** Cast off 4 sts. at beg. of next row, 2 sts. at same edge on next 3 alternate rows and 1 st. at same edge on next 4 alternate rows. Work 2 rows on remaining 22 (24, 26) sts. Now keeping front edge straight cast off for shoulder 7 (8, 9) sts. at beg. of next row and next alternate row. Work one row, cast off remaining 8 sts. ***

With No. 10 needles and V. cast on 23 sts. for pocket lining. Rep. first and 2nd rows of welt until work measures 3 in., ending with a first row.

Next row: rib 2, * p.2 tog., rib 4; rep. from * twice more, p.2 tog., k.1. Break yarn and leave remaining 19 sts. on a stitch holder.

With wrong side facing and No. 9 needles rejoin yarn to inner edge of left front sts. Work 7 (5, 3) rows in st.st., beg. with a p. row. You have thus ended at side edge. Work armhole shaping as on right front, then continue without shaping until work measures 25 in. from beg., ending with a p. row. Make pocket opening as follows:

Next row: k.8 (9, 10) slip off next 19 sts. on to a stitch holder, then with right side facing k. sts. of pocket lining, k. remaining 9 (10, 11) sts.

Continue in st.st. until work measures 28 (28¼, 28½) in. from beg., ending at the opening. Complete as for right front from *** to ***.

SLEEVES (make 2 alike)

With No. 10 needles and V. cast on 51 (55, 59) sts. and work 10 rows in rib as on Back. Change to No. 9 needles and beg. with a k. row work in st.st. for 4 rows, then inc. 1 st. at both ends of next row and every following 8th row until there are 75 (79, 83) sts. Work 7 rows after last inc. row, thus ending with a p. row.

Now work in stripe patt as follows:
Break off V., join on Y.

1st row: cast on 1, k. to last st., k.f.b.
Beg. with 2nd row work 7 rows in rib as on welt.

9th row: cast on 1, work in correct rib to last st., k.f.b. Work 1 more row in rib.

Change back to V. and work 6 rows in st.st., inc. 1 st. at both ends of next row, then work 3 more rows: 81 (85, 89) sts.

This completes incs. Break off V., join on P. K. 1 row, then beg. with 2nd row work 9 rows in rib.

Change back to V. and beg. with a k. row continue in st.st. until work measures 18½ in. from beg.

Place marker loops of contrast wool at each end of last row, then work 3 (5, 7) rows straight. Dec. 1 st. at both ends of next row, then work 3 rows straight.

Rep. last 4 rows 3 times more. Cast off 2 sts. at beg. of next 8 rows, 3 sts. at beg. of next 8 rows and 6 sts. at beg. of next 2 rows. Cast off remaining 21 (25, 29) sts.

FRONT BORDERS

With right side of work facing and No. 10 needles and P., pick up and k.41 sts. along right edge of front opening. Beg. with 2nd row work 4 rows in rib.

6th row (wrong side): rib 5, * p.2 tog. t.b.l., w.o.2 (see Abbreviations), p.2 tog., rib 6; rep. from * twice more, p.2 tog. t.b.l., w.o.2, p.2 tog., rib 2.

7th row: rib 3, * drop one loop of the double loop to make a long st. and work k.1, p.1 into this st., rib 8; rep. from * but ending last rep. rib 6, instead of rib 8.

Work 4 more rows in rib. Cast off ribwise. Work left front border to match but omitting buttonholes.

NECK BORDER

First join shoulder seams. With right side of work facing and No. 10 needles and P., pick up and k.9 sts. across top edge of right front border, 29 sts. along right front neck, 37 sts. across back neck, 29 sts. down left front neck edge and 9 sts. across border. Beg. with 2nd row work 4 rows in rib.

6th row (wrong side): rib to last 6 sts., p.2 tog. t.b.l., w.o.2, p.2 tog., rib. 2.

Change to No. 11 needles. Complete buttonhole on next row, then work 4 more rows in rib. Cast off ribwise.

POCKET BORDER

With right side of work facing and No. 10 needles and Y. work across sts. of pocket as follows: cast on 1 and k. this st., k.2, * k.f.b., k.3; rep. from * to last st., k.f.b.: 25 sts.

Beg. with 2nd row work 5 rows in rib. Cast off ribwise.

TO COMPLETE

Press st.st. sections, shoulder seams and sleeve stripes lightly on wrong side with warm iron and damp cloth. Sew in sleeves matching markers to beg. of armhole casting-off. Press seams. Remove markers.

Join side seams, then join sleeve seams matching stripes. Press seams. Neatly sew lower edge of right front border to centre cast-off edge. Catch left front border in place underneath. Press pocket lining to flatten slightly and slip-st. edges in place on wrong side. Neatly sew sides of pocket border in place on right side. Sew on buttons.

Knickerbocker suit
illustrated opposite

MATERIALS

35 (37, 39) oz. Lee Target Motoravia Double Knitting. One pair each Nos. 9, 10 and 11 knitting needles (USA sizes 5, 3 and 2). A 9-in. zip fastener. 1¼ yd. of elastic, 1 in. wide.

MEASUREMENTS

To fit bust size 32 (34, 36) in.; hip size 34 (36, 38) in.; length of jersey 27½ (28, 28½) in.; sleeve seam 17 in.; inside leg seam of knickerbockers including band 22 in.

TENSION

13 sts. to 2 in. over st.st. with No. 10 needles; 13 sts. over rib with No. 9 needles.

ABBREVIATIONS

See page 22; inc., increase (by working into the back and front of the same st.); dec., decrease (by working 2 sts. tog.).

JERSEY BACK

With No. 11 needles cast on 116 (122, 128) sts. and work in rib as follows:

1st row: k.3, * p.2, k.4; rep. from * ending last repeat with k.3.
2nd row: p.3 * k.2, p.4; rep. from * ending last repeat with p.3.
Repeat these 2 rows twice. Change to No. 10 needles and work in st.st. for 16 rows, then dec. 1 st. at each end of the next row and 2 following 20th rows. On 110 (116, 122) sts. work in st.st. for 9 rows. Change to No. 9 needles and work 90 rows in rib as given at beg. of Back.

To Shape Armholes
Cast off 6 sts. at the beg. of each of the next 2 rows, then dec. 1 st. at the beg. of the next 10 (12, 14) rows. Rib 4 rows. **
Change to No. 10 needles and work in st.st. for 38 rows.

To Slope Shoulders
Cast off 7 sts. at the beg. of each of the next 6 rows: 7 (8, 9) sts. on the following 2 rows. Leave the remaining 32 (34, 36) sts. on a spare needle for collar.

FRONT
Work as given for Back until ** is reached. Change to No. 10 needles and work in st.st. for 25 rows. Now divide the sts. for neck.
Next row: p.32 (34, 36) and leave for right front shoulder, p.24 and leave for collar, p. to end and work on these last 32 (34, 36) sts.

Left Front Shoulder
Dec. 1 st. at neck edge of the next row and 4 following alternate rows. Work 3 rows.

To Slope Shoulder
Cast off 7 sts. at the beg. of next row and 2 following alternate rows. Work 1 row then cast off the 7 (8, 9) remaining sts. With right side of work facing, rejoin yarn to the 32 (34, 36) sts. and k. to end of row.

Right Front Shoulder
Work as for left front shoulder.

SLEEVES (make 2 alike)
With No. 11 needles cast on 62 sts. and work 12 rows in rib as on Back. Change to No. 9 needles and work 2 rows more. Continue in rib and inc. 1 st. at each end of the next row and every following 6th row until the 17th (18th, 19th) inc. row has been worked: 96 (98, 100) sts.
Continue until sleeve measures 17 in. or length required.

To Shape Top
Cast off 6 sts. at the beg. of each of the next 2 rows, then dec. 1 st. at the beg. of the next 22 (24, 26) rows. Cast off 4 sts. at the beg. of the next 6 rows, 3 sts. on next 6 rows. Cast off remaining 20 sts.

TO COMPLETE
Join right shoulder seam.

Polo Collar
With right side of work facing and No. 11 needles, pick up and k.21 (20, 22) sts. down left neck edge, k. across the 24 sts. at centre front, pick up and k.21 (20, 22) sts. from right neck edge, k. across the 32 (34, 36) sts. of back: 98 (98, 104) sts. Beg. with first rib row, work 2 in. in rib as on back. Change to No. 10 needles and work 2 in. more. Change to No. 9 needles and work a further 1 in.
Cast off in rib.

To Make Up
Press lightly on the wrong side with a hot iron over a damp cloth. Join left shoulder seam and polo collar. Set in sleeves. Join sleeve and side seams. Press seams.

KNICKERBOCKERS LEFT FRONT LEG
With No. 11 needles cast on 49 (52, 55) sts. Work in st.st. for 8 rows. P.1 row on right side to mark hemline. Change to No. 10 needles and work in st.st. for 7 (7, 9) rows (when working right front leg work 8 (8, 10) rows here of st.st.).
Inc. 1 st. at end (side seam) of the next row and 5 following 6th rows, then on the 4 following 8th rows: 59 (62, 65) sts.
Work in st.st. for 1 (3, 5) rows.
Inc. 1 st. at beg. (centre front edge) of the next row and at the same edge on the 11 following rows. Place a marker at each end of row: 71 (74, 77) sts.
Work in st.st. for 4 rows.
Dec. 1 st. at centre front edge on the next row and 3 following 6th rows. Work in st.st. for 5 rows.
** Dec. 1 st. at each end of the next row and 2 following 8th rows. Work in st.st. for 9 rows. Inc. 1 st. at each end of the next row and 4 following 22nd rows. Work in st.st. for 15 rows. (Adjust length here if necessary.)
Dec. row: k. or p.2, * dec. 1, k. or p.1; rep. from * to end: 48 (50, 52) sts.
Work in st.st. for 3 rows, then cast off.

RIGHT FRONT LEG
Work as given for Left Front Leg, working the extra row where indicated.

RIGHT BACK LEG
With No. 11 needles cast on 43 (46, 49) sts. and work in st.st. for 8 rows.
P. 1 row on the right side to mark the hemline. Change to No. 10 needles and work in st.st. for 7 (7, 9) rows (8 (8, 10) rows here for left back leg).
Inc. 1 st. at each end of the next row and 4 following 6th rows. Work in st.st. for 5 rows, then inc. 1 st. at the beg. (centre back) of the next row and 4 following 8th rows.
Work in st.st. for 1 (3, 5) rows. Inc. 1 st. at centre back edge of next row and 3 following alternate rows. Work one row then cast on 12 sts. at the beg. of following row. Place marker at each end of last row. Work one row in st.st.
Dec. 1 st. at centre back edge of the next row and 6 following 4th rows. Work in st.st. for 3 rows.
Now work from ** to end as give for Left Front Leg.

LEFT BACK LEG
Work as given for Right Back Leg, working the extra row where indicated.

LEG BANDS (make 2 alike)
With No. 10 needles cast on 92 sts. and work in st.st. for 10 rows. P. 1 row on right side to mark the hemline. Work in st.st. for 9 rows, then cast off.

TO COMPLETE

Press as given for the jersey. Join front and back seams as far as markers, then join leg seams, leaving 8 in. free below hemline in left side seam. Fold top over at marked hemline and sew cast-on edge in position. Thread a waist length of elastic through hem and secure ends. Sew in zip fastener. Sew cast-on edge of band to dec. row on leg, easing in any fullness. Fold band in half and sew cast-off edge in position. Thread through elastic and secure ends to fit. Sew up opening. Press all seams.

Lacy-patterned sweater

MATERIALS
19 (20) balls ($\frac{3}{4}$ oz. each) Lee Target Lorette Double Crêpe. One pair each Nos. 9 and 11 knitting needles (USA sizes 5 and 2). A medium cable needle. One crochet hook International Standard Size 3.50.

MEASUREMENTS
To fit bust size 32/34 (36/38) in.; length 22 (22$\frac{1}{2}$) in.; sleeve seam 14$\frac{1}{2}$ in.

TENSION
1 patt. (14 sts.) to 1$\frac{3}{4}$ in.

ABBREVIATIONS
See page 22; bind 11, using the cable needle patt. the next 11 sts. as follows: k.2, y.fwd., sl.1, k.1, p.s.s.o., p.3, k.2, y.fwd., sl.1, k.1, p.s.s.o., wind yarn twice round these sts., then sl. them on to right-hand needle and take yarn to back of work; bobble, make crochet bobble as follows: work 5 tr. into next d.c. leaving last loop of each tr. on hook, yarn over hook and draw through all 6 loops tog.

BACK AND FRONT (both worked alike)
With No. 11 needles cast on 119 (131) sts.
Work 7 rows in k.1 t.b.l., p.1 rib, beg. alternate rows p.1.
Inc. row: * rib 4, inc. in next st.; rep. from * to last 4 (1) sts., for first size rib 3, inc. in last st.; for 2nd size rib 1: 143 (157) sts.
Change to No. 9 needles and patt. as follows:
1st row: p.3, * k.2, y.fwd., sl.1, k.1, p.s.s.o., p.3; rep. from * to end.
2nd and every following alternate row: k.3, * p.2, y.r.n., p.2 tog., k.3; rep. from * to end.
3rd and 5th rows: as first row.
7th row: p.3, * bind 11 (see Abbreviations), p.3; rep. from * to end.
9th, 11th, 13th, 15th and 17th rows: as first row.
19th row: p.3, k.2, y.fwd., sl.1, k.1, p.s.s.o., p.3, * bind 11, p.3; rep. from * to last 7 sts., k.2, y.fwd., sl.1, k.1, p.s.s.o., p.3
21st and 23rd rows: as first row.
24th row: as 2nd row.
These 24 rows form patt. Continue in patt. until work measures 14$\frac{1}{2}$ in.

Shape Armholes
Cast off 7 sts. at beg. of next 2 rows, then dec. 1 st. at both ends of every row until 115 (129) sts. remain. Continue in patt. until work measures 21 (21$\frac{1}{2}$) in., ending with a wrong-side row.

Shape Neck
Next row: patt. 42 (46), cast off 31 (37) sts., patt. to end.
Continue on last set of sts. only. Patt. 1 row.
** Cast off 3 sts. at beg. of next and following 3 alternate rows.

Shape Shoulder
Next row: cast off 8 (9) sts., patt. to end.
Next row: cast off 3 sts., patt. to end.
Rep. last 2 rows once more. Cast off remaining 8 (10) sts.
Rejoin yarn to neck edge of remaining sts. and work as for first side from ** to end.

SLEEVES (make 2 alike)
With No. 11 needles cast on 66 sts. Work 7 rows in k.1 t.b.l., p.1 rib.
Inc. row: * rib 2, inc. in next st.; rep. from * to last 3 sts., rib 3: 87 sts.
Change to No. 9 needles and patt., inc. 1 st. at both ends of 7th and then every following 6th row until there are 105 sts., then at both ends of every following 8th row until there are 115 sts., working the new sts. into patt. as they occur.
Continue straight until sleeve measures 14$\frac{1}{2}$ in.

Shape Top

Cast off 7 sts. at beg. of next 2 rows. Dec. 1 st. at beg. of next 8 (16) rows, then dec. 1 st. at both ends of every row until 57 sts. remain. Cast off 4 sts. at beg. of next 6 rows. Cast off remaining 33 sts.

TO COMPLETE

Press lightly with a warm iron. Join shoulder, side and sleeve seams. Set in sleeves.

Neck Edging

With crochet hook and with right side of work facing, work 90 (99) d.c. round neck edge, turn with 1 ch.
2nd row: 1 d.c. into first d.c., * 1 bobble into next d.c. (see Abbreviations), 1 d.c. into each of next 2 d.c.; rep. from * to last 2 d.c., 1 bobble into next d.c., 1 d.c. into last d.c.
Fasten off. Press seams.

Lime green and white sweater

illustrated in colour on page 88

MATERIALS

12 (13, 14) balls (25 gr. each) Patons Limelight 4-ply in main shade and 1 ball in a contrasting shade. One pair each Nos. 13 and 11 knitting needles (USA sizes 0 and 2). One set of No. 14 needles (USA size 0) with points at both ends.

MEASUREMENTS

To fit bust size 34 (36, 38) in.; length 25 ($25\frac{1}{4}$, $25\frac{1}{2}$) in.; length of sleeve seam 5 in.

TENSION

$7\frac{1}{2}$ sts. and $9\frac{1}{2}$ rows to 1 in. over st.st. with No. 11 needles.

ABBREVIATIONS

See page 22; tw.2, twist 2 by k. into 2nd st. on left-hand needle then into first st., then slip both sts. off needle tog.; M., main shade; C., contrast shade.

BACK

With No. 13 needles and C. cast on 146 (154, 162) sts. Work 5 rows in k.1, p.1 rib. Break C.
Join M. and p. 1 row. Change to No. 11 needles and work in twisted rib patt.
1st row: * k.2, p.2, tw.2, p.2; rep. from * to last 2 sts., k.2.
2nd row: * p.2, k.2; rep. from * to last 2 sts., p.2.
These 2 rows form patt.
Cont. straight in patt. until work measures $17\frac{1}{2}$ in.

Shape Armholes

Cast off 8 (9, 10) sts. at beg. of next 2 rows, then dec. 1 st. at each end of every alt. row until 112 (118, 124) sts. remain.
Cont. straight on these sts. until armholes measure 7 ($7\frac{1}{4}$, $7\frac{1}{2}$) in.

Shape Shoulders

Cast off 17 (18, 19) sts. at beg. of next 4 rows. Slip rem. 44 (46, 48) sts. on to a st. holder.

POCKETS (make 2 alike)

With No. 13 needles and M. cast on 34 (36, 38) sts. Work in k.1, p.1 rib for 4 in. Slip sts. on length of C. yarn.

FRONT

Work as Back until Front measures 17 in., ending with a wrong-side row.

Work Pocket Tops and Place Pockets

Next row: patt. 15 (17, 19), with No. 13 needles and C. k. next 34 (36, 38) sts.; turn and with C. work 2 rows in k.1, p.1 rib over these 34 (36, 38) sts., then cast off these sts. in rib and break C.; break M. and rejoin M. to rem. sts. then patt. to last 49 (53, 57) sts.; with No. 13 needles and C. k. next 34 (36, 38) sts.; turn and work on these sts. to match first pocket top; break M. and rejoin M. to last 15 (17, 19) sts., patt. to end.
Next row: patt. 15 (17, 19) sts.; slip 34 (36, 38) sts. from one Pocket on to left-hand needle, patt. over these sts. then patt. to last 15 (17, 19) sts., slip 34 (36, 38) sts. from 2nd pocket on to left-hand needle, patt. these sts. then patt. to end. Cont. in patt. until work matches Back to beg. of armhole shaping.

Shape Armholes

Work as Back: 112 (118, 124) sts. Cont. on these sts. until armholes measure $5\frac{1}{2}$ ($5\frac{3}{4}$, 6) in.

Shape Neck

Next row: patt. 43 (45, 47), patt. next 26 (28, 30) sts. on to st. holder, patt. 43 (45, 47).
Work on last set of sts. only, dec. 1 st. at neck edge on next and every alt. row until 34 (36, 38) sts. remain. Cont. straight on these sts. until work matches Back to beg. of shoulder shaping, ending at armhole edge.

Shape Shoulder

Cast off 17 (18, 19) sts. at beg. of next and foll. alt. row. Rejoin yarn to sts. for other side of neck, and work to match first side.

SLEEVES (make 2 alike)

With No. 13 needles and C. cast on 78 (82, 86) sts. Work 5 rows in k.1, p.1 rib. Break C. Join M.
Next row: p.10 (6, 11), * p. twice into next st., p.18 (9, 20); rep. from * 2 (6, 2) times, p. twice into next st., p. to end: 82 (90, 90) sts.
Change to No. 11 needles and work in rib patt. as for Back inc. 1 st. at each end of 4th row and every foll. 3rd (4th, 3rd) row until there are 104 (108, 112) sts. Cont. straight on these sts. until work measures 5 in.

Shape Top

Cast off 8 (9, 10) sts. at beg. of next 2 rows, then dec. 1 st. at each end of every alt. row until 70 (72, 74) sts. remain. Cast off 8 (7, 6) sts. at beg. of next 6 (8, 10) rows.
Cast off.

TO COMPLETE

Join shoulders.

Neckband

With right side facing and set of No. 14 needles and C. k. across sts. from back st. holder, pick up and k.20 (21, 22) sts. down side of front neck, k. sts. from centre front st. holder, pick up and k.20 (21, 22) sts. up other side of front neck: 110 (116, 122) sts. Work 6 rounds in k.1, p.1 rib. P. 2 rounds. Work 6 more rounds in k.1, p.1 rib. With No. 13 needle cast off.

To Make Up

St. pockets in position on wrong side and pocket tops on right side. Fold neckband at centre to inside and loosely st. cast-off edge to knitted-up edge. Using flat seam for rib, fine back st. for rem. join side and sleeve seams and sew Sleeves into position matching shapings. Very lightly press on wrong side.

Two-colour waistcoat

MATERIALS
9 (10) oz. Emu Scotch Double Knitting in main shade and 5 (6) oz. in a contrasting shade. One pair each No. 9 and No. 10 (No. 8 and No. 9) knitting needles (USA sizes 5 and 3 (6 and 5)). One crochet hook International Standard Size 3.00. Four buttons $\frac{5}{8}$ in. in diameter.

MEASUREMENTS
To fit bust size 35/36 (37/38) in.; length $22\frac{1}{4}$ ($22\frac{1}{2}$) in.

TENSION
$6\frac{1}{2}$ sts. to 1 in. over patt. with No. 9 needles.

ABBREVIATIONS
See page 22; M., main shade; C., contrasting shade.

BACK
With No. 10 (9) needles and M. cast on 122 sts. and work 2 rows in st.st. Join C. and change to No. 9 (8) needles and patt.

1st row (right side): k.: 1 M., * 6 C., 4 M.; rep. from * to last st., 1 M.

2nd row: p.: 1 M., * 3 M., 1 C., 1 M., 5 C.; rep. from * to last st., 1 M.

3rd row: k.: 1 M., * 5 C., 2 M., 1 C., 2 M.; rep. from * to last st., 1 M.

4th row: p.: 1 M., * 1 M., 1 C., 3 M., 5 C.; rep. from * to last st., 1 M.

5th row: k.: 1 M., * 5 C., 4 M., 1 C.; rep. from * to last st., 1 M.

6th row: p.: 1 M., * 5 M., 1 C., 4 M.; rep. from * to last st., 1 M.

7th row: k.: 1 M., * 3 M., 1 C., 6 M.; rep. from * to

last st., 1 M.

8th row: p.: 1 M., * 7 M., 1 C., 2 M.; rep. from * to last st., 1 M.

9th row: k.: 1 M., * 1 M., 1 C., 8 M.; rep. from * to last st., 1 M.

10th row: p.: 1 M., * 9 M., 1 C.; rep. from * to last st., 1 M.

These 10 rows form the patt. Cont. straight until work measures 13¼ in., ending with a wrong-side row.

Shape Armholes

Cast off 4 sts. at beg. of next 2 rows, then dec. 1 st. at each end of next 3 rows, then dec. 1 st. at each end of every alt. row until 96 sts. remain. Cont. straight until armholes measure 8 (8¼) in., ending with a wrong-side row.

Shape Shoulders

Cast off 5 sts. at beg. of next 8 rows. Cast off rem. sts.

LEFT FRONT

With No. 10 (9) needles and M., cast on 65 sts. and work 2 rows in st.st.

Join C. and change to No. 9 (8) needles and patt.

1st row: k.: 3 M., * 6 C., 4 M.; rep. from * to last 2 sts., 2 M.

2nd row: p.: 2 M., * 3 M., 1 C., 1 M., 5 C.; rep. from * to last 3 sts., 3 M.

Cont. in patt. as now set until work measures 11½ in., ending at front edge.

Shape Front Slope

Next row (wrong side): p.2 tog., patt. to end.

Work 3 rows straight. Now keeping 2 sts. in M. at front edge dec. 1 st. at front edge on next and every foll. 4th row until work measures 13¼ in., ending at armhole edge.

Shape Armhole

Still dec. at front edge as before, cast off 4 sts. at beg. of next row, then work 1 row.

Now dec. 1 st. at armhole edge on next 3 rows, then next 6 alt. rows.

Cont. straight at armhole edge, but dec. at front edge as before until 42 sts. remain, then dec. at front edge on every 3rd row until 36 sts. remain, then on every alt. row until 30 sts. remain. Cont. straight until armhole measures same as Back to shoulder ending at armhole edge.

Shape Shoulder

Cast off 5 sts. at beg. of next row and foll. 5 alt. rows.

RIGHT FRONT

With pins mark button positions on Left Front, the first ½ in. from lower edge, the 4th just below beg. of front slope and 2 more at equal distances between these 2 positions.

Work Right Front to match Left, reversing shapings and working buttonholes to matched marked positions as follows.

1st buttonhole row (right side): patt. 2 sts., cast off 4, patt. to end. Cast on 4 sts. on foll. row in place of those cast off.

TO COMPLETE

Join shoulder and side seams. With right side facing, with crochet hook and M., work 1 row firm d.c. all round edge of Waistcoat, beg. and ending at right side seam on lower edge of Back, ending s.s. to first d.c. Fasten off. Work 1 row of d.c. round armhole edges. Neaten buttonholes. Press work lightly on wrong side. Sew on buttons.

Sleeveless dress

MATERIALS

18 (19, 20, 21) oz. Lee Target Motoravia Double Knitting in main colour, 2 oz. in first contrasting and 1 oz. in second contrasting colour. One pair each Nos. 9 and 10 knitting needles (USA sizes 5 and 3). One crochet hook International Standard size 4.00.

MEASUREMENTS

To fit bust size 34 (36, 38, 40) in.; length 38 (38¼, 38½, 38¾) in.

TENSION

6 sts. to 1 in.

ABBREVIATIONS

See page 22; M., main colour; C., contrasting colour.

BACK

With No. 10 needles and M., cast on 139 (145, 153, 157) sts. Beg. with a k. row, work 9 rows in st.st.

Next row: k. to mark hemline.

Change to No. 9 needles and continue in st.st.

Work straight until back measures 4 (3½, 4, 4) in. from hemline. Dec. 1 st. at both ends of next and then every following 24th (14th, 32nd, 18th) row until 129 (129, 145, 145) sts. remain. Continue straight until back

measures 16½ in. from hemline, ending with a p. row.

Now join in first C. and work in patt. as follows:

1st row: with first C., k.1, * y.fwd., k.6, sl.1, k.2 tog., p.s.s.o., k.6, y.fwd., k.1; rep. from * to end.

2nd row: with first C., p.

Rep. last 2 rows once more. Join second C. and rep. first and 2nd rows twice, but use second C. Rep. last 8 rows once more, then rep. the first 2 rows twice. Break off first and second C. and continue with M. only. Work in st.st., dec. 1 st. at both ends of next and then every following 6th row until 109 (115, 121, 127) sts. remain.

Continue straight until back measures 31½ in. from hemline (measure with work hanging from needle).

Shape Armholes

Cast off 6 sts. at beg. of next 2 rows, then dec. 1 st. at both ends of every row until 83 (89, 93, 99) sts. remain. **

Continue straight until armhole measures 6½ (6¾, 7, 7¼) in., ending with a p. row.

Shape Shoulders and Back Neck

1st row: cast off 7 (7, 8, 8) sts., k.23 (25, 25, 27) including st. already on needle, cast off 23 (25, 27, 29) sts., k. to end.

Continue on last set of sts. only.

2nd row: cast off 7 (7, 8, 8) sts., p. to end.

3rd row: cast off 5 sts., k. to end.

Rep. last 2 rows once more. Cast off remaining 6 (8, 7, 9) sts.

Rejoin yarn to neck edge of remaining sts.

1st row: cast off 5 sts., p. to end.

2nd row: cast off 7 (7, 8, 8) sts., k. to end.

3rd row: as first row.

Cast off remaining 6 (8, 7, 9) sts.

FRONT
Work as for Back to **.
Continue straight until armhole measures 5 (5¼, 5½, 5¾) in., ending with a p. row.

Shape Neck
Next row: k.31 (33, 34, 36), cast off 21 (23, 25, 27) sts., k. to end.
Continue on last set of sts. only. P. 1 row.
*** Dec. 1 st. at neck edge on every row until 20 (22, 23, 25) sts. remain.

Shape Shoulder
Cast off 7 (7, 8, 8) sts. at beg. of next and following alternate row. Work 1 row. Cast off remaining 6 (8, 7, 9) sts. Rejoin yarn to neck edge of remaining sts. and work as for first side from *** to end.

TO COMPLETE
Press. Join shoulder and side seams. Turn up hem at lower edge and sl.st. to wrong side.

Neck Edging
With crochet hook and first C., work 85 (88, 91, 94) d.c. round neck edge, turn with 1 ch.
2nd row: 1 d.c. into first d.c., * 3 ch., miss 2 d.c., 1 d.c. into next d.c.; rep. from * to end.
3rd row: work 4 d.c. into each loop. Fasten off. Join ends of edging.

Arm Edgings
With first C. work 73 (73, 76, 76) d.c. round armhole edge. Turn with 1 ch. and work 2nd and 3rd rows as for neck edging. Fasten off and join ends of edgings.
Press seams, hem and edgings lightly.

Peasant-style suit
illustrated in colour on page 89

MATERIALS
20 (21, 22) balls (20 gr. each) Wendy Tricel Nylon Crêpe Double Knit for skirt, 12 (13, 13) balls for waistcoat. One pair each Nos. 9 and 11 knitting needles (USA sizes 5 and 2). A medium crochet hook. A 7-in. zip fastener. A waist length of elastic.

MEASUREMENTS
To fit bust size 34 (36, 38) in.; hip size 36 (38, 40) in.; length of waistcoat 21 (21½, 22) in.; length of skirt 30 in.

TENSION
6½ sts. to 1 in. over st.st. on No. 9 needles.

ABBREVIATIONS
See page 22; inc. 1, increase one st., by picking up loop between sts. and k. into back of it.

SKIRT
BACK AND FRONT (make 2 pieces alike)
With No. 11 needles cast on 85 (91, 97) sts.
1st row: k.1, * p.1, k.1; rep. from * to end.
2nd row: p.1, * k.1, p.1; rep. from * to end.
Rep. these 2 rows for 1¼ in., ending with 2nd row.
Change to No. 9 needles and beg. with a k. row work 4 rows in st.st.
Next row: k.2, inc. 1, k.25 (27, 29), inc. 1, k.2, inc. 1, k.27 (29, 31), inc. 1, k.2, inc. 1, k.25 (27, 29), inc. 1, k.2.
Work 7 rows in st.st.
Next row: k.2, inc. 1, k.27 (29, 31), inc. 1, k.2, inc. 1, k.29 (31, 33), inc. 1, k.2, inc. 1, k.27 (29, 31), inc. 1, k.2.
Cont. to inc. in this way on every 8th row until there are 127 (133, 139) sts., then omitting inc. at each end of row, cont. to inc. at each side of the 2 dart sts. on every 20th row until work measures 29½ in. from beg., or ½ in. less than final length required, ending with a p. row.
Change to No. 11 needles and work 2 rows in rib as at beg.
Cast off loosely in rib.

WAISTCOAT
BACK
With No. 11 needles cast on 135 (145, 153) sts. and work 2 rows in rib as on Skirt, inc. 1 st. at end of 2nd row on first and 3rd sizes only: 136 (145, 154) sts.
Change to No. 9 needles and beg. with a k. row cont. in st.st. until work measures 5 in. from beg., ending with a p. row.
Next row: k.1, * k.2 tog., k.1; rep. from * to end: 91 (97, 103) sts.
Cont. in st.st. for 5 rows.
Next row: k.2, * inc. 1, k.29 (31, 33); rep. from * twice more, inc. 1, k.2.
Work 7 rows.
Next row: k.2, inc. 1, k.30 (32, 34), inc. 1, k.31 (33, 35), inc. 1, k.30 (32, 34), inc. 1, k.2. Cont. to inc. in this way on every 8th row until there are 119 (125, 131) sts., then cont. straight until work measures 14 in. from beg. ending with a p. row.

Shape Armholes
Cast off 6 sts. at beg. of next 2 rows, then 2 sts. at beg. of next 4 rows.
Next row: k.1, sl.1, k.1, p.s.s.o., k. to last 3 sts., k.2 tog., k.1.
Next row: p. to end.
Rep. the last 2 rows 6 (7, 8) times more: 85 (89, 93) sts.
Cont. straight until armhole measures 7 (7½, 8) in., ending with a p. row.

Shape Shoulders
Cast off 6 sts. at beg. of next 6 rows, then 6 (7, 8) sts. at beg. of next 2 rows.
Change to No. 11 needles and work 2 rows in rib as at beg.
Cast off in rib.

LEFT FRONT
With No. 11 needles cast on 63 (67, 73) sts. and work 2 rows in rib as on Back, inc. 1 st. at end of 2nd row on first and 2nd sizes: 64 (68, 73) sts.
Change to No. 9 needles and cont. in st.st. until work measures 5 in. from beg., ending with a p. row.
Next row: k.1 (2, 1), * k.2 tog., k.1; rep. from * to end: 43 (46, 49) sts.
Cont. in st.st. for 5 rows.
Next row: k.2, inc. 1, k.29 (31, 33), inc. 1, k. to end.
Work 7 rows.
Next row: k.2, inc. 1, k.30 (32, 34), inc. 1, k. to end.
Cont. to inc. in this way on every 8th row until there are 57 (60, 63) sts., then cont. straight until work measures 12 rows less than Back to armholes, ending with a p. row.

Shape Front Edge
Next row: k. to last 3 sts., k.2 tog., k.1.
Work 3 rows straight.
Rep. the last 4 rows twice more.

Shape Armhole
Next row: cast off 6, k. to last 3 sts., k.2 tog., k.1.
Cont. to shape armhole to match Back, at the same time cont. to dec. at front edge on every 4th row until 25 (26, 27) sts. rem. Cont. straight, if necessary, until armhole measures the same as on Back, ending with a p. row.

Shape Shoulder
Cast off 6 sts. at beg. of next and foll. 2 alt. rows. P. 1 row, then cast off rem. 7 (8, 9) sts.

RIGHT FRONT
Work to match Left Front, reversing all shaping.

LEFT FRONT BORDER
With No. 11 needles and right side facing pick up and k. 131 (135, 139) sts. along front edge. Work 1 row rib as at beg.
Next row: rib 54 (58, 62) sts., m.1, work 2 tog., (rib 13, m.1, work 2 tog.) 3 times, rib to end.
Cast off in rib.

RIGHT FRONT BORDER
Work to match Left Front Border but ribbing 30 sts. at beg. of row of holes instead of 54 (58, 62) sts.

ARMHOLE BORDERS (make both alike)
Join shoulder seams.
With No. 11 needles and right side facing, pick up and k. 95 (101, 107) sts. along armhole edge. Work 2 rows in rib.
Cast off in rib.

TO COMPLETE
Press work very lightly with a cool iron over a slightly damp cloth.
Join side seams of skirt, leaving one side open for zip. Sew in zip. Sew elastic behind waist with herringbone sts.
Join side seams of waistcoat. Press all seams well. Make a crochet chain 60 in. long and thread through holes of Waistcoat to form lace-up fastening.

Roll-collar pullover
also illustrated in colour on page 61

MATERIALS
17 (18, 19) oz. Emu Scotch Double Knitting. One pair each No. 6 and No. 7 knitting needles (USA sizes 8 and 7). One cable needle. One medium-sized crochet hook. One 12-in. zip fastener.

MEASUREMENTS
To fit bust size 34/35 (36/37, 38/39) in.; length 23 (23, 24) in.; sleeve seam 18 in.

TENSION
7 sts. to 1 in. over rib (unstretched).

ABBREVIATIONS
See page 22.

FRONT
With No. 6 needles cast on 122 (128, 134) sts. and k. 1 row. Now work in rib.
1st row: k.2, * p.4, k.2; rep. from * to end.
2nd row: p.2, * k.4, p.2; rep. from * to end. Cont. in rib until work measures 10½ (10½, 11½) in., ending with a 2nd row. Change to honeycomb patt.
1st row: k.1, * sl. next st. on to cable needle and leave at front of work, p. next 2 sts. k. st. from cable needle, sl. next 2 sts. on to cable needle and leave at back of work, k.1, p. 2 sts. from cable needle; rep. from * to last st., k.1.
2nd and 4th rows: p.1, * k.2, p.2, k.2: rep. from * to last st., p.1.
3rd row: k.1, * p.2, k.2, p.2; rep. from * to last st., k.1.
5th row: k.1, * sl. next 2 sts. on to cable needle and leave at back of work, k.1, p. sts. from cable needle, sl. next st. on to cable needle and leave at front of work, p.2, k. st. from cable needle; rep. from * to last st., k.1.
6th row: p.2, * k.4, p.2; rep. from * to end.
These 6 rows from the patt. Cont. straight until Front is 15 (15, 16) in., ending with a wrong-side row.

Shape Armholes
Cast off 4 sts. at beg. of next 2 rows, then 3 sts. at beg. of next 2 rows.

Divide for Opening
Next row: cast off 2 sts., patt. 52 (55, 58) sts. (including st. used in casting off); turn and leave rem. sts. on st. holder.
Working on first sts. only, dec. 1 st. at armhole edge on next 2 rows: 50 (53, 56) sts.
Work straight until armhole measures 7½ in. ending at opening edge.

** Shape Shoulder
Next 2 rows: patt. to last 11 (12, 12) sts.; turn and patt. back.
Next 2 rows: patt. to last 22 (24, 24) sts.; turn and patt. back.
Next 2 rows: patt. to last 33 (36, 36) sts.; turn and patt. back.
Work 1 row back to armhole edge. Cast off 33 (36, 36) sts. ** Leave rem. sts. on st. holder.
Rejoin yarn to sts. for other side of opening, and work to match first side, reversing shapings.

BACK
Work as Front until Back measures 15 (15, 16) in., ending with a wrong-side row.

Shape Armholes
Cast off 4 sts. at beg. of next 2 rows, 3 sts. at beg. of

next 2 rows and 2 sts. at beg. of next 2 rows, then dec. 1 st. at beg. of next 2 rows. Cont. straight until work measures 20½ (20½, 21½) in.

Shape Neck
Next row: patt. 38 (41, 44) sts.; turn and leave rem. sts. on st. holder. Cast off 2 sts. at beg. of next and next alt. row.
For size 38/39. Cast off 3 sts. at beg. of next alt. row.
For all sizes. Dec. 1 st. at neck edge on next row. Cont. straight until armhole measures same as Front to shoulder.

Shape Shoulder
Work as Front from ** to **.
Return to rem. sts. Slip centre 26 sts. on st. holder then work to match other side of neck on rem. sts.

SLEEVES (make 2 alike)
With No. 7 needles cast on 56 sts. and k. 1 row, then work in rib as for Front for 3 in.
Change to No. 6 needles and cont. in rib, inc. 1 st. at each end of next and every foll. 6th row until there are 86 sts. Cont. straight until Sleeve measures 18 in. (or length required).

Shape Top
Cast off 4 sts. at beg. of next 2 rows, 3 sts. at beg. of next 2 rows and 2 sts. at beg. of next 2 rows. Rep. last 6 rows once.
Now dec. 1 st. at beg. of every row until 26 sts. remain, then cast off 2 sts. at beg. of next 6 rows. Cast off.

TO COMPLETE
Collar
Join shoulder seams. With No. 7 needles, beg. at opening edge of right front and k. across sts. from st. holder, pick up and k. 2 sts. to shoulder and 16 sts. down side of back neck, then k. across centre back neck sts., pick up and k. 16 sts. to shoulder and 2 sts. down front neck, then k. across sts. from st. holder on left front.
Work in p.4, k.2 rib (so right side is inside) for 6 in. Cast off in rib.

To Make Up
Join side and sleeve seams and sew in Sleeves.
Work 2 rows of d.c. all round front opening. Sew zip down front opening. Press seams lightly.

Pinafore dress

MATERIALS
19 (20, 21) oz. Lister Lochinvar Double Knitting. One pair No. 9 knitting needles (USA size 5). One crochet hook International Standard Size 3.50.

MEASUREMENTS
To fit bust size 34 (36, 38) in.; length 41 (41$\frac{1}{4}$, 41$\frac{1}{2}$) in.

TENSION
6 sts. to 1 in.

ABBREVIATIONS
See page 22.

BACK
Cast on 156 (162, 168) sts. Work 2$\frac{1}{2}$ in. in st.st.
Continue in st.st., dec. 1 st. at both ends of next and every following 8th row until 106 (112, 118) sts. remain. * Continue straight until Back measures 33$\frac{1}{2}$ in.

Shape Armholes
Cast off 6 sts. at beg. of next 2 rows, then dec. 1 st. at both ends of every row until 78 (84, 88) sts. remain. Continue straight until armhole measures 7$\frac{1}{4}$ (7$\frac{1}{2}$, 7$\frac{3}{4}$) in., ending with a p. row.

Shape Shoulders and Back Neck
Next row: cast off 5 (5, 6) sts., k.19 (21, 22) including st. already on needle, cast off 30 (32, 32) sts., k. to end. Continue on last set of sts. only.
1st row: cast off 5 (5, 6) sts., p. to end.
2nd row: cast off 5 sts., k. to end.
Rep. last 2 rows once more. Cast off remaining 4 (6, 6) sts. Rejoin yarn to neck edge of remaining sts.
1st row: cast off 5 sts., p. to end.
2nd row: cast off 5 (5, 6) sts., k. to end.

3rd row: as first row. Cast off remaining 4 (6, 6) sts.

FRONT
Work as for Back to *.
Continue straight until Front measures 32 in., ending with a p. row.

Shape Neck
Next row: k.53 (56, 59); turn and continue on these sts. only.
** Dec. 1 st. at neck edge on next and every following 4th row until front is 33½ in., ending at side edge.

Shape Armhole
Continue to dec. at front edge on every 4th row and at the same time cast off 6 sts. at beg. of next row, then dec. 1 st. at armhole edge on following 8 (8, 9) rows. Keeping armhole edge straight, continue to dec. at neck edge on every 4th row until 14 (16, 18) sts. remain. Continue straight until armhole measures 7¼ (7½, 7¾) in., ending at armhole edge.

Shape Shoulder
Cast off 5 (5, 6) sts. at beg. of next and following alternate row. Work 1 row. Cast off rem. 4 (6, 6) sts.
Rejoin yarn to neck edge of remaining sts. and k. 1 row. Now work as for first side from ** to end.

TO COMPLETE
Press. Join shoulder and side seams. Using crochet hook, work 2 rows of double crochet along lower edge, round neck and armholes. Join ends of edgings. Press seams and edgings.

Poncho, skirt and helmet – knitted on a circular needle
illustrated on page 108

MATERIALS
39 (41, 43, 45) oz. Wendy Double Knit Nylonised for poncho and skirt, 4 oz. for the helmet. One Twin Pin (circular needle) No. 7, 24 in. long; one pair No. 7 knitting needles (USA size 7). ¾ yd. facing ribbon, 1 in. wide. A 7-in. zip fastener. A waist length of elastic, 1 in. wide. Two press studs.

MEASUREMENTS
Poncho: to fit bust size 32–40 in.; length 30¼ in.
Skirt: to fit hip size 36 (38, 40, 42) in.; length 18½ in.

TENSION
6 sts. and 11 rows to 1 in.

ABBREVIATIONS
See page 22; PU1, pick up and knit into loop before next stitch.

SKIRT
Using the circular needle, cast on 264 (276, 288, 300) sts. and work as follows:
1st round: k. **2nd round:** p.
Rep. these 2 rounds once. Now begin pattern:
1st round: * p.1, keeping yarn at front sl.1 purlwise; rep. from * to end. **2nd round:** k.
3rd round: * yarn at front, sl.1 purlwise, p.1; rep. from * to end. **4th round:** k.
These 4 rounds form patt. Cont. in patt. until skirt is 6 in., ending with a first or 3rd round.
(Note. Length can be adjusted here.)
Next round: * k.42 (44, 46, 48), sl.1, k.2 tog., p.s.s.o., k.42 (44, 46, 48); rep. from * to end.
Work 11 rounds without shaping.

Next round: * k.41 (43, 45, 47), sl.1, k.2 tog., p.s.s.o., k.40 (42, 44, 46), sl.1, k.2 tog., p.s.s.o., k.41 (43, 45, 47); rep. from * to end.
Work 11 rounds without shaping.
Cont. to dec. in this manner noting that there will be 1 st. fewer in side panels and 2 sts. fewer in centre panel after each dec. until there are 192 (204, 216, 228) sts. Now dec. every 8th round until there are 160 (172, 184, 196) sts. Work straight until skirt is 18½ in. or desired length. Cast off.

HELMET
With pair of No. 7 needles cast on 104 sts. and work 2 rows in k.1, p.1 rib. Change to patt. (Note. 2nd and 4th rows will be p.) and cont. till work is 2 in. ending with 1st or 3rd row.
Next row: p.50, PU1, p.1, PU1, p.2, PU1, p.1, PU1, p.50. **Next row:** patt. 1 row.
Next row: p.51, PU1, p.1, PU1, p.4, PU1, p.1, PU1, p.51.

Cont. to inc. in this way, with 1 extra st. at each end and 2 extra sts. between incs. in centre, on each inc. row until there are 128 sts.
Cont. straight till work is 4 in.

Shape Face
Slip first 12 sts. on spare needle. Rejoin yarn to next st., work to last 12 sts. Leave these on spare needle. Cont. straight until work is 8 in., ending with a p. row.

Shape Top
1st row: patt. 65, k.2 tog. t.b.l., turn.
Next row: p.27, p.2 tog., turn.
Next row: patt. 27, k.2 tog. t.b.l., turn.
Work last 2 rows until all sts. have been worked off.

Edging
With right side of work facing, k.12 sts. from spare needle at right end, pick up and k.26 sts. along right side of face edging, k.28 across centre, pick up and k.26 sts. down left side, k.12 sts. on spare needle: 104 sts.
Work 4 rows in k.1, p.1 rib. Cast off in rib.

PONCHO
With the circular needle cast on 384 sts. and work as for Skirt until poncho is 6 in. ending with a first or 3rd round. (Note. Length can be adjusted here.)
Next round: * k.2, sl.1, k.2 tog., p.s.s.o., k.182, sl.1, k.2 tog., p.s.s.o., k.2; rep. from * to end. Work 37 rounds without shaping.
Next round: * k.2, sl.1, k.2 tog., p.s.s.o., k.178, sl.1, k.2 tog., p.s.s.o., k.2; rep. from * to end. Work 24 rounds without shaping and break off yarn. Slip first 68 sts. from left-hand point to right point. Slip next 48 sts. on spare needle for front panel. Rejoin yarn to next st. and using a separate No. 7 needle work across all sts. working backwards and forwards thus noting that 2nd and 4th rows will be p.
1st row: k.6, patt. to last 6 sts., k.6.
2nd row: k.6, p. to last 6 sts., k.6.
Rep. these 2 rows 5 times then first row once.
Next row: k.6, p.57, sl.1, p.2 tog., p.s.s.o., p.4, sl.1, k.2 tog., p.s.s.o., p.4, sl.1, p.2 tog., p.s.s.o., p.57, k.6.
Work 30 rows without shaping.
Break yarn and leave these sts. on spare needle. Slip 48 sts. of front panel on to No. 7 needles and cast on 6 at beg. of next 2 rows. Work 40 rows in patt. Cast off 6 sts. at beg. of next 2 rows. Break yarn. Slip front panel sts. on to left-hand side of circular needle, then slip the first 66 sts. from right-hand end of needle to left. Rejoin yarn and cont. in rounds, working 7 without shaping.

Next round: * k.2, sl.1, k.2 tog., p.s.s.o., k.170, sl.1, k.2 tog., p.s.s.o., k.2; rep. from * to end. Work 5 rounds straight. Cont. to dec. thus every 6th round to 256 sts.

Divide for Front Opening
Break yarn and slip 85 sts. from left side of needle to the right. Mark beg. with a contrast thread, rejoin yarn and work backwards and forwards as follows:
1st row: k.6, patt. to coloured thread, turn.
2nd row: cast on 3 sts., p. to last 6 sts., k.6. Rep. these 2 rows once then the first row once.
6th row: p.59, sl.1, p.2 tog., p.s.s.o., p.4, sl.1, p.2 tog., p.s.s.o., p.118, sl.1, p.2 tog., p.s.s.o., p.4, sl.1, p.2 tog., p.s.s.o., p.56, k.6.
Work 5 rows without shaping. Cont. to dec. thus every 6th row keeping 6 k. sts. at border on right front until

there are 227 sts. Then dec. every alt. row until there are 107 sts. Work 11 rows garter st. Cast off.

TO COMPLETE
Skirt
Join elastic for waist into a circle; place inside waistband and attach with herringbone stitches.

Helmet
Backstitch neck seam.

Poncho
Slip st. facing ribbon to inside of neckband and right front. Catch down under-wraps of neck and armhole openings. Sew in zip, attaching right edge to inside edge of facing ribbon. Finish collar with 2 press studs.

Winter-warm outfits—duffle coat with hood (see opposite) and matching poncho, skirt and helmet (see previous page).

Duffle coat with hood

MATERIALS
29 balls (50 gr. each) Wendy Diabolo. One pair No. 4 knitting needles (USA size 10). Five medium buttons. Ten press fasteners. 10 yd. braid, 1 in. wide.

MEASUREMENTS
To fit bust size 34—36 in.; length 40 in.; sleeve seam 16 in.

TENSION
4 sts. and 5 rows to 1 in. over st.st.

ABBREVIATIONS
See page 22; inc. 1, increase one st., by picking up loop between sts. and k. into back of it.

BACK
With No. 4 needles cast on 120 sts. and work in st.st. for 14 rows.
Next row: k.29, sl.1, k.1, p.s.s.o., k.2, k.2 tog., k.50, sl.1, k.1, p.s.s.o., k.2, k.2 tog., k.29. Work 13 rows in st.st.
Next row: k.28, sl.1, k.1, p.s.s.o., k.2, k.2 tog., k.48, sl.1, k.1, p.s.s.o., k.2, k.2 tog., k.28.
Cont. to dec. in this way on every 14th row until 80 sts. rem., then work 9 rows after last dec.

Shape Armholes
Cast off 4 sts. at beg. of next 2 rows.
Next row: k.1, k.2 tog., k. to last 3 sts., sl.1, k.1, p.s.s.o., k.1.
Next row: p.1, p.2 tog. t.b.l., p. to last 3 sts., p.2 tog., p.1.
Rep. the last 2 rows 3 times more.
Cont. to dec. on next and every foll. 3rd row until 42 sts. rem., work 2 rows after last dec., then dec. on next and every alt. row until 22 sts. rem., ending with a p. row. Cast off.

LEFT FRONT
With No. 4 needles cast on 62 sts. and work in st.st. for 14 rows.
Next row: k.29, sl.1, k.1, p.s.s.o., k.2, k.2 tog., k.27. Work 13 rows in st.st.
Next row: k.28, sl.1, k.1, p.s.s.o., k.2, k.2 tog., k.26.
Cont. to dec. in this way on every 14th row until 42 sts. rem., then work 9 rows after last dec.

Shape Armhole
Cast off 4 sts. at beg. of next row.
Next row: p. to end.
Next row: k.1, k.2 tog., k. to end.
Next row: p. to last 3 sts., p.2 tog., p.1.
Rep. the last 2 rows 3 times more.
Cont. to dec. at armhole edge on next and every foll. 3rd row until 23 sts. rem. then work 2 rows after last dec. Dec. at armhole edge on next and every alt. row until 18 sts. rem., ending with a k. row.

Shape Neck
Next row: cast off 6, p. to end.
Next row: k.1, k.2 tog., k. to last 2 sts., k. 2 tog.
Next row: p. to end.
Rep. the last 2 rows 3 times more: 4 sts.
Next row: k.1, k.2 tog., k.1.
Next row: p.2 tog., p.1.
Cast off rem. 2 sts.

RIGHT FRONT
Work to match Left Front, reversing all shaping.

SLEEVES (make 2 alike)
With No. 4 needles cast on 44 sts. and work in st.st., inc. 1 st. at each end of 9th and every foll. 8th row until there are 60 sts., then cont. straight until sleeve measures 17 in., ending with a p. row. (Note. The last inch is set into armhole shaping and is not included in sleeve seam measurement.)

Shape Top
Dec. as on Back at each end of next and every foll. 4th row until 52 sts. rem., then work 3 rows after last dec. Dec. at each end of next and every alt. row until 22 sts. rem., ending with a p. row. Dec. at each end of next 6 rows.
Cast off rem. 10 sts.

POCKETS (make 2 alike)
With No. 4 needles cast on 24 sts. and work in st.st. for 6 in. Cast off.

HOOD
With No. 4 needles cast on 74 sts. and beg. with a k. row work 6 rows in st.st.
Next row: k.2, * k.2 tog., k.2; rep. from * to end: 56 sts.
Cont. in st.st. for 3 in., ending with a k. row.
Next row: cast off 4, p. to last 4 sts., cast off 4.
With right side facing rejoin yarn.
Next row: k.1, * inc. 1, k.2; rep. from * to last st., inc. 1, k.1: 72 sts.
Cont. in st.st. for 11 in., ending with a k. row.
Next row: cast off 20, p. to last 20 sts., cast off 20.
With right side facing rejoin yarn and cont. on the 32 sts. in st.st. for 5 in.
Cast off.

TO COMPLETE
Press work with a warm iron over a damp cloth. Join raglan seams, sewing the last inch of sleeve seams to the cast-off sts. at armholes. Join side and sleeve seams. Sew braid down each raglan seam, then round neck edge, lower edge of coat and sleeves and up each front. Make buttonhole tabs in braid on right front. Sew braid along top edge of pockets, then sew on pockets. Press seams. Sew on buttons. Sew press fasteners underneath braid to correspond with each button.
Sew on braid around face edge of hood and down two front edges. Sew on button tab and button and two press fasteners — one at top and one at bottom. Also one press fastener on each shoulder and at centre back to attach hood to coat.

Brown and white coat
illustrated in colour on page 93

MATERIALS
27 (29, 31) oz. Wendy Double Knit Nylonised in main colour, 3 (4, 4) in a contrasting colour. One pair each Nos. 9 and 11 knitting needles (USA sizes 5 and 2). 1 (1¼, 1¼) yards petersham ribbon, 2 in. wide. One large button. Two press fasteners.

MEASUREMENTS
To fit bust size 34 (36, 38) in.; length from top of shoulder 42 (42½, 43) in.; sleeve seam 17½ (18, 18) in.

TENSION
6 sts. and 7 rows to 1 in.

ABBREVIATIONS
See page 22; M., main shade; C., contrasting shade.

BACK
With No. 9 needles and M., cast on 140 (146, 152) sts. Work in st.st. Dec. 1 st. at each end of every 8th row 14 times, then every 6th row 5 times and then every 4th row 6 times. Now inc. 1 st. at each end of every 8th row 5 times: 100 (106, 112) sts. When work measures 32 (32, 32½) in. from beg. shape armholes as follows. Cast off 6 sts. at beg. of next 2 rows, then dec. 1 st. at each end of every row until 76 (80, 84) sts. remain. When armholes measure 7 (7½, 7½) in., shape shoulders and neck as follows:
Next row: cast off 5, work 24 (25, 26) including st. on needle, place rem. sts. on a st. holder. Cast off at neck edge 3 sts. 3 times and continue to cast off at armhole edge 5 sts. twice more and 5 (6, 7) sts. once. Go back to sts. left on st. holder and join yarn at centre edge. Cast off the first 18 (20, 22) sts. then work on rem. sts. to correspond with other side of neck. With No. 11 needles and C., pick up and k.138 (144, 150) sts. along cast-on edge. Work in garter st. for 11 rows. Change to M. Work in garter st. for 11 rows. Cast off on wrong side.

LEFT FRONT
With No. 9 needles and M., cast on 74 (77, 80) sts. Work in st.st. Work 7 rows. Dec. 1 st. at end of next row. Rep. this dec. at this edge every 8th row 13 times more, then every 6th row 5 times and then every 4th row 6 times. Now inc. 1 st. at this edge every 8th row 5 times. At the same time when work measures 27 in. from beg., finishing at centre edge, shape neck as follows.
Dec. 1 st. at beg. of next row. Rep. this dec. at this edge every 4th row 21 (22, 23) times more. At the same time when work measures 32 (32, 32½) in. from beg., finishing at outside edge, shape armhole as follows. Cast off 6 sts. at beg. of next row then dec. 1 st. at this edge on every row 6 (7, 8) times. When armhole measures 7 (7½, 7½) in., shape shoulder as follows. Cast off at armhole edge 5 sts. 3 times and 5 (6, 7) sts. once.
With No. 11 needles and C., pick up and k. 73 (76, 79) sts. along cast-on edge. Work in garter st. Work 11 rows C., 11 rows M., inc. 1 st. at centre edge on every alternate row. Cast off.

RIGHT FRONT
Work as for Left Front, reversing shapings.

SLEEVES (make 2 alike)
With No. 9 needles and M., cast on 48 (52, 52) sts. Work in st.st. Inc. 1 st. at each end of every 6th row until there are 76 (80, 80) sts. When sleeve measures 15½ (16, 16) in. from beg., shape top of sleeve as follows.

Cast off 6 sts. at beg. of next 2 rows, dec. 1 st. at beg. only of foll. 16 (20, 20) rows, then dec. 1 st. at each end of every row until 20 sts. remain. Cast off. With No. 11 needles and C., pick up and k.46 (50, 50) sts. along cast-on edge then work border as for lower edge of Back.

BELT
With No. 9 needles and M., cast on 28 sts. Work in st.st. Work straight for 30 (32, 34) in., finishing with a p. row.

Next row: k.14; turn.
Work 6 rows on these sts. Break yarn. Rejoin yarn at centre and work 7 rows on rem. sts. Work 3 rows across all sts. Shape point as follows.
Next row: k.7; turn.
Dec. 1 st. at beg. of next row. Rep. this dec. at this edge on every alternate row twice more.
Cast off rem. sts. Rejoin yarn, k. across next 14 sts. Work on these sts., dec. 1 st. at each end of next row. Rep. this dec. on every alternate row twice more. Cast off. K. across rem. 7 sts. Dec. 1 st. at inside edge on every alternate row 3 times. Cast off.

TO COMPLETE
Press all pieces under a damp cloth. Back st. side, shoulder and sleeve seams, oversewing garter st. borders. Set in Sleeves.

Front Borders
Beg. at bottom of Right Front, with No. 11 needles and C., pick up and k. 163 (163, 163) sts. along straight edge of Right Front, 73 (77, 81) sts. along shaped edge of neck and 21 (22, 23) sts. to centre back of neck. Work in garter st. Work 11 rows C., 11 rows M., inc. 1 st. at bottom of coat on every alternate row. Cast off. In a similar way, work border for Left Front. Join borders tog. at centre back of neck. Place the petersham on to the wrong side of belt and join side edges of belt tog. in the centre of the petersham. Cut a space in the petersham to correspond with buttonhole and shape point. Work round buttonhole. Press seams, front borders and belt. Sew 2 press studs to borders of coat at waist. Sew button to belt.

Skinny rib sweater

MATERIALS
10 (10, 11, 11, 12, 12) oz. Twilleys Cortina Super Crochet Wool. One pair No. 11 knitting needles (USA size 2). One crochet hook International Standard Size 2.50.

MEASUREMENTS
To fit bust size 34 (36, 38, 40, 42, 44) in.; length from shoulder 25½ (25½, 26, 26, 26½, 26½) in.

TENSION
8 sts. to 1 in. over rib when slightly stretched.

ABBREVIATIONS
See page 22.

BACK AND FRONT (make 2 pieces alike)
Cast on 146 (154, 162, 170, 178, 186) sts.
1st rib row: k.3, * p.4, k.4; rep. from * to last 7 sts.,
p.4, k.3.
2nd rib row: k.1, p.2, * k.4, p.4; rep. from * to last 7 sts.,
k.4, p.2, k.1.
Rep. the 2 rib rows until work measures 19 in.

To Shape Armholes
Cast off 8 (8, 9, 9, 10, 10) sts. at start of next 2 rows,
then dec. 1 st. at each end of next 8 (10, 10, 12, 12, 14)
rows and the foll. 4 (4, 5, 5, 6, 6) alt. rows.
Cont. on rem. 106 (110, 114, 118, 122, 126) sts. until
work measures 23½ (23½, 24, 24, 24½, 24½) in.

Shape Neck
Next row: rib 45 (46, 47, 48, 49, 50) sts.; turn.
Leave rem. sts. on a spare needle.
Dec. 1 st. at neck edge on next 9 rows and the foll. 3 alt.
rows.

Cont. on rem. 33 (34, 35, 36, 37, 38) sts. until work
measures 25½ (25½, 26, 26, 26½, 26½) in., finishing at
armhole edge.

To Shape Shoulder
Cast off 7 sts. at start of next row and the foll. 3 alt. rows.
Work 1 row, then cast off rem. 5 (6, 7, 8, 9, 10) sts.
With right side of work facing, join yarn to inner end of
sts. on spare needle, cast off next 16 (18, 20, 22, 24, 26)
sts. Rib to end. Complete to match first side.

TO COMPLETE
Join shoulder and side seams.
With right side of work facing, join yarn to a shoulder
seam at neck edge and using crochet hook, work a
row of d.c. all round neck.
Picot row: work 1 d.c. in first d.c., * make 3 ch., then
work 1 d.c. in last d.c. to form a picot, 1 d.c. in each of
next 3 d.c.; rep. from * all round neck. Fasten off.
Work a similar edging round each armhole.

Chapter eight
PARTY SPECIALS

Bolero
illustrated opposite

MATERIALS
6 (6, 7, 7) balls (20 gr. each) Emu Filigree in main shade and 1 ball in a contrasting shade. One pair each Nos. 5 and 6 knitting needles (USA sizes 9 and 8).

MEASUREMENTS
To fit bust size 34 (36, 38, 40) in.; length 15¼ (15½, 15½, 15¾) in.; sleeve seam 5 in.

TENSION
4 sts. to 1 in. with No. 5 needles.

ABBREVIATIONS
See page 22; M., main shade; C., contrasting shade.

BACK
With No. 6 needles and C. cast on 60 (64, 68, 72) sts. and k. 3 rows.
Break C. Join M.
Next row: k.
Change to No. 5 needles and cont. with M. in reversed st.st., beg. with a k. row (wrong side). Inc. 1 st. at each end of the 2nd and every foll. 4th row until there are 78 (82, 86, 90) sts. Cont. straight until work measures 8 in.

Shape Armholes
Cast off 3 (4, 5, 5) sts. at beg. of next 2 rows, 2 sts. at beg. of next 2 rows, then dec. 1 st. at beg. of every row until 60 (62, 64, 66) sts. remain. Cont. straight until armholes measure 6¾ (7, 7, 7¼) in.

Shape Shoulders
Cast off 7 (8, 9, 9) sts. at beg. of next 2 rows.
Next row: cast off 5 sts., patt. 10 sts. (including st. used in casting off), cast off 26 (26, 26, 28) sts., patt. to end.
Working on last set of sts., cast off 5 sts. at armhole edge on next and next alt. row, and 5 sts. at neck edge on 2nd row.
Rejoin yarn to first set of sts., cast off at neck 5 sts. on first row and 5 sts. at armhole edge on 2nd row.

RIGHT FRONT
With No. 6 needles and C. cast on 32 (35, 38, 41) sts. and k. 3 rows. Break C.
Join M. and k. 1 row. Change to No. 5 needles, then beg. with a k. row (wrong side), cont. with M. in reversed st.st., inc. 1 st. at end of the 2nd row (a p. row) and every foll. 4th row until there are 41 (44, 47, 50) sts. Cont. straight until work measures 8 in. ending at side edge.

Shape Armhole
Cast off 3 (4, 5, 5) sts. at beg. of next row, 2 sts. at beg. of next alt. row and 1 st. at beg. of next 4 (4, 4, 5) alt. rows: 32 (34, 36, 38) sts. Cont. straight until armhole measures 5 (5, 5, 5¼) in., ending at front edge.

Shape Neck
Cast off 3 (4, 4, 5) sts. at beg. of next row, 2 sts. at beg. of next 5 (5, 5, 6) alt. rows and 1 st. at neck edge on next

2 (2, 3, 2) rows, and at the same time when armhole measures 6¾ (7, 7, 7¼) in. end at side edge.

Shape Shoulder
Cast off 7 (8, 9, 9) sts. at beg. of next row and 5 sts. at beg. of next 2 alt. rows.

LEFT FRONT
Work to match Right Front, reversing all shapings.

SLEEVES (make 2 alike)
With No. 6 needles and C. cast on 42 (44, 48, 52) sts. and k. 3 rows. Break off C.
Join M. and k. 1 row. Change to No. 5 needles and cont. in reversed st.st. beg. with a k. row (wrong-side), inc. 1 st. at each end of the 2nd and every foll. 4th row until there are 56 (60, 64, 68) sts. Cont. straight until Sleeve measures 5 in.

Shape Top
Cast off 3 (4, 5, 5) sts. at beg. of next 2 rows, 2 sts. at beg. of next 2 rows, then dec. 1 st. at beg. of every row until 12 (12, 14, 14) sts. remain. Cast off 2 sts. at beg. of next 2 rows. Cast off rem. sts.

TO COMPLETE
Border
Join shoulders. With right side facing, No. 6 needles and C. pick up and k. 66 sts. up front edge of Right Front from lower edge to neck shaping, 24 (26, 28, 30) sts. round front neck, 32 (33, 34, 35) sts. round back neck, 24 (26, 28, 30) sts. round front neck of Left Front and 66 sts. down front edge of Left Front.
K. 3 rows. Cast off purlwise.

To Make Up
Press work lightly on wrong side with a cool iron over a slightly damp cloth. Sew in sleeves. Join sleeve and side seams, then press seams.

Yellow skirt
illustrated in colour on page 116

MATERIALS
20 (21, 22) oz. Hayfield Gaylon Double Knitting in gold, 6 balls in navy and 3 balls in red. One pair each Nos. 9 and 10 knitting needles (USA sizes 5 and 3). ¾ yd. boned petersham ribbon, 1½ in. wide. An 8-in. gold zip fastener. Two large hooks and eyes.

MEASUREMENTS
To fit hip size 36 (38, 40) in.; length 41 in.

TENSION
6 sts. and 8 rows to 1 in. over st.st. with No. 9 needles.

ABBREVIATIONS
See page 22; G., gold; N., navy; R., red.

FRONT AND BACK (make 2 pieces alike)
With No. 10 needles and N. cast on 186 sts. and work 1 in. in st.st., beg. and ending with a k. row.
K. 1 row for hemline.

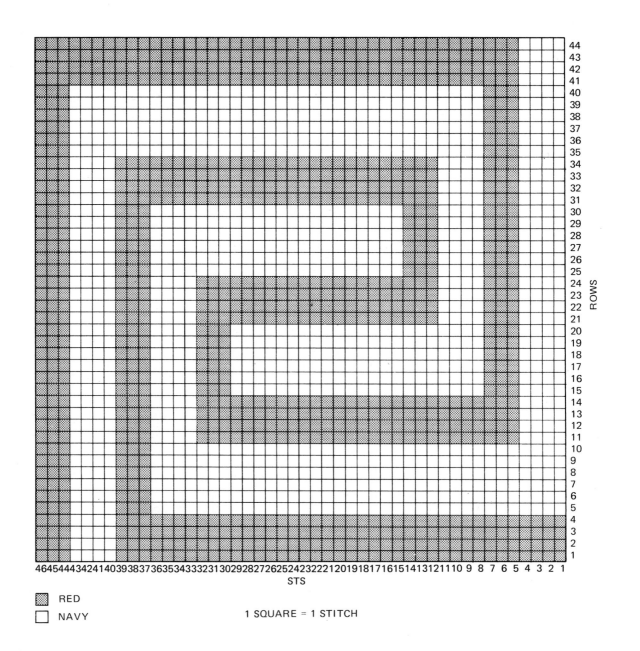

44
43
42
41
40
39
38
37
36
35
34
33
32
31
30
29
28
27
26
25
24
23
22
21
20
19
18
17
16
15
14
13
12
11
10
9
8
7
6
5
4
3
2
1

ROWS

46 45 44 43 42 41 40 39 38 37 36 35 34 33 32 31 30 29 28 27 26 25 24 23 22 21 20 19 18 17 16 15 14 13 12 11 10 9 8 7 6 5 4 3 2 1

STS

▦ RED

☐ NAVY

1 SQUARE = 1 STITCH

Now beg. with a k. row, work 1 in. more.

Change to No. 9 needles and border patt. as given in chart above. Beg. each row with a k. st. worked in same colour as first st. of patt. and ending each row with a k. st. worked in same colour as last st. of patt., work 4 reps. of the 46-st. chart patt. between, in st.st. Read chart from right to left for k. rows and from left to right for p. rows. Weave yarn not in use at back of work.

When the 44 patt. rows have been completed work 4 rows in N. in st.st. Cont. in N. and st.st.

1st dec. row: * k.6, k.2 tog. t.b.l., k.46, k.2 tog., k.6; rep. from * twice: 180 sts.

Work 3 more rows in N. then change to G. and work 18 (22, 26) rows straight.

2nd dec. row: * k.6, k.2 tog. t.b.l., k.44, k.2 tog., k.6; rep. from * twice: 174 sts.

Work 17 (21, 25) rows straight.

3rd dec. row: * k.6, k.2 tog. t.b.l., k.42, k.2 tog., k.6; rep. from * twice: 168 sts.

Work 17 (17, 21) rows straight.

4th dec. row: * k.6, k.2 tog. t.b.l., k.40, k.2 tog., k.6; rep. from * twice: 162 sts.

Work 15 rows straight.

5th dec. row: * k.6, k.2 tog. t.b.l., k.38, k.2 tog., k.6; rep. from * twice: 156 sts.

Work 15 rows straight.

6th dec. row: * k.6, k.2 tog. t.b.l., k.36, k.2 tog., k.6; rep. from * twice: 150 sts.

Work 15 (13, 15) rows straight.

7th dec. row: * k.6, k.2 tog. t.b.l., k.34, k.2 tog., k.6; rep. from * twice: 144 sts.

Work 15 (13, 13) rows straight.

8th dec. row: * k.6, k.2 tog. t.b.l., k.32, k.2 tog., k.6; rep. from * twice: 138 sts.

Work 15 (13, 13) rows straight.

9th dec. row: * k.6, k.2 tog. t.b.l., k.30, k.2 tog., k.6; rep. from * twice: 132 sts.

Work 11 (13, 13) rows straight.

10th dec. row: * k.6, k.2 tog. t.b.l., k.28, k.2 tog., k.6; rep. from * twice: 126 sts.

Work 11 (13, 13) rows straight.
11th dec. row: * k.6, k.2 tog. t.b.l., k.26, k.2 tog., k.6;
rep. from * twice: 120 sts.
Work 11 (13, 13) rows straight.
12th dec. row: * k.6, k.2 tog. t.b.l., k.24, k.2 tog., k.6;
rep. from * twice: 114 sts.
Work 11 (11, 13) rows straight.
13th dec. row: * k.6, k.2 tog. t.b.l., k.22, k.2 tog., k.6;
rep. from * twice: 108 sts.
Work 11 rows straight.
14th dec. row: * k.6, k.2 tog. t.b.l., k.20, k.2 tog., k.6;
rep. from * twice: 102 sts.
Work 11 rows straight.
15th dec. row: * k.6, k.2 tog. t.b.l., k.18, k.2 tog., k.6;
rep. from * twice: 96 sts.
Work 11 (11, 7) rows straight.
16th dec. row: * k.6, k.2 tog. t.b.l., k.16, k.2 tog., k.6;
rep. from * twice: 90 sts.
Work 11 (7, 3) rows straight.
For size 40 hip only. Cast off.
For sizes 36 and 38 hip only. 17th dec. row: * k.6,
k.2 tog. t.b.l., k.14, k.2 tog., k.6; rep. from * twice:
84 sts.
Work 7 (3) rows straight.
For size 38 hip only. Cast off.
For size 36 hip only. 18th dec. row: * k.6, k.2 tog.
t.b.l., k.12, k.2 tog., k.6; rep. from * twice: 78 sts.
Work 3 rows. Cast off.

TO COMPLETE
Press well under damp cloth. Join side seams leaving
left seam open for 8 in. from top. Insert zip in opening.
Attach petersham ribbon to inside of top of Skirt with
herringbone casing. Close with 2 large hooks and eyes.
Turn up hem and slip st. in place.

Tartan skirt
illustrated in colour on page 117

MATERIALS
21 (23, 25) oz. Hayfield Gaylon Double Knitting in
green, 8 (9, 9) oz. in red, 4 oz. in each of yellow and
white and 3 oz. in blue. One pair each Nos. 10 and 11
knitting needles (USA sizes 3 and 2). One medium-sized
crochet hook. Waist length elastic, 1 in. wide. Two large
hooks and eyes. An 8-in. green zip fastener.

MEASUREMENTS
To fit hip size 36 (38, 40) in.; length 40-41 in.

TENSION
6 sts. and 8 rows to 1 in. over st.st. with No. 10 needles.

ABBREVIATIONS
See page 22; G., green; R., red; Y., yellow; W., white;
B., blue.

BACK AND FRONT (make 2 pieces alike)
With No. 11 needles and G., cast on 188 sts. and work
1 in. in st.st. K. 1 row for hemline.
Now begin patt. as follows, joining in R. and changing
to No. 10 needles after 1 in. has been worked.
1st row: k.1G., (k.6G., p.1G., k.5G., p.1G., k.1G., k.3R.,
k.1G., p.1G., k.9G., p.1G., k.2G.) 6 times, k.1G.
2nd row: p.1G., (p.2G., k.1G., p.9G., k.1G., p.1G.,
p.3R., p.1G., k.1G., p.5G., k.1G., p.6G.) 6 times, p.1G.
3rd to 6th rows: work first and 2nd rows twice.
7th row: as first row but use B. only.
8th row: as 2nd row.
9th to 18th rows: work first and 2nd rows 5 times.
19th row: as first row but use W. only.
20th row: as 2nd row.

21st row: with R. only, k.
22nd row: with R. only, p.
23rd and 24th rows: as 21st and 22nd rows.
25th row: as first row.
26th row: as 2nd row but use W. only.
27th to 38th rows: work first and 2nd rows 6 times.
39th row: as first row but use Y. only.
40th row: as 2nd row but use Y. only.
41st to 46th rows: work first and 2nd rows 3 times.
These 46 rows form patt. Continue in patt. throughout.
When 54 rows of patt. have been worked begin dec.
rows, being careful to keep continuity of patt. correct.
1st dec. row: k.1, k.2 tog., (patt. 58, k.2 tog. t.b.l., k.2
tog.) twice, patt. 58, k.2 tog. t.b.l., k.1: 182 sts.
Work 31 (33, 35) rows.
2nd dec. row: k.1, k.2 tog., (patt. 56, k.2 tog. t.b.l.,
k.2 tog.) twice, patt. 56, k.2 tog. t.b.l., k.1: 176 sts.
Work 27 (29, 31) rows.
3rd dec. row: k.1, k.2 tog., (patt. 54, k.2 tog. t.b.l., k.2
tog.) twice, patt. 54, k.2 tog. t.b.l., k.1: 170 sts.
Work 23 (25, 27) rows.
4th dec. row: k.1, k.2 tog., (patt. 52, k.2 tog. t.b.l.,
k.2 tog.) twice, patt. 52, k.2 tog. t.b.l., k.1: 164 sts.
Work 19 (21, 21) rows.
5th dec. row: k.1, k.2 tog., (patt. 50, k.2 tog. t.b.l., k.2
tog.) twice, patt. 50, k.2 tog. t.b.l., k.1: 158 sts.
Work 15 (15, 17) rows.
6th dec. row: k.1, k.2 tog., (patt. 48, k.2 tog. t.b.l., k.2
tog.) twice, patt. 48, k.2 tog. t.b.l., k.1: 152 sts.
Work 15 (15, 17) rows.
7th dec. row: k.1, k.2 tog., (patt. 46, k.2 tog. t.b.l., k.2
tog.) twice, patt. 46, k.2 tog. t.b.l., k.1: 146 sts.
Work 15 (15, 15) rows.
8th dec. row: k.1, k.2 tog., (patt. 44, k.2 tog. t.b.l., k.2
tog.) twice, patt. 44, k.2 tog. t.b.l., k.1: 140 sts.
Work 15 (15, 15) rows.
9th dec. row: k.1, k.2 tog., (patt. 42, k.2 tog. t.b.l., k.2
tog.) twice, patt. 42, k.2 tog. t.b.l., k.1: 134 sts.
Work 15 (13, 15) rows.
10th dec. row: k.1, k.2 tog., (patt. 40, k.2 tog. t.b.l., k.2
tog.) twice, patt. 40, k.2 tog. t.b.l., k.1: 128 sts.
Work 9 (11, 11) rows.
11th dec. row: k.1, k.2 tog., (patt. 38, k.2 tog. t.b.l., k.2
tog.) twice, patt. 38, k.2 tog. t.b.l., k.1: 122 sts.
Work 7 (7, 11) rows.   8 8 8
12th dec. row: k.1, k.2 tog., (patt. 36, k.2 tog. t.b.l., k.2
tog.) twice, patt. 36, k.2 tog. t.b.l., k.1: 116 sts.
Work 7 (7, 7) rows.
13th dec. row: k.1, k.2 tog., (patt. 34, k.2 tog. t.b.l.,
k.2 tog.) twice, patt. 34, k.2 tog. t.b.l., k.1: 110 sts.
Work 7 (7, 7) rows.
14th dec. row: k.1, k.2 tog., (patt. 32, k.2 tog. t.b.l., k.2
tog.) twice, patt. 32, k.2 tog. t.b.l., k.1: 104 sts.
Work 7 (7, 3) rows.
15th dec. row: k.1, k.2 tog., (patt. 30, k.2 tog. t.b.l., k.2
tog.) twice, patt. 30, k.2 tog. t.b.l., k.1: 98 sts.
Work 7 (7, 3) rows.
16th dec. row: k.1, k.2 tog., (patt. 28, k.2 tog. t.b.l., k.2
tog.) twice, patt. 28, k.2 tog. t.b.l., k.1: 92 sts.
For size 36 only: work 7 rows.
For size 38 only: work 3 rows.
For size 40 only: cast off.
17th dec. row: k.1, k.2 tog., (patt. 26, k.2 tog. t.b.l., k.2
tog.) twice, patt. 26, k.2 tog. t.b.l., k.1.
Work 3 rows.
For size 38 only: cast off.
For size 36 only: 18th dec. row: k.1, k.2 tog., (patt.
24, k.2 tog. t.b.l., k.2 tog.) twice, patt. 24, k.2 tog. t.b.l.,
k.1.
Work 3 rows.
Cast off.

continued on page 117

Below and left: yellow skirt, with close-up of red and navy border pattern (see page 112).
Opposite: tartan skirt, with close-up of the colour pattern (see page 115).

TO COMPLETE
Press both pieces well with warm iron over damp cloth.

Tartan Pattern
With crochet hook, work a line of ch. in B. right up first p. line of patt. on Back. Work a line of ch. in W. up 2nd p. line of patt. Work another line of ch. in W. up 3rd p. line of patt.

Work 2 rows of ch. in Y. up 4th p. line of patt. Rep. these ch. lines across Back and then Front. When p. sts. stop because of skirt shapings, then stop the line of ch. being worked—i.e. the only ch. lines which will go all the way up to the waist are 3 B. lines and 3 double Y. lines.

Join side seams of Skirt, leaving left one open at waist edge for 8 in. Insert zip in opening. Attach elastic to inside top of Skirt with herringbone casing. Fasten ends with 2 large hooks and eyes. Turn up hem and slip st. in place on wrong side of work. Press again, paying special attention to lines of crochet and also to seams.

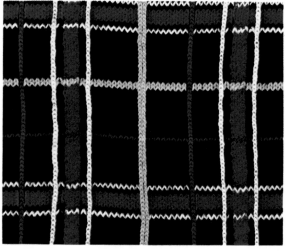

Party tunic

also illustrated in colour on page 120

MATERIALS
16 (17, 18, 19) oz. Twilleys Goldfingering.
One pair each Nos. 9 and 11 knitting needles (USA sizes 5 and 2).

MEASUREMENTS
To fit bust size 32 (34, 36, 38) in.; length 27 (27, 28, 28) in.; sleeve seam 18½ in.

TENSION
6 sts. and 9 rows to 1 in. over main patt.

ABBREVIATIONS
See page 22; m.1, make 1 st. by picking up loop before next st. and k. into back of it.

BACK
With No. 9 needles cast on 117 (125, 133, 141) sts. and k. 4 rows. Work in patt. as follows:
1st row (right side): k.1, * p.1, y.b., y.o.n., k.2 tog., k.1; rep. from * to end.
2nd row: k.1, * p.2, k.2; rep. from * to end.
These 2 rows form main patt. Continue in patt. until work measures 8½ (8½, 9, 9) in. from beg., ending with a 2nd row and inc. 1 st. at end of last row: 118 (126, 134, 142) sts.
Now work smock patt. thus:
1st row: p.2, * k.2, p.2; rep. from * to end.
2nd row: k.2, * p.2, k.2; rep. from * to end.
3rd row: p.2, * k.2, m.1 (see Abbreviations), p.2, k.2, insert point of left-hand needle into 7th st. from point of right-hand needle and lift this st. over last 6 sts. and off needle, p.2 *; rep. from * to * to last 4 sts., k.2, p.2. Rep. 2nd row then first and 2nd rows again.
7th row: p.2, k.2, p.2, now rep. from * to * of 3rd row to end.
8th row: as 2nd row.
These 8 rows form smock patt. Continue in smock patt. until work measures 12 (12, 12½, 12½) in. from beg., ending with a 4th or 8th patt. row and dec. 1 st. at end of last row: 117 (125, 133, 141) sts. Now work in main

patt., beg. with a first patt. row, until work measures 19½ (19½, 20, 20) in. from beg.

Armhole Shaping
Keeping main patt. correct, cast off 4 sts. at beg. of next 2 rows then dec. 1 st. each end of next 12 rows: 85 (93, 101, 109) sts.
Continue in main patt. until work measures 27 (27, 28, 28) in. from beg.

Shoulder Shaping
Cast off 6 (7, 8, 9) sts. loosely at beg. of next 8 rows. Cast off remaining 37 sts. loosely.

FRONT
Work as for Back until work measures 22 (22, 23, 23) in. from beg.

Front dividing row: patt. 41 (45, 49, 53) sts.: turn. Leave remaining sts. on st. holder or spare needle. Work in main patt. on these sts. until work measures 25 (25, 26, 26) in. from beg., ending at inner edge.

Neck Shaping
Cast off 9 sts. loosely at beg. of next row then dec. 1 st. at neck edge on next 8 rows: 24 (28, 32, 36) sts.
Continue straight until work measures 27 (27, 28, 28) in. from beg., ending at armhole edge.

Shoulder Shaping
Cast off 6 (7, 8, 9) sts. loosely at beg. of next and following 3 alternate rows. Return to remaining sts., place centre 3 sts. on a safety pin or st. holder, rejoin yarn and patt. across remaining 41 (45, 49, 53) sts. Complete to match other side of front.
Place 3 sts. from safety pin on to a No. 11 needle. With right side facing k. into front then into back of each st.: 6 sts.
Next row: inc. in first st., p.1, k.1; turn.
Work on these sts. only for right front band.
Work in p.1, k.1 rib for 3 in. Cast off.
Rejoin yarn to wrong side of remaining 3 sts., k.1, p.1, inc. in last st. Work 3 in. in k.1, p.1 rib for left front band. Cast off.

SLEEVES (make 2 alike)
With No. 11 needles cast on 52 (52, 58, 58) sts.
Work 2 in. in k.1, p.1 rib.
Next row: k.1 (1, 2, 2), * inc. in next st.; rep. from * to end: 103 (103, 114, 114) sts.
Next row: p.3 (3, 6, 6), * inc. in next st., p.1; rep. from * to end: 153 (153, 169, 169) sts.
Change to No. 9 needles and work in main patt. as for Back, beg. with a first patt. row, until work measures 11 in. from beg., ending with a 2nd patt. row.
Next row: k.1, * k.2 tog.; rep. from * to end: 77 (77, 85, 85) sts.
K. 7 rows. Now continue in main patt., beg. with a first patt. row, until work measures 18½ in. from beg.
To shape top continue in main patt., casting off 4 sts. at beg. of next 2 rows then dec. 1 st. each end of every alternate row until 33 (33, 37, 37) sts. remain. Dec. 1 st. each end of next 10 rows. Cast off.

NECKBAND AND TIE
With No. 11 needles cast on 5 sts. Work 60 in. in k.1, p.1 rib, beg. 2nd row p.1. Cast off.

TO COMPLETE
Press lightly, omitting rib and smocking. Join shoulder, side and sleeve seams. Set in sleeves.
Sew on front bands. Sew on neckband and tie, leaving 20 in. approx. free at each end to tie. Press seams.

Gold dress

also illustrated in colour on page 121

MATERIALS
16 (17, 18) balls (50 gr. each) Lister Bel-Air Starspun 4-ply.
One pair each Nos. 12 and 13 knitting needles (USA sizes 1 and 0).

MEASUREMENTS
To fit bust size 34 (36, 38) in.; length $34\frac{1}{2}$ ($34\frac{3}{4}$, 35) in.; sleeve seam 18 in.

TENSION
8 sts. and 11 rows to 1 in. over st.st. with No. 12 needles.

ABBREVIATIONS
See page 22; m.b., make bobble: into next st. work k.1, y.f., k.1; turn; p. these 3 sts., turn; k.3; turn; p.3; turn; now slip 2nd st. of bobble over first st. and off needle then k. tog. t.b.l. rem. 2 sts.

BACK AND FRONT (make 2 pieces alike)
With No. 13 needles cast on 166 (174, 182) sts.
1st row: k.2, * p.1, k.1; rep. from * to end.
Rep. this row once. Now, beg. with a k. row, work in st.st. for 15 rows. K. next row to make a ridge on right side for hemline.
Change to No. 12 needles and, beg. with another k. row, cont. in st.st. Cont. straight until work measures $2\frac{1}{2}$ in. from hemline.
Dec. 1 st. at each end of next row and every foll. 12th row until 138 (146, 154) sts. remain, then cont. straight until work measures 18 in. from hemline. Place marker loops of contrast yarn at each end of last row to indicate waistline. Cont. in st.st., inc. 1 st. at each end of row when work measures 20 in., 22 in. and 24 in. from hemline. Cont. on these 144 (152, 160) sts. until work measures 27 in. from hemline.

Shape Armholes
Cast off 5 sts. at beg. of next 4 rows and 5 (6, 7) sts. at beg. of next 4 rows.
Cont. straight on rem. 104 (108, 112) sts. until work measures 33 ($33\frac{1}{4}$, $33\frac{1}{2}$) in. from hemline, ending with a p. row.

Shape Neck and Shoulders
1st row: k.44 (46, 48) and leave these sts. on a st. holder, cast off 16, k. to end.
Cont. on last 44 (46, 48) sts. and work 1 row straight.
** Cast off 4 sts. at beg. of next row and 3 sts. at same (neck) edge on next 7 alt. rows. Cast off 8 sts. at armhole edge at beg. of next row and 3 sts. at neck edge on foll. row. Cast off rem. 8 (10, 12) sts. **
With wrong side facing rejoin yarn to inside edge of sts. on st. holder. Complete to match first side from ** to **.

SLEEVES (make 2 alike)
With No. 13 needles cast on 63 (67, 71) sts. Beg. with a k. row work 5 rows in st.st. K. next row to make hemline ridge.
Change to No. 12 needles and patt.
1st row: k.4, * m.b., k.3; rep. from * to last 3 sts., m.b., k.2.
2nd row: p., but pull the st. above each bobble fairly tightly to prevent bobble slipping through.
3rd row: k.2, * m.b., k.3; rep. from * to last st., k.1.
4th row: as 2nd row.
Now work in st.st., working next (5th) row straight, inc. 1 st. at each end of 6th row, then working 5 rows straight. Rep. last 6 rows twice more, then inc. 1 st. at each end of next row.

These 24 rows form 1 patt: 4 sts. inc. at each side.
Cont. to rep. these 24 rows until there are 111 (115, 119) sts. and 6th patt. is completed. Cont. in patt. without any incs. until work measures 18 in. from hemline. Place marker loops at each end to indicate end of sleeve seam.
Cont. in patt., work 28 (31, 34) rows straight.
Keeping patt. correct cast off 6 sts. at beg. of next 16 rows. Cast off 15 (19, 23) sts.

NECKBANDS (make 2 alike)
With No. 12 needles cast on 87 sts. Beg. with a k. row work 2 rows in st.st. Now work the first patt. row of Sleeves.
Change to No. 13 needles and work 2nd, 3rd and 4th patt. rows of Sleeves. Now p. the next row to make a ridge on right side. P. 1 more row, dec. 1 st. at end of row. Now work the rib row given at beg. of Back 5 times. Cast off ribwise.

BELT
With No. 13 needles cast on 8 sts. and rep. the rib row given at beg. of Back until strip measures 54 (56, 58) in. Cast off.

TO COMPLETE
Press st.st. sections on wrong side with cool iron. Join shoulder seams, using back st. for these and all seams. Press seams.
Sew cast-off edges of Sleeves to sides of armholes and straight rows of Sleeves above markers to armhole casting-off. Remove markers. Press seams.
Join side seams matching shapings and waistline markers, ending seam just below hemline ridge. Remove markers. Press seams.
Turn up hem to wrong side along the ridge and slip st. cast-on edge in place. At side seams catch the sides of hems in place next to the seams but do not sew them over seams.
Join sleeve seams matching patt. Turn up hems on Sleeves and slip st. in place.
Join ends of neckbands. With right sides together sew cast-on edge to neck edge. Press seam carefully using point of iron. Fold the last 6 rows inside and slip st. over first seam.

Silver and gold evening bag
illustrated left

MATERIALS
Of Twilleys Double Gold—one ball each (50 gr. each) in gold and silver. One pair No. 9 knitting needles (USA size 5). An 8-in. evening bag frame. ½ yd. lining material, 36 in. wide.

MEASUREMENTS
Finished bag measures 8 in. by 8 in.

TENSION
5 sts. and 10 rows to 1 in.

ABBREVIATIONS
See page 22.

TO MAKE TRIANGLE MOTIF (make 4 in silver, 4 in gold)
Cast on 40 sts.

1st row: k.
2nd row: cast off 1 st., k. to last 2 sts., k.2 tog. Cont. to dec. 1 st. at both ends of every alt. row until there are 2 sts. Cast off.

TO COMPLETE

Place 4 triangles to form a square, alternating the colours. Sew tog. on the wrong side. Stitch other 4 triangles tog. in a similar way. Place the 2 squares tog., right sides facing. Sew the bottom edges tog., then open bag out flat, and use as a pattern to cut out lining material. Add $\frac{1}{2}$ in. to all edges on lining for seam allowances. Sew up the side seams on the bag and the lining, leaving 2 in. of the seam unstitched at the top. Sew bag to the frame along the open edges and along the top. Place lining inside bag, wrong sides together, and trim remaining open edges to $\frac{1}{4}$ in., turn in and stitch lining neatly in place to inside of knitted fabric.

Opposite: party tunic (see page 118).
Below and right: gold dress (see page 119).

Frilled top and ribbon-trimmed blouse (see opposite for both patterns).

Frilled top

MATERIALS
8 (9, 10, 11) balls (20 gr. each) Emu Tricel Nylon Double Knitting in main shade and one ball in a contrasting shade. One pair each Nos. 8, 9 and 10 knitting needles (USA sizes 6, 5 and 3). One set of four No. 8 needles (USA size 6) with points at both ends. Shirring elastic.

MEASUREMENTS
To fit bust size 32 (34, 36, 38) in.; length 14 (14, 14½, 14½) in.; sleeve seam 3 in.

TENSION
5 sts. to 1 in. with No. 8 needles.

ABBREVIATIONS
See page 22; M., main shade; C., contrasting shade.

Note. Patt. is reversible, so either side can be right side.

BACK AND FRONT (make 2 pieces alike)
With No. 9 needles and M., cast on 80 (85, 90, 95) sts. and k. 3 rows. Work in patt.
1st row: * k.1, (y.f., k.2 tog.) twice; rep. from * to end. This row forms the patt. Cont. in patt. Cont. until work measures 2 in.
Change to No. 10 needles and cont. for a further 3 in.
Change to No. 8 needles and cont. straight until work measures 11 (11, 11½, 11½) in.

Shape Armholes
Dec. 1 st. at each end of next and every alt. row until 64 (69, 74, 79) sts. remain.
Join shirring elastic and still dec. as before work in k.1, p.1 rib for 7 rows. Break shirring elastic; leave sts. on a st. holder.

SLEEVES (make 2 alike)
With No. 9 needles and M. cast on 60 (65, 65, 65) sts. and work in garter st. (every row k.) for 1 in.
Change to No. 8 needles and cont. in patt. until work measures 3 in.

Shape Top
Dec. 1 st. at each end of next and every alt. row until 44 (49, 49, 49) sts. remain.
Join shirring elastic and still dec. as before work in k.1, p.1 rib for 7 rows. Break shirring elastic; leave sts. on st. holder.

TO COMPLETE
Neckband
With set of No. 8 needles with points at both ends and C., k. across front sts. from st. holder then one set of sleeve sts., then back sts. then 2nd sleeve sts.; turn.
Next row: * k.1, k. twice into next st.; rep. from * to end.
Work 1 in. in garter st., ending with a wrong-side row. Break C. Join M. and work in garter st. for 3 rows. Cast off.

To Make Up
Press very lightly on wrong side with a cool iron over a dry cloth. Sew in Sleeves, then sew up sleeve and side seams. Turn over neckband to right side and catch in position with shirring elastic.

Ribbon-trimmed blouse

MATERIALS
14 (14, 15, 16) balls (20 gr. each) Emu Tricel Nylon Double Knitting in main shade and one ball in a contrasting shade. One pair each Nos. 10 and 8 knitting needles (USA sizes 3 and 6). 2 yd. narrow ribbon.

MEASUREMENTS
To fit bust size 32 (34, 36, 38) in.; length 21 (21½, 22, 22½) in.; sleeve seam 4½ in.

TENSION
5½ sts. and 8 rows to 1 in. with No. 8 needles.

ABBREVIATIONS
See page 22; M., main shade; C., contrasting shade.

BACK
With No. 10 needles and M. cast on 90 (96, 102, 108) sts. Work in k.1, p.1 rib for 7 in., inc. 3 (5, 3, 5) sts. evenly over last row: 93 (101, 105, 113) sts.
Change to No. 8 needles and patt.
1st row (right side): k.1, p.1, * y.r.n. twice, p.2 tog., p.2; rep. from * to last 3 sts., y.r.n. twice, p.2 tog., k.1.
2nd row: k.2, * y.f., sl. next st. purlwise dropping extra loop, keep y.f., k.3; rep. from * to last 3 sts., y.f., sl. next st. purlwise dropping extra loop, keep y.f., k.2.
3rd row: k.1, p.1, * sl. next 2 loops purlwise, y.r.n., p.3; rep. from * to last 3 sts., sl. next 2 loops purlwise, y.r.n., p.1, k.1.

4th row: k.2, * p. next 3 loops tog., k.3; rep. from * to last 3 sts., p. next 3 loops tog., k.2.
5th row: k.1, p.3, * y.r.n. twice, p.2 tog., p.2; rep. from * to last st., k.1.
6th row: k.4, * y.f., sl. next st. purlwise dropping extra loop, keep y.f., k.3; rep. from * to last st., k.1.
7th row: k.1, p.3, * sl. next 2 loops purlwise, y.r.n., p.3; rep. from * to last st., k.1.
8th row: k.4, * p. next 3 loops tog., k.3; rep. from * to last st., k.1.
These 8 rows form patt. Cont. in patt. until the Back measures 14 in. or desired length to armholes, ending with a 4th or 8th row of patt.

continued on page 126

Above: a set of matching three-colour cushions, from left to right—oblong cushion, diagonal cushion, square cushion (see page 141).
Opposite: sleeveless slip-on has front button fastening, two pockets and feather pattern panels (see page 132).

Shape Armholes
Keeping patt. correct cast off 4 (4, 4, 5) sts. at beg. of the next 2 rows. Dec. 1 st. at each end of the next and every foll. alt. row until 75 (81, 85, 89) sts. remain.
Cont. straight in patt. until armhole measures 7 (7½, 8, 8½) in., ending with a 4th or 8th row of patt.

Shape Shoulders
Cast off 6 sts. at the beg. of the next 4 rows. Cast off 5 (6, 6, 7) sts. at the beg. of the next 2 rows. Cast off 5 (6, 7, 7) sts. at the beg. of the next 2 rows. Cast off rem. 31 (33, 35, 37) sts.

FRONT
Work as Back until armhole measures 2½ (3, 3½, 4) in., ending with a 4th or 8th row of patt.

Divide for Front Opening
Next row: patt. 37 (40, 42, 44); turn and leave rem. sts. on a st. holder.
Cont. in patt. on this first set of sts. until armhole measures 5 (5½, 6, 6½) in., ending at neck edge.

Shape Neck
Cast off 8 (9, 10, 11) sts. at the beg. of the next row, then dec. 1 st. at neck edge on the next and every foll. alt. row until 22 (24, 25, 26) sts. remain.
Cont. straight until Front measures same as Back to shoulder shaping, ending at armhole edge.

Shape Shoulder
Cast off 6 sts. at the beg. of the next and foll. alt. row. Work 1 row. Cast off 5 (6, 6, 7) sts. at the beg. of the next row. Work 1 row. Cast off the rem. 5 (6, 7, 7) sts.
Rejoin yarn to rem. sts., cast off centre st. then patt. to end of row.
Complete 2nd side of opening to match first, reversing shapings.

SLEEVES (make 2 alike)
With No. 10 needles and C. cast on 68 (68, 74, 74) sts. K. 5 rows.
Next (eyelet) row (right side): k.2, * y.f., k.2 tog., k.1; rep. from * to end.
K. 5 rows. Change to M. and k. 1 row.
Next row: k.22 (20, 24, 24), (k. twice into next st.) 25 (29, 27, 27) times, k.21 (19, 23, 23): 93 (97, 101, 101) sts.
Change to No. 8 needles and patt. as given for Back. Cont. in patt. until Sleeve measures 4½ in. or desired length, ending with a 4th or 8th row of patt.

Shape Top
Cast off 4 (4, 4, 5) sts. at the beg. of the next 2 rows. Work 0 (0, 0, 2) rows. Dec. 1 st. at each end of the next and every foll. alt. row until 55 (59, 59, 59) sts. remain, and then every now until 45 (49, 49, 49) sts. remain. Keeping the patt. correct cont. as follows:
1st row: patt. 40 (44, 44, 44); turn.
2nd row: patt. 35 (39, 39, 39); turn.
3rd row: patt. 30 (34, 34, 34); turn.
4th row: patt. 25 (29, 29, 29); turn.
5th row: patt. 20 (24, 24, 24); turn.
6th row: patt. 15 (19, 19, 19); turn.
7th row: patt. 10 (14, 14, 14); turn.
8th row: patt. 5 (9, 9, 9); turn.
9th row: p. to end. **10th row:** k.
11th row: p.0 (1, 1, 1), * p.3 tog.; rep. from * to end: 15 (17, 17, 17) sts. Cast off knitwise.

TO COMPLETE
Front Opening
With No. 10 needles and M. and right side facing pick up and k. 38 sts. around front opening. Cast off knitwise.

Neckband
Join shoulder seams, using a back st. With No. 10 needles and C. and right side facing, pick up and k. 92 (92, 98, 98) sts. evenly around neck. K. 5 rows.
Next (eyelet) row: k.2, * y.f., k.2 tog., k.1; rep. from * to end.
K. 4 rows. Cast off knitwise.

To Make Up
Pin out all pieces to correct measurements and press lightly with a cool iron over a dry cloth, omitting ribbing. Using a flat seam for ribbing and back st. for rem. join side and sleeve seams. Set in Sleeves. Press seams lightly. Thread ribbon through eyelet holes and tie in bows.

Victorian-style evening jumper — with 'leg-of-mutton' sleeves

MATERIALS
21 oz. Hayfield Gaylon Double Knitting. One pair each Nos. 9 and 11 knitting needles (USA sizes 5 and 2). A set each of four double-pointed Nos. 10 and 11 knitting needles (USA sizes 3 and 2).

MEASUREMENTS
To fit bust size 34/36 in.

TENSION
25 sts. to 4 in. and 10 rows to 1 in. on No. 9 needles over rib pattern.

ABBREVIATIONS
See page 22.

BACK
With No. 11 needles cast on 108 sts. and work 4 rows in k.1, p.1 rib, inc. 1 st. at end of row: 109 sts.
Change to No. 9 needles and work in the foll. rib patt.:
1st row (wrong side): p. across sts.
2nd row: k.1, * p.2, k.1, sl.1, k.1; rep. from * to last 3 sts., p.2, k.1.
These 2 rows form rib patt. Work in rib patt. until Back measures 14 in. from cast-on edge, ending on wrong-side row.

Shape Armholes
At beg. of next 2 rows cast off 6 sts. At beg. of every row dec. 1 st. until 83 sts. remain. Keeping rib patt. correct work straight until armholes measure 8 in. from beg. of armhole shaping, ending with a wrong-side row.

Shape Shoulders
At beg. of next 6 rows, cast off 8 sts. Leave rem. 35 sts. on a stitch holder or spare needle.

FRONT
Work exactly as for Back until 83 sts. remain in armhole. Work straight until armholes measure 5½ in. from beg. of armhole shaping, ending with a wrong-side row.

Shape Neck
Patt. 35 sts., turn and leave rem. sts.
Work in patt. on the 35 sts., dec. 1 st. at beg. of every neck edge row until 24 sts. remain. Work straight until armhole is 8 in. from beg. of armhole shaping, ending at side edge.

Shape Shoulder

At beg. of next and alt. row cast off 8 sts. Work 1 row. Cast off rem. 8 sts.
Rejoin yarn to rem. sts. at neck edge, cast off 13 sts., work on rem. 35 sts. to match other side.

SLEEVES (make 2 alike)

With No. 11 needles cast on 56 sts. Rib in k.1, p.1 for 4 in. **Next row:** rib, inc. both ends of row.
Rib straight for 2 in., inc. both ends of next row: 60 sts. Rib straight until 11 in. from cast-on edge.
Change to No. 9 needles and k., inc. 3 times into every st.: 180 sts.
Next row: p. to last st., inc. 1: 181 sts.
Now work in the foll. patt.:
1st row: k.3, * p.1, k.5; rep. from * to last 4 sts., p.1, k.3.
2nd row: p.2, * k.1, p.1, k.1, p.3; rep. from * to last 5 sts., k.1, p.1, k.1, p.2.
3rd row: * k.1, p.1, k.3, p.1; rep. from * to last st., k.1.
4th row: * k.1, p.5; rep. from * to last st., k.1.
5th row: as 3rd row.
6th row: as 2nd row.
These 6 rows form the diamond patt. and are repeated throughout.
Work in patt. until sleeve measures 17½ in. from cast-on edge, ending on wrong side of work.

Shape Top

At beg. of next 2 rows cast off 6 sts. At both ends of every row dec. 1 st. until 113 sts. remain. At beg. of next 8 rows cast off 8 sts.: 49 sts. remain.
K. 2 tog. across row: 25 sts. remain. Cast off rem. sts.

TO COMPLETE

Join shoulder seams of Back and Front.
With right side of work facing, and set of four No. 11 needles, slip the 35 sts. from back neck on to one needle, k., inc. evenly to 42 sts., then pick up and k. 26 sts. down left front of neck, pick up and k. 13 sts. across centre front neck, then k. up 25 sts. along right front neck: 106 sts.
Work in rounds of k.1, p.1 for 2 in.
Change to set of No. 10 needles and rib in k.1, p.1 until collar measures 5 in. from beg. Cast off ribwise.

To Make Up

Press pieces very lightly. Do not open rib. Join side and sleeve seams.
To set in sleeves, run a length of yarn through the top of sleeve head beg. at the first set of 8 sts. cast off and ending at last set of 8 sts. Pin sleeve into armhole drawing up the top of sleeve to fit into top of armhole. This forms a slightly gathered sleeve top.
Sew into armhole in usual way with a neat backstitch seam. Press all seams.

Chapter nine
MEN ONLY

Aran cardigan

MATERIALS
25 (26, 26) balls (50 gr. each) Mahony's Blarney Bainin (USA Blarneyspun). One pair each Nos. 7, 8 and 10 knitting needles (USA sizes 7, 6 and 3). Two cable needles. Five buttons $\frac{5}{8}$ in. in diameter.

MEASUREMENTS
To fit chest size 41/42 (42$\frac{1}{2}$/43$\frac{1}{2}$, 44/55) in. loosely; length 27$\frac{1}{2}$ (27$\frac{3}{4}$, 28) in.; sleeve seam 20 in.

TENSION
5 sts. and 6$\frac{1}{2}$ rows to 1 in. over rice st.

ABBREVIATIONS
See page 22; claw patt. 7, slip next 2 sts. on to a cable needle and leave at back of work, k.1 then k.2 from cable needle, k. next st., now slip foll. st. on to cable needle and leave at front of work, k.2 then k.1 from cable needle; k.f.b. (or p.f.b.), knit (or purl) into front and back of next st.; cable 6 back (or cable 6 front), slip next 3 sts. on to a cable needle and leave at back (or front) of work, k.3, then k.3 from cable needle; cross 6 right, slip next 4 sts. on to a cable needle and leave at

back of work, k.2, now pass the 2 p. sts. from other end of cable needle back on to left-hand needle, bring cable needle to front, p.2 from left-hand needle and lastly k.2 from cable needle; cross 6 left, slip next 2 k. sts. on to one cable needle and leave at front of work, slip next 2 p. sts. on to 2nd cable needle and leave at back of work, k.2, now p.2 from back needle and lastly k.2 from front needle.

BACK
With No. 10 needles cast on 113 (117, 121) sts. and work in rib.
1st row: k.2, * p.1, k.1; rep. from * to last st., k.1.
2nd row: k.1, * p.1, k.1; rep. from * to end.
Rep. these 2 rows 5 times more, then first row again.
Inc. row (wrong side): k.f.b., k.11 (13, 15), * k.f.b., p.2, (p.f.b., p.1) twice, p.f.b., p.2, (k.f.b., p.2) 4 times, k.f.b., p.2, (p.f.b., p.1) twice, p.f.b., p.2, k.f.b. *, then ** p.1, (p.f.b., p.1) twice, k.f.b. **; rep. from ** to ** twice more, p.1, (p.f.b., p.1) twice; rep. from * to *, k.11 (13, 15), k.f.b.: 152 (156, 160) sts.
Change to No. 7 needles and patt.
1st patt. row: k.1 t.b.l., (p.1, k.1 t.b.l.) 6 (7, 8) times, * p.2, k.12, p.2, (k.2, p.2) 4 times, k.12, p.2, * (k.7, p.2) 3 times, k.7; rep. from * to *, (k.1 t.b.l., p.1) 6 (7, 8) times, k.1 t.b.l.
2nd and alt. patt. rows: k.13 (15, 17), * k.2, p.12, k.2, (p.2, k.2) 4 times, p.12, k.2 *, (p.7, k.2) 3 times, p.7; rep. from * to *, k.13 (15, 17).
This forms rice st. patt. over the 13 (15, 17) sts. at each end.
Cont. to work these sts. in rice st. patt.
3rd patt. row: rice st. 13 (15, 17), * p.2, k.12, p.2, k.2, p.2, cross 6 right, p.2, k.2, p.2, k.12, p.2 *, (claw patt. 7, p.2) 3 times, claw patt. 7; rep. from * to *, rice st. 13 (15, 17).
5th patt. row: rice st. 13 (15, 17), * p.2, cable 6 back, cable 6 front, p.2, (k.2, p.2) 4 times, cable 6 back, cable 6 front, p.2 *, (k.7, p.2) 3 times, k.7; rep. from * to *, rice st. 13 (15, 17).
7th patt. row: rice st. 13 (15, 17), work from * to * of first patt. row, (claw patt. 7, p.2) 3 times, claw patt. 7; work from * to * again, rice st. 13 (15, 17).
9th patt. row: rice st. 13 (15, 17), * p.2, k.12, p.2, (cross 6 left, p.2) twice, k.12, p.2 *, (k.7, p.2) 3 times, k.7; rep. from * to *, rice st. 13 (15, 17).
11th patt. row: rice st. 13 (15, 17) * p.2, cable 6 back, cable 6 front, p.2, (k.2, p.2) 4 times, cable 6 back, cable 6 front, p.2 *, (claw patt. 7, p.2) 3 times, claw patt. 7; rep. from * to *, rice st. 13 (15, 17).
13th patt. row: as first patt. row.
15th patt. row: as 3rd patt. row.
17th patt. row: rice st. 13 (15, 17), * p.2, cable 6 front, cable 6 back, p.2, (k.2, p.2) 4 times, cable 6 front, cable 6 back, p.2 *, (k.7, p.2) 3 times, k.7; rep. from * to *, rice st. 13 (15, 17).
19th patt. row: as 7th patt. row.
21st patt. row: as 9th patt. row.
23rd patt. row: rice st. 13 (15, 17), * p.2, cable 6 front, cable 6 back, p.2, (k.2, p.2) 4 times, cable 6 front, cable 6 back, p.2 *, (claw patt. 7, p.2) 3 times, claw patt. 7; rep. from * to *, rice st. 13 (15, 17).
24th patt. row: as 2nd patt. row.
These 24 rows form 1 patt. Cont. straight in patt. until work measures 18 in. from beg.
Cont. in patt.

Shape Armholes
Cast off 6 (8, 10) sts. at beg. of next 2 rows and 7 sts. at beg. of next 2 rows. (There are now no sts. in rice st.) Cont. straight on rem. 126 sts. until work measures 27½ (27¾, 28) in. from beg.

Shape Shoulders
Cast off rather tightly over cables and claw patt. Cast off 13 sts. at beg. of next 2 rows, 9 sts. at beg. of next 4 rows and 8 sts. at beg. of next 2 rows. Cast off rem. 48 sts.

POCKET LININGS (make 2 alike)
With No. 8 needles cast on 33 sts. and work 29 rows in rib as for Back welt.
Next row: work from * to * of the inc. row of Back: 46 sts.
Change to No. 7 needles and patt.
1st row: work from * to * of first patt. row.
2nd row: work from * to * of 2nd patt. row.
Break yarn and leave sts. on a st. holder.

RIGHT FRONT
With No. 10 needles cast on 69 (71, 73) sts. and work 13 rows in rib as for Back welt.
Inc. row: k.f.b., k.11 (13, 15), work from * to * of the inc. row of Back, then work from ** to ** twice; turn and slip rem. 12 sts. on to a safety pin for front border. Change to No. 7 needles and work in patt. on 77 (79, 81) sts. of main part.
1st row: (p.2, k.7) twice, work from * to * of first patt. row, (k.1 t.b.l., p.1) 6 (7, 8) times, k.1 t.b.l.
2nd and alt. rows: k.13 (15, 17), work from * to * of 2nd patt. row, (p.7, k.2) twice.
Cont. in patt. as now set until the 8th row of 2nd patt. has been worked.

Pocket Opening
Next row: (p.2, k.7) twice, slip next 46 sts. on to a st. holder, with right side facing work from * to * of 9th patt. row across sts. of 1 pocket lining, then rice st. 13 (15, 17).
*** Cont. in patt. across all sts. until work measures 17 in. from beg., ending at front edge. Dec. 1 st. at beg. of next row and every alt. row and at same time when work measures 18 in. from beg. end at side edge.

Shape Armhole
Cast off 6 (8, 10) sts. at beg. of next row and 7 sts. at beg. of next alt. row. Now keeping side edge straight cont. with front decs. on every alt. row until 46 sts. remain, then dec. 1 st. at same edge on every foll. 3rd row until 39 sts. remain. Cont. straight until work measures 27½ (27¾, 28) in. from beg., ending at side edge.

Shape Shoulder
Cast off 13 sts. at beg. of next row and 9 sts. at beg. of next 2 alt. rows. Work 1 row.
Cast off rem. 8 sts.

LEFT FRONT
With No. 10 needles cast on 69 (71, 73) sts. and work 5 rows in rib as for Back welt, then make buttonhole.
6th row: rib 4, cast off 4, rib to end.
Next rows: rib to last 4 sts.; turn; cast on 4; turn; rib 4. Work 6 more rows in rib.
Inc. row: rib 12 and slip these sts. on to a safety pin for border, cont. along row, k.f.b., work from ** to ** of the inc. row of Back, p.1, (p.f.b., p.1) twice, then work from * to * of Back inc. row, k.11 (13, 15), k.f.b.: 77 (79, 81) sts.
Change to No. 7 needles and patt.
1st row: k.1 t.b.l., (p.1, k.1 t.b.l.) 6 (7, 8) times, work from * to * of first patt. row, (k.7, p.2) twice.
Cont. in patt. as now set until the 8th row of 2nd patt. has been worked.

Pocket Opening

Next row: rice st. 13 (15, 17), slip next 46 sts. on to a st. holder, with right side facing work from * to * of 9th patt. row across sts. of pocket lining, (k.7, p.2) twice. Complete as Right Front from *** to end working all shapings at opposite edges.

SLEEVES (make 2 alike)

With No. 10 needles cast on 53 (57, 57) sts. and work 13 rows in rib as for Back welt.
Inc. row: p.2 (4, 4), k.f.b., p.7, work from * to * of the inc. row of Back, p.7, k.f.b., k.2 (4, 4): 68 (72, 72) sts.
Change to No. 7 needles and patt.
1st row: k.2 (4, 4), p.2, k.7, work from * to * of first patt. row, k.7, p.2, k.2 (4, 4).
2nd row: p.2 (4, 4), k.2, p.7, work from * to * of 2nd patt. row, p.7, k.2, p.2 (4, 4).
3rd row: k.2 (4, 4), p.2, claw patt. 7, work from * to * of 3rd patt. row, claw patt. 7, p.2, k.2 (4, 4).
Cont. in patt. as now set but inc. 1 st. at each end of 5th, 10th, 15th, 20th, and 24th rows of every patt. until there are 112 (116, 118) sts., taking extra sts. into patt. as follows: the first 5 (3, 3) sts. added each side form another claw patt. with the 2 (4, 4) already at each end, the next 2 sts. each side form a rib (p.2 on right side) then rem. 15 (17, 18) sts. added each side are worked in rice st.
Cont. straight until work measures 20 in. from beg. Place marker loops of contrast yarn at each end, then work 16 (19, 22) rows straight. Cast off 5 (7, 8) sts. at beg. of next 2 rows, 5 sts. at beg. of next 4 rows, 9 sts. at beg. of next 4 rows and 14 sts. at beg. of next 2 rows. Cast off rem. 18 sts.

TO COMPLETE
Front Borders

Slip sts. of left front border on to a No. 10 needle with point at inner edge, join yarn, cast on 1, rib to end. Cont. in rib on these 13 sts. making further buttonholes in same way as before when work measures 4½ in., 8 in., 11½ in., and 15 in. from beg., then cont. in rib until strip is long enough to fit along front edge to shoulder when slightly stretched. Work another 2¾ in.
Cast off ribwise.
Work right front border in same way but omit buttonholes.

Pocket Tops (make 2 alike)

Slip sts. from holder at one pocket opening on to a No. 10 needle so that right side will be facing for first row, join yarn.
1st row: k.f.b., p.1, * k.1, p.1, (k.2 tog., p.1) 3 times, k.1 *, (p.2 tog., k.1, p.1, k.2 tog., p.1, k.1) twice, p.2 tog.; rep. from * to *, p.1, k.f.b.: 37 sts.
Beg. with 2nd row work 5 more rows in rib as for Back welt.
Cast off ribwise.

To Make Up

Do not press. Join shoulder seams matching patt. and using back st. for these and all seams. Press seams on wrong side with warm iron and damp cloth. Sew cast-off edges of Sleeves to sides of armholes and straight sides of Sleeves above markers to armhole casting-off. Press seams. Remove markers. Join side and sleeve seams and press. Join ends of front borders with a flat seam. Back st. borders in place stretching them to fit so that join comes at centre back neck. Press seams using point of iron so as not to flatten rib. Slip st. sides of pocket linings to wrong side of Fronts and neatly catch sides of pocket tops in place on right side of work.
Sew buttons on to Right Front to correspond with buttonholes on Left Front.

Summer shirt

MATERIALS

14 (15, 15, 16, 17, 17) balls (25 gr. each) Twilleys Cortina Super Crochet Wool. One pair each Nos. 11 and 13 knitting needles (USA sizes 2 and 0). Three medium buttons.

MEASUREMENTS

To fit chest size 36 (38, 40, 42, 44, 46) in.; length 26 (26, 27, 27, 28, 28) in.; sleeve seam 4½ in.

TENSION

7 sts. and 10 rows to 1 in.

ABBREVIATIONS

See page 22.

BACK

With No. 13 needles cast on 133 (141, 149, 157, 165, 173) sts. Work 2 in. in k.1, p.1 rib, beg. 2nd row p.1 and ending with a 2nd row.
Change to No. 11 needles and work in patt. as follows:
1st row (right side): p.2, k.1, * p.3, k.1; rep. from * to last 2 sts., p.2.
2nd row: k.2, * p.1, k.3; rep. from * to last 3 sts., p.1, k.2.
These 2 rows form rib patt. Continue in patt. until work measures 17 (17, 17½, 17½, 18, 18) in. from beg.

Armhole Shaping

Cast off 5 sts. at beg. of next 2 rows then dec. 1 st. each end of next 10 rows: 103 (111, 119, 127, 135, 143) sts. Continue in patt. until work measures 26 (26, 27, 27, 28, 28) in. from beg., ending with a wrong-side row.

Shoulder Shaping

Cast off 6 (7, 8, 9, 10, 11) sts. at beg. of next 8 rows. Leave remaining 55 sts. on a spare needle.

FRONT

Work as for Back until work measures 15 (15, 16, 16, 17, 17) in. from beg., ending with a 2nd patt. row.

Front dividing row: patt. 62 (66, 70, 74, 78, 82); turn, leaving remaining 71 (75, 79, 83, 87, 91) sts. on a st holder.
Continue in patt. until work measures 17 (17, 17½, 17½, 18, 18) in. from beg. ending with a wrong-side row.

Armhole Shaping

Cast off 5 sts. at beg. of next row then dec. 1 st. at armhole edge on next 10 rows: 47 (51, 55, 59, 63, 67) sts. Continue until work measures 24½ (24½, 25½, 25½, 26½, 26½) in. from beg., ending with a right-side row.

Neck Shaping

Next row: patt. 11 and place these 11 sts. on a st. holder, patt. to end. Dec. 1 st. at neck edge on next 12 rows: 24 (28, 32, 36, 40, 44) sts.
Work 2 rows straight.

Shoulder Shaping

Cast off 6 (7, 8, 9, 10, 11) sts. at beg. of next and following 3 alternate rows. Return to sts. on st. holder, place

centre 9 sts. on another st. holder, rejoin yarn to remaining 62 (66, 70, 74, 78, 82) sts. and patt. to end. Complete to match other side of Front, reversing all shapings.

SLEEVES (make 2 alike)
With No. 13 needles cast on 84 (84, 92, 92, 100, 100) sts. Work 14 rows in k.1, p.1 rib. Change to No. 11 needles and continue in st.st., inc. 1 st. each end of 2nd and then every following 4th row until there are 100 (100, 108, 108, 116, 116) sts. Continue until work measures $4\frac{1}{2}$ in. from beg. To shape top cast off 5 sts. at beg. of next 2 rows then dec. 1 st. each end of every alternate row until 52 (52, 56, 56, 60, 60) sts. remain. Dec. 1 st. each end of next 12 rows. Cast off.

FRONT BANDS
Right Front Band
With No. 13 needles cast on 12 sts. Work $11\frac{1}{2}$ in. in k.1, p.1 rib. Cast off firmly ribwise.

Left Front Band
Place 9 sts. at centre front on to a No. 13 needle. With right side facing, k.9, cast on 10.
Next row: p. **Next row:** k.9, sl.1, k.9.
Work 15 rows more in st.st. with sl.st. at centre of k. rows.
Next row (buttonhole row): k.3, cast off 3, k.3, sl.1, k.3, cast off 3, k.3.
Next row: p.3, cast on 3, p.7, cast on 3, p.3.
Continue in st.st. with sl.st., making another buttonhole as before, $4\frac{1}{2}$ in. from the first (measure from base of previous buttonhole). Work 4 in. more, ending with a p. row. Break yarn and leave sts. on a st. holder.

NECKBAND
Join shoulders. Place 11 sts. at right front edge on to a No. 13 needle then pick up and k. 22 sts. up right side of front neck, k. sts. from back neck, pick up and k. 22 sts. down left side of front neck, k. 11 sts. from st. holder then work across 19 sts. of left front band as follows:

k.9, sl.1, k.9: 140 sts.
Work 5 rows st.st., beg. with a p. row, and keeping sl. st. in line as before.
Next row (buttonhole row): k. to last 16 sts., cast off 3, k.3, sl.1, k.3, cast off 3, k.3.
Next row: p.3, cast on 3, p.7, cast on 3, p. to end.
Work 5 rows more in st.st. with sl. st. as before.
Next row (wrong side): cast off 19, k. to end. (This row marks hemline.)
Work 12 rows in st.st., beg. with a k. row.
Cast off loosely knitwise.

TO COMPLETE
Press st.st. parts only. Set in sleeves. Join side and sleeve seams. Fold neckband in half at hemline and sew down. Fold left front band in half at slip st., join top and lower edges then sew down on wrong side. Sew on right front band, joining lower edge behind left front band. Press seams. Sew on buttons.

Sleeveless slip-on
illustrated in colour on page 125

MATERIALS
11 (12, 13) balls (25 gr. each) Patons Limelight Crêpe 4-ply. One pair each Nos. 13, 12 and 11 knitting needles (USA sizes 0, 1 and 2). Seven medium-sized buttons. Two small buttons. Two press studs.

MEASUREMENTS
To fit chest size 38 (40, 42) in.; length 25 (25¼, 25½) in.

TENSION
7½ sts. and 9½ rows to 1 in. over st.st. with No. 11 needles.

ABBREVIATIONS
See page 22; k. (or p.) 1 b., k. (or p.) into back of st.; m. 1, make 1: pick up loop between st. just worked and foll. st. and k. it t.b.l.

FEATHER PATT. (23 sts.)
1st row: p.2, k.1 b., k.17, k.1 b., p.2.
2nd row: p.2, p.1 b., p.17, p.1 b., p.2.
3rd row: p.2, k.1 b., (k.2 tog.) 3 times, (m.1, k.1), 5 times, m.1, (k.2 tog. t.b.l.) 3 times, k.1 b., p.2.
4th row: p.2, p.1 b., p.17, p.1 b., p.2.

POCKETS (make 2 alike)
With No. 12 needles cast on 37 (39, 41) sts. Work in st.st. for 5 in. Leave sts. on a st. holder.

FRONT
With No. 13 needles cast on 151 (159, 167) sts. K. 8 rows. Change to No. 11 needles and work in st.st. until front measures 6½ in. from cast-on edge, ending with a p. row.

Place Pockets
Next row: k.18 (19, 20), k. next 37 (39, 41) sts. on to st. holder, k.41 (43, 45), k. next 37 (39, 41) sts. on to st. holder, k.18 (19, 20).
Next row: p.18 (19, 20), slip 37 (39, 41) sts. of one pocket to left-hand needle, p.37 (39, 41), p.17 (18, 19), cast off 7, p.17 (18, 19) including st. used in casting off, slip 37 (39, 41) sts. from 2nd pocket on to left-hand needle, p. to end.
Work on first group of 72 (76, 80) sts. only.
1st row: k.25 (27, 29), work first row of feather patt.

over next 23 sts., k.24 (26, 28).
2nd row: k.1, p.23 (25, 27), work 2nd row of feather patt., p.25 (27, 29).
3rd and 4th rows: keeping feather patt. correct as 3rd and 4th rows work rem. as first and 2nd rows.
These 4 rows form patt.
Cont. straight in patt. until work measures 16 in. from beg., ending with a wrong-side row.

Shape Armhole
Cast off 7 (8, 9) sts. at beg. of next row, 3 sts. at beg. of foll. alt. row, then 2 sts. at beg. of foll. alt. row. Now dec. 1 st. at armhole edge on every alt. row until 55 (58, 61) sts. remain. Cont. on these sts. until armhole measures 5 (5¼, 5½) in. ending at inside edge.

Shape Neck
Cast off 9 (10, 11) sts. at beg. of next row, then dec. 1 st. at neck edge on every alt. row until 39 (41, 43) sts. remain.
Cont. on these sts. until armhole measures 8 (8¼, 8½) in. ending at armhole edge.
Change to No. 13 needles.

Shape Shoulder
1st row: cast off 13 (13, 14), patt. to end.
2nd and 4th rows: patt. to end.
3rd row: cast off 13 (14, 14), patt. to end.
Cast off rem. sts.

Pocket Top
Slip the 37 (39, 41) sts. from st. holder on to No. 13 needle with right side facing. K. 4 rows.
Next row: k.18 (19, 20), y.f., k.2 tog., k.17 (18, 19). K. 3 rows. Cast off.
Slip the 2nd set of 72 (76, 80) sts. on to No. 11 needle with point at inside edge.
1st row: k.24 (26, 28), work first row of feather patt. over next 23 sts., k.25 (27, 29).
2nd row: p.25 (27, 29), work 2nd row of feather patt., p.23 (25, 27), k.1.
3rd and 4th rows: keeping feather patt. correct as 3rd and 4th rows work rem. as first and 2nd rows.
Complete to match first half reversing all shapings.

LEFT FRONT BAND
With No. 13 needles cast on 10 sts. K.14 (16, 18) rows.
1st row: k.4, cast off 2, k. to end.
2nd row: k.4, cast on 2, k.4.
3rd to 24th rows: k.
Rep first to 24th rows 4 times more, then work first to 20th rows again.
Leave sts. on st. holder.

RIGHT FRONT BAND
With No. 13 needles cast on 10 sts. K. 154 (156, 158) rows. Leave sts. on st. holder.

BACK
With No. 13 needles cast on 151 (159, 167) sts. K. 8 rows. Change to No. 11 needles and work in st.st. until Back matches Front to beg. of armholes.

Shape Armholes
Cast off 7 (8, 9) sts. at beg. of next 2 rows, 3 sts. at beg. of next 2 rows, 2 sts. at beg. of next 2 rows. Then dec. 1 st. at each end of every alt. row until 117 (123, 129) sts. remain. Cont. on these sts. until work matches Front to beg. of shoulders.
Change to No. 13 needles.

Shape Shoulders
1st and 2nd rows: cast off 13 (13, 14), patt. to end.

3rd and 4th rows: cast off 13 (14, 14), patt. to end.
5th and 6th rows: cast off 13 (14, 15), patt. to end.
Cast off.

TO COMPLETE
Armbands
Join shoulders. With No. 13 needles pick up and k. 173 (179, 185) sts. round one armhole. Work 12 rows in k.1, p.1 rib. Cast off.
Work round other armhole in same way.

Neckband
Slip 10 sts. from top of Right Front Band on to No. 13 needle with point at outside edge, rejoin yarn and k. 10 sts. of band, then with same needle pick up and k. 109 (115, 121) sts. round neck, then slip sts. from top of Left Front Band on to left-hand needle with point to end of last row and k.10 sts. of band.
1st row: k.10, * p.1, k.1; rep. from * to last 11 sts., p.1, k.10.
2nd row: k.11, * p.1, k.1; rep. from * to last 10 sts., k.10.
3rd and 4th rows: as first and 2nd rows.
5th row: k.4, cast off 2, k.4, p.1, rib to last 11 sts., p.1, k.10.
6th row: k.11, * p.1, k.1; rep. from * to last 4 sts. before buttonhole, k.4, cast on 2, k.4.
7th to 11th rows: rep. first and 2nd rows twice, then first row again.
Cast off in rib.

To Make Up
Omitting ribbing block and press on wrong side using warm iron and dry cloth. St. pockets down on wrong side and pocket tops on right side. St. front bands in position; now st. ends of Left Front Band over Right Front Band, then st. to 7 cast-off sts. at centre Front. Join side seams and ends of armbands.
Sew medium-sized buttons on Right Front Band to match buttonholes. Sew 2 press studs at top of bands. Sew small buttons to match buttonholes on top of pockets. Lightly press seams.

Leather jerkin with knitted sleeves and borders
illustrated on page 134

MATERIALS
9 balls (50 gr. each) Hayfield Brig Aran-type yarn. One pair each Nos. 8 and 10 knitting needles (USA sizes 6 and 3). Three leather skins. A 22-in. open-ended zip fastener.

MEASUREMENTS
To fit chest size 40–42 in.; length 23 in.; sleeve seam 18 in.

TENSION
6 sts. to 1 in. over rib patt. on No. 8 needles.

ABBREVIATIONS
See page 22; inc. 1, increase 1 st. by picking up loop between sts. and k. into the back of it.

SLEEVES (make 2 alike)
With No. 10 needles cast on 45 sts. and work in st.st. for 1 in., ending with a p. row. Change to No. 8 needles.
Next row: p.2, k.1, p.2, * inc. 1, p.2, k.1, p.2; rep. from * to end: 53 sts.
Next row: k.2, * p.1, k.2; rep. from * to end.
Next row: p.2, * y.b., sl.1 purlwise, y.fwd., p.2; rep. from * to end.

The last 2 rows form the rib patt. and are repeated throughout.
Cont. in patt., inc. 1 st. at each end of 7th and every foll. 8th row until there are 89 sts., working the extra sts. into patt., then cont. straight until sleeve measures 19 in. from beg., or length required, ending with a wrong-side row.

Shape Top
Cast off 4 sts. at beg. of next 2 rows, then 2 sts. at beg. of next 4 rows: 73 sts.
P.2 tog. at each end of next and foll. 9 alt. rows, ending with a wrong-side row: 53 sts.
Cast off 2 sts. at beg. of next 12 rows, 3 sts. at beg. of next 4 rows, then 4 sts. at beg. of next 2 rows.
Cast off rem. 9 sts.

NECKBAND
With No. 10 needles cast on 92 sts.
1st row: k.2, * p.1, k.2; rep. from * to end.
2nd row: p.2, * y.b., sl.1 purlwise, y.fwd., p.2; rep. from * to end.
Rep. these 2 rows 4 times more, and then the first row again.
Cast off loosely in rib.

LARGE POCKETS (make 2 alike)
With No. 8 needles cast on 35 sts. and work in rib patt. as on Sleeves for 6 in. Cast off in patt.

SMALL POCKETS (make 2 alike)
With No. 8 needles cast on 26 sts. and work in rib patt. as on Sleeves for 4½ in. Cast off in patt.

TO COMPLETE
The diagrams below show the pattern pieces you will need to cut out the leather front and back sections for the jerkin. Each square on the miniature diagrams represents 1 in. Prepare your own full-size pattern on strong white or brown paper. Now use the pattern pieces

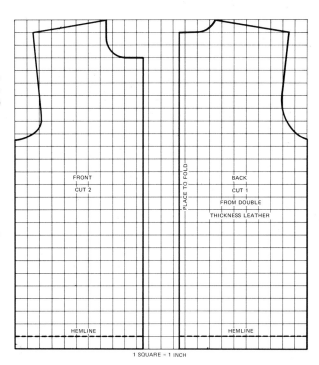

FRONT
CUT 2

PLACE TO FOLD

BACK
CUT 1
FROM DOUBLE
THICKNESS LEATHER

HEMLINE   HEMLINE

1 SQUARE = 1 INCH

to cut out the leather; cut 2 front sections then cut back from double thickness leather, being sure to place centre back edge on fold of leather. A word of warning when working with leather — never use pins on an area which will show on the finished garment, as the pin marks will remain even after the pins are removed. Use transparent self-adhesive tape instead of pins to secure pattern to the leather skins when cutting out. Machine-stitch zip to centre fronts. Join shoulder and side seams, with $\frac{1}{2}$-in. turnings. Sew in knitted sleeves and join sleeve seams. Stitch on collar, fold in half to outside and sl.st. in place.

Sew on pockets as in picture above. Turn up lower hem and stick in place with a little fabric glue.

Chapter ten
HOME COMFORT

Traditional table mats – in three sizes

MATERIALS
4 balls (20 gr. each) Coats Mercer-Crochet No. 20 (this quantity is sufficient to make one coffee table mat, two place mats, and two glass mats). One set of four double-pointed No. 12 knitting needles, and one No. 12 circular knitting needle, 30 in. long (USA size 1). One steel crochet hook International Standard Size 1.25.

MEASUREMENTS
Coffee table mat: 21 in. in diameter. **Place mat:** 12 in. in diameter. **Glass mat:** 6 in. in diameter.

TENSION
8 sts. and 9 rows to 1 in. over st.st.

ABBREVIATIONS
See page 22.

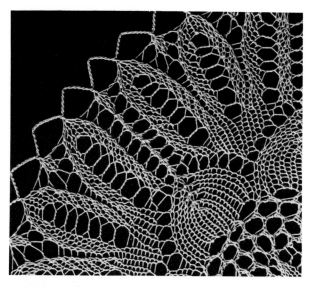

COFFEE TABLE MAT

With set of needles cast on 8 sts., 3 sts. on each of 2 needles and 2 sts. on 3rd needle and work in rounds as follows:

1st and 2nd rounds: k.

3rd round: * into next st. work k.1, p.1 and k.1; rep. from * to end: 24 sts.

4th and following alternate rounds: k.

5th round: k.

7th round: * y.fwd., k.3; rep. from * to end: 32 sts.

9th round: * y.fwd., k.1, y.fwd., k.3; rep. from * to end: 48 sts.

11th round: * y.fwd., k.2 tog., y.r.n. twice, k.1, y.fwd., sl.1, k.2 tog., p.s.s.o.; rep. from * to end: 56 sts.

12th and following alternate rounds: k., working k.1 and p.1 into each y.r.n. twice.

13th round: * k.1, y.r.n. twice, sl.1, k.1, p.s.s.o., k.2 tog., y.r.n. twice, sl.1, k.1, p.s.s.o.; rep. from * to end: 64 sts.

15th round: * y.r.n. twice, sl.1, k.1, p.s.s.o., k.2 tog.; rep. from * to end: 64 sts.

17th round: before commencing round, k. one st. from left-hand needle on to right-hand needle, * k.2 tog., y.r.n. twice, sl.1, k.1, p.s.s.o.; rep. from * to end: 64 sts.

19th round: as 15th round: 64 sts.

21st round: as 17th round: 64 sts.

23rd round: as 15th round: 64 sts.

24th round: k., working k.1, p.1 and k.1 into each y.r.n. twice: 80 sts.

25th to 28th rounds: k.: 80 sts.

29th round: * y.fwd., k.10; rep. from * to end: 88 sts.

30th and following alternate rounds: k.

31st round: * y.fwd., k.1, y.fwd., k.10; rep. from * to end: 104 sts.

33rd round: * y.fwd., k.3, y.fwd., k.4, sl.1, k.1, p.s.s.o., k.4; rep. from * to end: 112 sts.

35th round: * y.fwd., k.5, y.fwd., k.3, sl.1, k.2 tog., p.s.s.o., k.3; rep. from * to end: 112 sts.

37th round: * y.fwd., k.7, y.fwd., k.2, sl.1, k.2 tog., p.s.s.o., k.2; rep. from * to end: 112 sts.

39th round: * y.fwd., k.9, y.fwd., k.1, sl.1, k.2 tog., p.s.s.o., k.1; rep. from * to end: 112 sts.

41st round: * k.2, (y.r.n. twice, k.3) twice, y.r.n. twice, sl.1, k.1, p.s.s.o., k.1, y.fwd., sl.1, k.2 tog., p.s.s.o., y.fwd.; rep. from * to end: 152 sts.

42nd and following alternate rounds: k. working k.1 and p.1 into each y.r.n. twice.

43rd round: * k.3, (y.r.n. twice, k.5) twice, y.r.n. twice, k.3, y.fwd., sl.1, k.2 tog., p.s.s.o., y.fwd.; rep. from * to end: 200 sts.

45th round: * sl.1, k.1, p.s.s.o., k.2, y.r.n. twice, k.2, k.2 tog., k.3, y.r.n. twice, k.3, sl.1, k.1, p.s.s.o., k.2, y.r.n. twice, k.2, k.2 tog., y.fwd., sl.1, k.2 tog., p.s.s.o., y.fwd.; rep. from * to end: 216 sts.

47th round: * (sl.1, k.1, p.s.s.o., k.2, y.r.n. twice, k.2, k.2 tog.) 3 times, y.fwd., sl.1, k.2 tog., p.s.s.o., y.fwd.; rep. from * to end: 216 sts.

49th and 51st rounds: as 47th round: 216 sts.

53rd round: * (sl.1, k.1, p.s.s.o., k.2, y.r.n. twice, k.2, k.2 tog., y.fwd.) 3 times, sl.1, k.2 tog., p.s.s.o., y.fwd.; rep. from * to end: 232 sts.

55th round: * (sl.1, k.1, p.s.s.o., k.4, k.2 tog., y.fwd., k.1, y.fwd.) twice, sl.1, k.1, p.s.s.o., k.4, k.2 tog., y.fwd., sl.1, k.2 tog., p.s.s.o., y.fwd.; rep. from * to end: 216 sts.

56th round: k.: 216 sts.

Now change to circular knitting needle and mark beginning of round with a coloured thread.

57th round: * sl.1, k.1, p.s.s.o., k.2, k.2 tog., y.fwd., k.2 tog., y.r.n. twice, k.1, y.fwd.; rep. from * to end: 240 sts.

58th round: k., working k.1 and p.1 into each y.r.n. twice: 240 sts.

59th round: * sl.1, k.3 tog., p.s.s.o., k.1, y.r.n. twice, sl.1, k.1, p.s.s.o., k.2 tog., y.r.n. twice, k.1, y.fwd.; rep. from * to end: 264 sts.

60th round: as 58th round: 264 sts.

61st round: * (k.2 tog., y.r.n. twice, sl.1, k.1, p.s.s.o.) twice, k.2 tog., y.r.n. twice, k.1; rep. from * to end: 288 sts.

62nd round: as 12th round.

63rd to 71st rounds: as 15th to 23rd rounds.

72nd round: as 12th round.

73rd to 75th rounds: k.

76th round: * y.fwd., k.12; rep. from * to end: 312 sts.

77th and following alternate rounds: k.

78th round: * y.fwd., k.1, y.fwd., k.5, sl.1, k.1, p.s.s.o., k.5; rep. from * to end: 336 sts.

80th round: * y.fwd., k.3, y.fwd., k.4, sl.1, k.2 tog., p.s.s.o., k.4; rep. from * to end: 336 sts.

82nd to 103rd rounds: as 35th to 56th rounds.

104th round: * sl.1, k.1, p.s.s.o., k.2, k.2 tog., y.fwd., k.3, y.fwd.; rep. from * to end: 648 sts.

105th round: k.: 648 sts.

Edging

With crochet hook, * work 1 d.c. into next 4 sts. and slip off, 12 ch., 1 d.c. into next 5 sts. and slip off, 12 ch.; rep. from * ending with 1 s.s. into first d.c. Fasten off.

PLACE MAT

With set of needles, cast on 8 sts. and work as for Coffee Table Mat for 56 rounds: 216 sts.

57th round: * sl.1, k.1, p.s.s.o., k.2, k.2 tog., y.fwd., k.3, y.fwd.; rep. from * to end: 216 sts.

58th round: k.: 216 sts.

Work edging as for Coffee Table Mat.

GLASS MAT

With set of needles cast on 8 sts. and work as Coffee Table Mat for 4 rounds.

5th round: * y.fwd., k.3; rep. from * to end: 32 sts.

7th round: * y.fwd., k.1, y.fwd., sl.1, k.2 tog., p.s.s.o.; rep. from * to end: 32 sts.

9th round: * k.2 tog., y.r.n. twice, sl.1, k.1, p.s.s.o.; rep. from * to end: 32 sts.

10th round: k., working k.1 and p.1 into each y.r.n. twice: 32 sts.

11th round: * y.r.n. twice, sl.1, k.1, p.s.s.o., k.2 tog.; rep. from * to end: 32 sts.

12th round: k., working k.1, p.1 and k.1 into each y.r.n. twice: 40 sts.

13th and following alternate rounds: k.

14th round: * y.fwd., k.5; rep. from * to end: 48 sts.

16th round: * y.fwd., k.1, y.fwd., k.5; rep. from * to end: 64 sts.
18th round: * y.fwd., k.3, y.fwd., k.1, sl.1, k.2 tog., p.s.s.o., k.1; rep. from * to end: 64 sts.
20th round: * k.5, y.fwd., sl.1, k.2 tog., p.s.s.o., y.fwd.; rep. from * to end: 64 sts.
22nd round: * k.1, y.r.n. twice, k.2, y.r.n. twice, sl.1, k.1, p.s.s.o., y.fwd., sl.1, k.2 tog., p.s.s.o., y.fwd.; rep. from * to end: 88 sts.
23rd and following alternate rounds: k. working k.1 and p.1 into each y.r.n. twice.
24th round: * k.2, y.r.n. twice, k.4, y.r.n. twice, k.2, y.fwd., sl.1, k.2 tog., p.s.s.o., y.fwd.; rep. from * to end: 120 sts.
26th round: * (sl.1, k.1, p.s.s.o., k.1, y.r.n. twice, k.1, k.2 tog.) twice, y.fwd., sl.1, k.2 tog., p.s.s.o., y.fwd.; rep. from * to end: 120 sts.
28th round: * (sl.1, k.1, p.s.s.o., k.1, y.r.n. twice, k.1, k.2 tog., y.fwd.) twice, sl.1, k.2 tog., p.s.s.o., y.fwd.; rep. from * to end: 128 sts.
30th round: * sl.1, k.1, p.s.s.o., k.2, k.2 tog., y.fwd., k.1, y.fwd., sl.1, k.1, p.s.s.o., k.2, k.2 tog., y.fwd., sl.1, k.2 tog., p.s.s.o., y fwd.; rep. from * to end: 112 sts.
31st round: k.: 112 sts.

Edging
With crochet hook, * work 1 d.c. into next 4 sts. and slip off, 10 ch., 1 d.c. into next 3 sts., and slip off, 10 ch.; rep. from * ending with 1 s.s. into first d.c. Fasten off. Damp and pin out to measurements.

Five lace edgings

MATERIALS
Each edging is worked in Coats Mercer-Crochet No. 20—the exact quantity will depend on how much edging you want to make. For edgings 1, 3 and 5 you will need one pair No. 14 knitting needles (USA size 0); for edging 2 you will need one pair No. 13 knitting

needles (USA size 1); and for edging 4 you will need a set of four double-pointed No. 13 knitting needles (USA size 1). Edgings 2 and 4 also require one steel crochet hook International Standard Size 1.25.

MEASUREMENTS
See start of each edging pattern.

TENSION
A tension check can be made by working a small section of the edging, and then checking its size against the measurement quoted in the pattern.

ABBREVIATIONS
See page 22.

EDGING 1
Depth of edging: 1⅛ in.
Cast on 8 sts.
1st row: k.3, y.fwd., k.2 tog., y.r.n. twice, k.2 tog., k.1.
2nd row: k.2, k.1, p.1 into 'y.r.n. twice', k.2, y.fwd., k.2 tog., k.1.
3rd row: k.3, y.fwd., k.2 tog., k.1, y.r.n. twice, k.2 tog., k.1.

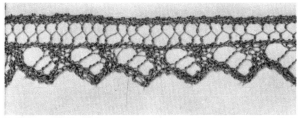

4th row: k.2, (k.1, p.1) into 'y.r.n. twice', k.3, y.fwd., k.2 tog., k.1.
5th row: k.3, y.fwd., k.2 tog., k.2, y.r.n. twice, k.2 tog., k.1.
6th row: k.2, (k.1, p.1) into 'y.r.n. twice', k.4, y.fwd., k.2 tog., k.1
7th row: k.3, y.fwd., k.2 tog., k.6.
8th row: cast off 3 sts., k.4 (5 sts. on right-hand needle), y.fwd., k.2 tog., k.1.
These 8 rows form the pattern and are repeated for length required.

EDGING 2
Depth of edging: 2 in.
Width of pattern repeat: 3 in. approx.
Cast on a number of sts. divisible by 21 plus 1.
P. 1 row.
Begin Pattern
1st row: k.2 tog., * y.fwd., sl.1, k.1, p.s.s.o., k.2, y.fwd., sl.1, k.1, p.s.s.o., k.3, y.r.n. twice, k.3, k.2 tog., y.fwd., k.2, k.2 tog., y.fwd., sl.1, k.2 tog., p.s.s.o.; repeat from * ending last repeat sl.1, k.1, p.s.s.o.
2nd and every following alternate row: p., working p.1, k.1. into 'y.r.n. twice'.
3rd row: as first row.
5th row: k.2 tog., * y.fwd., sl.1, k.1, p.s.s.o., k.2, y.fwd., sl.1, k.1, p.s.s.o., k.6, k.2 tog., y.fwd., k.2, k.2 tog., y.fwd., sl.1, k.2 tog., p.s.s.o.; rep. from * ending last repeat sl.1, k.1, p.s.s.o.
7th row: k.2, * y.fwd., sl.1, k.1, p.s.s.o., k.2, y.fwd., sl.1, k.1, p.s.s.o., k.4, k.2 tog., y.fwd., k.2, k.2 tog., y.fwd., k.3; rep. from * ending last repeat k.2.
9th row: k.3, * (y.fwd., sl.1, k.1, p.s.s.o., k.2) twice, k.2 tog., y.fwd., k.2, k.2 tog., y.fwd., k.5; repeat from * ending last repeat k.3.
11th row: k.1, (y.r.n. twice, k.1) 3 times, * y.fwd., sl.1, k.1, p.s.s.o., k.2, y.fwd., sl.1, k.3 tog., p.s.s.o., y.fwd., k.2, k.2 tog., y.fwd., (k.1, y.r.n. twice) 6 times, k.1; repeat from * ending last repeat (k.1, y.r.n. twice) 3 times, k.1.

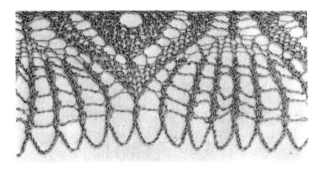

13th row: k.2 tog., (y.r.n. twice, sl.1, k.2 tog., p.s.s.o.) 3 times, * y.fwd., sl.1, k.1, p.s.s.o., k.5, k.2 tog., y.fwd., (sl.1, k.2 tog., p.s.s.o., y.r.n. twice) 6 times, sl.1, k.2 tog., p.s.s.o.; repeat from * to last 20 sts., y.fwd., sl.1, k.1, p.s.s.o., k.5, k.2 tog., y.fwd., (sl.1, k.2 tog., p.s.s.o., y.r.n. twice) 3 times, sl.1, k.1, p.s.s.o.
15th row: k.2 tog., (y.r.n. twice, sl.1, k.2 tog., p.s.s.o.) 3 times, * y.fwd., sl.1, k.1, p.s.s.o., k.3, k.2 tog., y.fwd., (sl.1, k.2 tog., p.s.s.o., y.r.n. twice) 6 times, sl.1, k.2 tog., p.s.s.o.; repeat from * to last 18 sts., y.fwd., sl.1, k.1, p.s.s.o., k.3, k.2 tog., y.fwd., (sl.1, k.2 tog., p.s.s.o., y.r.n. twice) 3 times, sl.1, k.1, p.s.s.o.
17th row: k.2 tog., (y.r.n. twice, sl.1, k.2 tog., p.s.s.o.) 3 times, * y.fwd., sl.1, k.1, p.s.s.o., k.1, k.2 tog., y.fwd., (sl.1, k.2 tog., p.s.s.o., y.r.n. twice) 6 times, sl.1, k.2 tog., p.s.s.o.; rep. from * to last 16 sts., y.fwd., sl.1, k.1, p.s.s.o., k.1, k.2 tog., y.fwd., (sl.1, k.2 tog., p.s.s.o., y.r.n. twice) 3 times, sl.1, k.1, p.s.s.o.
19th row: k.2 tog., * y.r.n. twice, sl.1, k.2 tog., p.s.s.o.; repeat from * to last 2 sts., y.r.n. twice, sl.1, k.1, p.s.s.o.
20th row: as 2nd row.

Edging
Using crochet hook, work 1 d.c. into first 2 sts., * 10 ch., 1 d.c. into next 3 sts.; repeat from * to last 2 sts., 10 ch., 1 d.c. into last 2 sts.
Fasten off.

EDGING 3
Depth of edging: 3¾ in.
Cast on 32 sts.
1st row: (k.2 tog.) twice, y.r.n. 3 times, sl.1, k.2 tog., p.s.s.o., k.1, (y.fwd., k.2 tog.) 3 times, k.2 tog., y.r.n. 3 times, sl.1, k.2 tog., p.s.s.o., (k.1, k.2 tog., y.fwd.) twice, k.2 tog., y.r.n. twice, k.2 tog., k.3: 31 sts.
2nd and every following alternate row: k.4, p. to end working (p.1, k.1, p.1) into 'y.r.n. 3 times', and (p.1, k.1) into 'y.r.n. twice'.
3rd row: y.fwd., k.2 tog., k.6, (y.fwd., k.2 tog.) twice k.9, k.2 tog., y.fwd., k.8.

5th row: y.fwd., k.2 tog., y.r.n. 3 times, sl.1, k.3 tog., p.s.s.o., y.r.n. 3 times, k.2 tog., k.1, y.fwd., (k.2 tog.) twice, y.r.n. 3 times, sl.1, k.2 tog., p.s.s.o., k.4, k.2 tog., y.fwd., k.2, k.2 tog., y.r.n. twice, k.2 tog., k.3: 33 sts.
7th row: y.fwd., k.2 tog., k.19, k.2 tog., y.fwd., k.1, k.2 tog., y.fwd., k.7.
9th row: y.fwd., k.2 tog., y.r.n. 3 times, k.2 tog., k.1, y.fwd., (k.2 tog.) twice, y.r.n. 3 times, sl.1, k.3 tog., p.s.s.o., y.r.n. 3 times, sl.1, k.2 tog., p.s.s.o., k.7, k.2 tog., y.fwd., k.1, k.2 tog., y.r.n. twice, k.2 tog., k.3: 35 sts.
11th row: y.fwd., k.2 tog., k.4, (y.fwd., k.2 tog.) twice, k.14, k.2 tog., y.fwd., k.9.
13th row: y.fwd., k.2 tog., y.r.n. 3 times, (k.2 tog., y.fwd.) 3 times, (k.2 tog.) twice, y.r.n. 3 times, sl.1, k.3 tog., p.s.s.o., k.2 tog., k.5, k.2 tog., y.fwd., k.1, k.2 tog., y.fwd., k.2 tog., y.r.n. twice, k.2 tog., k.3.
15th row: k.2 tog., k.6, (y.fwd., k.2 tog.) twice, k.13, k.2 tog., y.fwd., k.8: 34 sts.
17th row: (k.2 tog.) twice, y.r.n. 3 times, sl.1, k.2 tog., p.s.s.o., k.1, y.fwd., (k.2 tog.) twice, y.r.n. 3 times, sl.1, k.3 tog., p.s.s.o., y.r.n. 3 times, k.2 tog., k.5, k.2 tog., y.fwd., k.2, k.2 tog., y.r.n. twice, k.2 tog., k.3.
19th row: k.2 tog., k.20, k.2 tog., y.fwd., k.1, k.2 tog., y.fwd., k.7: 33 sts.
21st row: (k.2 tog.) twice, y.r.n. 3 times, sl.1, k.3 tog., p.s.s.o., y.r.n. 3 times, sl.1, k.2 tog., p.s.s.o., k.1, y.fwd., k.2 tog., k.1, y.r.n. 3 times, sl.1, k.2 tog., p.s.s.o., k.5, k.2 tog., y.fwd., k.1, k.2 tog., y.r.n. twice, k.2 tog., k.3.
23rd row: k.2 tog., k.8, (y.fwd., k.2 tog.) twice, k.8, k.2 tog., y.fwd., k.9: 32 sts.
24th row: k.4, p. to end.
These 24 rows form the pattern and are repeated for length required.

EDGING 4
Depth of edging: 2¼ in.
Width of pattern repeat: 2¼ in. approx.
Cast on a number of sts. divisible by 16 plus 2 for each side. K. 1 row.

Begin Pattern
1st row: * y.fwd., k.1, (y.fwd., sl.1, k.1, p.s.s.o.) 3 times, y.fwd., sl.1, k.2 tog., p.s.s.o., (y.fwd., k.2 tog.) 3 times; rep. from * along side, y.fwd., k.1, y.fwd., k.1 (centre st. at corner).

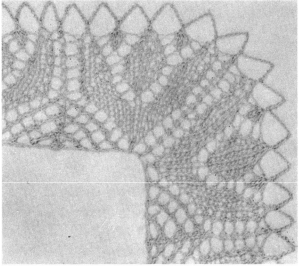

2nd and every following alternate row: k.
3rd row: * y.fwd., k.3, (y.fwd., sl.1, k.1, p.s.s.o.) 3 times, k.1, (k.2 tog., y.fwd.) twice, k.2 tog.; rep. from * along side, y.fwd., k.3, y.fwd., k.1.

5th row: * y.fwd., k.5, (y.fwd., sl.1, k.1, p.s.s.o.) twice, y.fwd., sl.1, k.2 tog., p.s.s.o., (y.fwd., k.2 tog.) twice; rep. from * along side, y.fwd., k.5, y.fwd., k.1.

7th row: * y.fwd., k.7, (y.fwd., sl.1, k.1, p.s.s.o.) twice, k.1, k.2 tog., y.fwd., k.2 tog.; rep. from * along side, y.fwd., k.7, y.fwd., k.1.

9th row: * y.fwd., k.9, y.fwd., sl.1, k.1, p.s.s.o., y.fwd., sl.1, k.2 tog., p.s.s.o., y.fwd., k.2 tog.; rep. from * along side, y.fwd., k.9, y.fwd., k.1.

11th row: * y.fwd., k.3, k.2 tog., y.fwd., k.1, y.fwd., sl.1, k.1, p.s.s.o., k.3, y.fwd., sl.1, k.1, p.s.s.o., k.1, k.2 tog.; rep. from * along side, y.fwd., k.3, k.2 tog., y.fwd., k.1, y.fwd., sl.1, k.1, p.s.s.o., k.3, y.fwd., k.1.

13th row: * y.fwd., sl.1, k.1, p.s.s.o., (k.3, y.fwd.) twice, k.3, k.2 tog., y.fwd., sl.1, k.2 tog., p.s.s.o.; rep. from * along side, y.fwd., sl.1, k.1, p.s.s.o., (k.3, y.fwd.) twice, k.3, k.2 tog., y.fwd., k.1.

15th row: * y.fwd., sl.1, k.1, p.s.s.o., k.3, y.fwd., k.5, k.3, k.2 tog., y.fwd., k.1; rep. from * to end.

17th row: * (y.fwd., sl.1, k.1, p.s.s.o., k.3) twice, k.2 tog., y.fwd., k.3, k.2 tog., y.fwd., k.1; rep. from * to end.

19th row: * y.fwd., sl.1, k.1, p.s.s.o., k.1, k.2 tog., y.fwd., sl.1, k.1, p.s.s.o., k.3, k.2 tog., y.fwd., sl.1, k.1, p.s.s.o., k.1, k.2 tog., y.fwd., k.1; rep. from * to end.

21st row: * y.fwd., sl.1, k.1, p.s.s.o., k.2, y.fwd., k.1, y.fwd., k.5, y.fwd., k.1, y.fwd., k.2, k.2 tog., y.fwd., k.1; rep. from * to end.

23rd row: * sl.1, k.1, p.s.s.o., k.2 tog., y.fwd., k.3, y.fwd., sl.1, k.1, p.s.s.o., k.1, k.2 tog., y.fwd., k.3, y.fwd., sl.1, k.1, p.s.s.o., k.2 tog., y.fwd., k.1, y.fwd.; rep. from * to end.

24th row: k.

Edging

Using crochet hook, work 1 d.c. into first 2 sts., * 10 ch., 1 d.c. into next 5 sts., 10 ch., 1 d.c. into next 3 sts., 10 ch., 1 d.c. into next 5 sts., 10 ch., 1 d.c. into next 2 sts., 10 ch., 1 d.c. into next 3 sts., 10 ch., 1 d.c. into next 2 sts.; rep. from * omitting 1 d.c. at end of last repeat, 1 s.s. into first d.c.
Fasten off.

EDGING 5

Depth of edging: $3\frac{1}{4}$ in.
Cast on 20 sts.

1st row: k.9, (k.2 tog., y.fwd., k.1) 3 times, y.fwd., sl.1, k.1, p.s.s.o.

2nd row: y.fwd., sl.1, k.1, p.s.s.o., k.18.

3rd row: k.8, (k.2 tog., y.fwd., k.1) 3 times, y.fwd., k.1, y.fwd., sl.1, k.1, p.s.s.o.: 21 sts.

4th row: (y.fwd., sl.1, k.1, p.s.s.o.) twice, k.17: 21 sts.

5th row: k.7, (k.2 tog., y.fwd., k.1) 3 times, y.fwd., k.1, (y.fwd., sl.1, k.1, p.s.s.o.) twice: 22 sts.

6th row: (y.fwd., sl.1, k.1, p.s.s.o.) 3 times, k.16: 22 sts.

7th row: k.6, (k.2 tog., y.fwd., k.1) 3 times, y.fwd., k.1, (y.fwd., sl.1, k.1, p.s.s.o.) 3 times: 23 sts.

8th row: (y.fwd., sl.1, k.1, p.s.s.o.) 4 times, k.15: 23 sts.

9th row: k.5, (k.2 tog., y.fwd., k.1) 3 times, y.fwd., k.1, (y.fwd., sl.1, k.1, p.s.s.o.) 4 times: 24 sts.

10th row: (y.fwd., sl.1, k.1, p.s.s.o.) 5 times, k.14: 24 sts.

11th row: k.4, (k.2 tog., y.fwd., k.1) 3 times, y.fwd., k.1, (y.fwd., sl.1, k.1, p.s.s.o.) 5 times: 25 sts.

12th row: (y.fwd., sl.1, k.1, p.s.s.o.) 6 times, k.13: 25 sts.

13th row: k.3, (k.2 tog., y.fwd., k.1) 3 times, y.fwd., k.12, (y.fwd., sl.1, k.1, p.s.s.o.) 6 times: 26 sts.

14th row: (y.fwd., sl.1, k.1, p.s.s.o.) 7 times, k.12: 26 sts.

15th row: k.2, (k.2 tog., y.fwd., k.1) 3 times, y.fwd., k.1, (y.fwd., sl.1, k.1, p.s.s.o.) 7 times: 27 sts.

16th row: (y.fwd., sl.1, k.1, p.s.s.o.) 8 times, k.11: 27 sts.

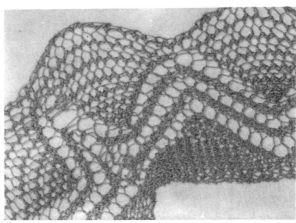

17th row: k.4, (y.fwd., k.2 tog., k.1) twice, y.fwd., sl.1, k.2 tog., p.s.s.o., (y.fwd., sl.1, k.1, p.s.s.o.) 7 times: 26 sts.

18th row: (y.fwd., sl.1, k.1, p.s.s.o.) 7 times, k.12: 26 sts.

19th row: k.5, (y.fwd., k.2 tog., k.1) twice, y.fwd., sl.1, k.2 tog., p.s.s.o., (y.fwd., sl.1, k.1, p.s.s.o.) 6 times: 25 sts.

20th row: (y.fwd., sl.1, k.1, p.s.s.o.) 6 times, k.13: 25 sts.

21st row: k.6 (y.fwd., k.2 tog., k.1) twice, y.fwd., sl.1, k.2 tog., p.s.s.o., (y.fwd., sl.1, k.1, p.s.s.o.) 5 times: 24 sts.

22nd row: (y.fwd., sl.1, k.1, p.s.s.o.) 5 times, k.14: 24 sts.

23rd row: k.7 (y.fwd., k.2 tog., k.1) twice, y.fwd., sl.1, k.2 tog., p.s.s.o., (y.fwd., sl.1, k.1, p.s.s.o.) 4 times: 23 sts.

24th row: (y.fwd., sl.1, k.1, p.s.s.o.) 4 times, k.15: 23 sts.

25th row: k.8, (y.fwd., k.2 tog., k.1) twice, y.fwd., sl.1, k.2 tog., p.s.s.o., (y.fwd., sl.1, k.1, p.s.s.o.) 3 times: 22 sts.

26th row: (y.fwd., sl.1, k.1, p.s.s.o.) 3 times, k.16: 22 sts.

27th row: k.9, (y.fwd., k.2 tog., k.1) twice, y.fwd., sl.1, k.2 tog., p.s.s.o., (y.fwd., sl.1, k.1, p.s.s.o.) twice: 21 sts.

28th row: (y.fwd., sl.1, k.1, p.s.s.o.) twice, k.17: 21 sts.

29th row: k.10, (y.fwd., k.2 tog., k.1) twice, y.fwd., sl.1, k.2 tog., p.s.s.o., (y.fwd., sl.1, k.1, p.s.s.o.): 20 sts.

30th row: y.fwd., sl.1, k.1, p.s.s.o., k.18: 20 sts.
These 30 rows form the pattern. Work in pattern for length required, ending with a 15th pattern row.

Corner

1st row: (y.fwd., sl.1, k.1, p.s.s.o.) 8 times, k.10, turn.

2nd row: sl.1, k.2, (k.2 tog., k.1) twice, y.fwd., sl.1, k.2 tog., p.s.s.o., (y.fwd., sl.1, k.1, p.s.s.o.) 7 times.

3rd row: (y.fwd., sl.1, k.1, p.s.s.o.) 7 times, k.9, turn.

4th row: sl.1, k.1, (y.fwd., k.2 tog., k.1) twice, y.fwd., sl.1, k.2 tog., p.s.s.o., (y.fwd., sl.1, k.1, p.s.s.o.) 6 times.

5th row: (y.fwd., sl.1, k.1, p.s.s.o.) 6 times, k.8, turn.

6th row: sl.1, (y.fwd., k.2 tog., k.1) twice, y.fwd., sl.1, k.2 tog., p.s.s.o., (y.fwd., sl.1, k.1, p.s.s.o.) 5 times.

7th row: (y.fwd., sl.1, k.1, p.s.s.o.) 5 times, k.7, turn.

8th row: sl.1, k.2, y.fwd., k.2 tog., k.1, y.fwd., sl.1, k.2 tog., p.s.s.o., (y.fwd., sl.1, k.1, p.s.s.o.) 4 times.

9th row: (y.fwd., sl.1, k.1, p.s.s.o.) 4 times, k.6, turn.

10th row: sl.1, k.1, y.fwd., k.2 tog., k.1, y.fwd., sl.1, k.2 tog., p.s.s.o., (y.fwd., sl.1, k.1, p.s.s.o.) 3 times.

11th row: (y.fwd., sl.1, k.1, p.s.s.o.) 3 times, k.5, turn.

12th row: sl.1, k.2 tog., k.1, y.fwd., sl.1, k.2 tog., p.s.s.o., (y.fwd., sl.1, k.1, p.s.s.o.) twice.

13th row : (y.fwd., sl.1, k.1, p.s.s.o.) twice, k.3, turn.
14th row : sl.1, k.1, y.fwd., sl.1, k.2 tog., p.s.s.o., y.fwd., sl.1, k.1, p.s.s.o.
15th row : y.fwd., sl.1, k.1, p.s.s.o., k.2, turn.
16th row : sl.1, k.1, y.fwd., sl.1, k.1, p.s.s.o.
17th row : y.fwd., sl.1, k.1, p.s.s.o., k.3, turn.
18th row : sl.1, (y.fwd., k.1) twice, y.fwd., sl.1, k.1, p.s.s.o.
19th row : (y.fwd., sl.1, k.1, p.s.s.o.) twice, k.3, turn.
20th row : sl.1, k.1, y.fwd., k.1, (y.fwd., sl.1, k.1, p.s.s.o.) twice.
21st row : (y.fwd., sl.1, k.1, p.s.s.o.) 3 times, k.3, turn.
22nd row : sl.1, k.2, (y.fwd., sl.1, k.1, p.s.s.o.) 3 times.
23rd row : (y.fwd., sl.1, k.1, p.s.s.o.) 4 times, k.4, turn.
24th row : k.2 tog., (y.fwd., k.1) twice, (y.fwd., sl.1, k.1, p.s.s.o.) 4 times.
25th row : as 7th row.
26th row : sl.1, k.2, k.2 tog., (y.fwd., k.1) twice, (y.fwd., sl.1, k.1, p.s.s.o.) 5 times.
27th row : (y.fwd., sl.1, k.1, p.s.s.o.) 6 times, k.7, turn.
28th row : sl.1, k.1, y.fwd., k.1, k.2 tog., (y.fwd., k.1) twice, (y.fwd., sl.1, k.1, p.s.s.o.) 6 times.
29th row : (y.fwd., sl.1, k.1, p.s.s.o.) 7 times, k.9, turn.
30th row : sl.1, k.1, (k.2 tog., y.fwd., k.1) twice, y.fwd., k.1, (y.fwd., sl.1, k.1, p.s.s.o.) 7 times.
The corner is now complete. Beginning with 16th pattern row, continue in pattern to next corner and turn as before. Work other two sides to correspond. Overcast cast-on and cast-off edges together.

Cotton bathmat

MATERIALS
Of Twilleys Bubbly—7 oz. in black, 6 oz. in white and 3 oz. in kingfisher. One pair No. 2 knitting needles (USA size 11).

MEASUREMENTS
Finished bathmat measures approx. 25½ in. by 19½ in.

TENSION
6 sts. and 7 rows to 2 in.

ABBREVIATIONS
See page 22; W., white; B., black; K., kingfisher.

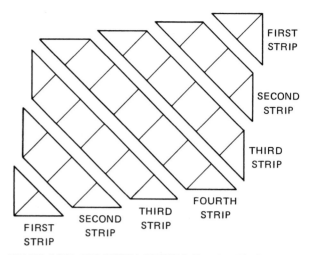

FIRST AND SEVENTH STRIPS (both alike)
** With 4 strands of W. cast on 3 sts.
1st row : k.1, p.1, k.1.
2nd row : inc. in first st., p.1, k.1.
3rd row : k.1, p.1, k.1, inc. in last st.
4th row : k.1, (p.1, k.1) twice.
5th row : * k.1, p.1; rep. from * to last st., inc. in last st.
6th row : inc. in first st., k.1, * p.1, k.1; rep. from * to end.
7th row : k.1, * p.1, k.1; rep. from * to end.
8th row : inc. in first st., * p.1, k.1; rep. from * to end.
9th row : k.1, * p.1, k.1; rep. from * to last st., inc. in last st.
10th row : k.1, * p.1, k.1; rep. from * to end.
Rep. 5th–10th rows again: 13 sts. Break off 3 strands of W. and join 1 strand B. and 2 strands K. **
*** Using the 4 strands tog., k. 1 row.
Next row : k.2 tog., k.1, * p.1, k.1; rep. from * to end.
Next row : * k.1, p.1; rep. from * to last 2 sts., k.2 tog.
Next row : k.1, * p.1, k.1; rep. from * to end.
Continue in m.st., dec. 1 st. at dec. edge on next 2 rows. Work 1 row straight. Rep. last 3 rows until 3 sts. remain. Work 1 row. Cast off. ***

SECOND AND SIXTH STRIPS (both alike)
Work as first and seventh strips from ** to **. K. 1 row.
Next row : k.1, * p.1, k.1; rep. from * to end.
Rep. last row 18 times more. Break off 1 strand of B. and 2 strands of K. and join 3 more strands of W. K. 1 row.
Next row : k.1, * p.1, k.1; rep. from * to end.
Rep. last row 18 times more. Break off 3 strands of W. and join 1 strand of B. and 2 strands of K. ****.
Rep. from *** to *** as first and seventh strips.

THIRD AND FIFTH STRIPS (both alike)
Work as second and sixth strips to ****. Now rep. last 40 rows again (i.e. one more K., W. and B. square and one more W. square). Break off 3 strands of W. and join 1 strand of B. and 2 strands of K. and rep. from *** to *** as first and seventh strips.

FOURTH STRIP
With 2 strands of K., 1 B. and 1 W., cast on 3 sts.
1st row : k.1, p.1, k.1.
2nd row : k.1, p.1, inc. in last st.
3rd row : inc. in first st., k.1, p.1, k.1.
4th row : k.1, (p.1, k.1) twice.
Working in m.st., inc. at same edge as before on next 2 rows then work 1 row straight until there are 13 sts. Work 1 row. Break 1 strand of B. and 2 strands of K. and join 3 strands of W.
Now work (one square W., one square K., W. and B.) twice, then one square W. again. Break off 3 strands W. and join 1 strand B. and 2 strands K. Rep. from *** to *** as first and seventh strips.

BORDERS

With 4 strands of B. cast on 1 st.
1st row: inc. twice in st.
2nd row: k.1, p.1, k.1.
3rd row: inc. in first st., p.1, inc. in last st.
4th row: p.1, (k.1, p.1) twice.
5th row: inc. in first st., k.1, p.1, k.1, inc. in last st.
6th row: k.1, (p.1, k.1) 3 times.
Rep. last row for m. st. for 22 in., straight. Now inc. 1 st. each end of next and following alternate row. Work one row. K.3 tog. Fasten off.
Work another band to match then work 2 more bands each only 16½ in. long.

TO COMPLETE

Press pieces lightly. Sew in ends. Join strips in order as in diagram, left. Sew on borders, join mitred corners then fold border in half and slip st. down. Press seams and borders.

Rug

MATERIALS

5 hanks (4 oz. each) Twilleys D42 dishcloth cotton. One pair No. 2 knitting needles (USA size 11).

MEASUREMENTS

Finished rug measures approx. 19 in. by 33½ in.

TENSION

4 sts. to 1½ in.

ABBREVIATIONS

See page 22.

TO MAKE

Note. Use yarn double throughout.
Cast on 74 sts.
1st row: k.
2nd row: k.6, p. to last 6 sts., k.6.
3rd and 4th rows: as first and 2nd rows.
5th and 6th rows: as first and 2nd rows.
Next row: k.1, * k.2 tog., y.fwd.; rep. from * to last st., k.1. Beg. with a p. row work another 6 rows in st.st., keeping 6 sts. at each end of row in garter st.
Now begin pattern as follows:
1st row: k.6, * p.2, k.1; rep. from * to last 8 sts., p.2, k.6.
2nd row: k.6, * k.2, p.1; rep. from * to last 8 sts., k.8.
3rd row: k.6, * p.2, y.fwd., k.1, p.2, k.1, sl. the y.fwd. over these last 4 sts.; rep. from * to last 8 sts., p.2, k.6.
4th row: as 2nd row.
5th row: as first row.
6th row: as 2nd row.
7th row: k.6, p.2, k.1, * p.2, y.fwd., k.1, p.2, k.1, sl. the y.fwd. over these last 4 sts.; rep. from * to last 11 sts., p.2, k.1, p.2, k.6.

8th row: as 2nd row.
These 8 rows form the patt. Cont. in patt. until work measures 35 in. from line of holes at beg.
Work 6 rows in st.st. with the 6 sts. at each end of row in garter st.
Next row: k.1, * k.2 tog., y.fwd.; rep. from * to last st., k.1. Beg. with a p. row work another 5 rows in st.st., keeping 6 sts. at each end of row in garter st. Cast off.

TO COMPLETE

Press work on the wrong side with a warm iron over a damp cloth. Fold hem in half along the row of holes at each end and sew to wrong side.

Three-way cushions

illustrated in colour on page 124

MATERIALS

For all three cushions: 5 balls (50 gr. each) Hayfield Brig in each of three contrasting shades. One pair No. 9 knitting needles (USA size 5). **For oblong cushion**: cushion pad 18 in. by 12 in. One medium-sized crochet hook. **For diagonal cushion**: one cushion pad 15 in. square. One extra ball Hayfield Brig in third contrasting shade and one crochet hook International Standard Size 5.00 *or* 1⅔ yd. cord to match third yarn shade. **For square cushion**: cushion pad 15 in. square. One extra ball Hayfield Brig in third contrasting shade and one crochet hook International Standard Size 5.00 *or* 4 yd. cord to match third yarn shade.

MEASUREMENTS

Oblong cushion: 17 in. by 12½ in. **Diagonal cushion**: 14 in. square. **Square cushion**: 14 in. square.

TENSION

5 sts. and 7 rows to 1 in.

ABBREVIATIONS

See page 22; first shade; B, 2nd shade; C, 3rd shade.

141

OBLONG CUSHION
MAIN PIECE (make 2 alike)
With B cast on 56 sts. Beg. with a k. row, work in st.st. in foll. stripes.
Work 22 rows in B.
Work 22 rows in A.
Work 28 rows in C.
Work 22 rows in A.
Work 22 rows in B.
Cast off loosely.

TO COMPLETE
Pin out firmly to size and press under a damp cloth with a hot iron. Leave in position until dry.

Fringe
Cut 4-in. lengths of C. Use 2 lengths to each knot. Fold yarn in half and insert crochet hook into the first st. along the cast-on edge of one piece of knitting and pull through folded end of yarn. Pull the ends through this loop and knot tightly. Rep. into each st. along the edge. Trim the ends evenly. Work along the opposite edge in the same way.
Right sides facing, join the 2 pieces of knitting tog., leaving one end open. Turn to right side. Insert the cushion pad and join opening.

DIAGONAL CUSHION
MAIN PIECE (make 2 pieces alike)
With C, cast on 2 sts.
Next row: p.2.
Beg. with a k. row, work in st.st., inc. 1 st. at the beg. and end of every row in foll. stripes.
Work 22 rows in C: 46 sts.
Work 22 rows in B: 90 sts.
Work 22 rows in A: 134 sts.
Now k.2 tog. at the beg. and end of every row.
Work 22 rows in C: 90 sts.
Work 22 rows in B: 46 sts.
Work 22 rows in A: 2 sts.
Cast off.

TO COMPLETE
Press as for Oblong Cushion, taking care to pin work to an even square.
Right sides facing, place 2 pieces tog., and sew round the edges leaving an opening to insert the pad. Turn to right side and press if required. Insert pad and sew up opening.
If ready-made cord is used, sew round the edge making a loop at each corner.
For crochet cord, with crochet hook and 2 strands of C tog. make a crochet ch. 60 in. in length. Complete as for ready-made cord.

SQUARE CUSHION
SQUARES (make 8 alike)
With B cast on 40 sts.
Work in st.st. beg. with a k. row.
Work 16 rows in B.
Work 16 rows in A.
Work 16 rows in C.
Cast off.

TO COMPLETE
Press as for Oblong Cushion. Join 4 pieces for each side of the cushion. Arrange the first piece with the C stripe across the top of square and the 2nd piece with the C stripe on the inside facing this square and join along the edge. Sew the other 2 pieces like this. Sew the 2 sides tog. so that the C stripes meet in the centre. Work the other side of the cushion in the same way. Press as before. Join 2 sides tog. right sides facing, leaving an

opening for inserting the pad. Turn to right side and insert pad. Sew up opening. Using ready-made or crochet cord made in same way as for Diagonal Cushion sew cord along each join on both sides. Sew cord round the edge making a loop at each corner and at each joining: 8 loops round the cushion.

Lacy-edged tablecloth

MATERIALS
4 balls (20 gr. each) Coats Mercer-Crochet No. 20. One No. 12 circular knitting needle, 30 in. long (USA size 1). One steel crochet hook International Standard Size 1.25. 1½ yd. fine linen, 54 in. wide.

MEASUREMENTS
Finished tablecloth measures 51½ in. in diameter; width of edging 4½ in.

TENSION
8 sts. and 9 rows to 1 in.

ABBREVIATIONS
See page 22; k.4 tog., sl.2, k. next 2 sts. tog., then pass the 2 sl. sts. over; work butterfly: cast on 5 sts., drop the next 5 sts., then insert right-hand needle under the 6 strands thus formed and k. 1 st., cast on 5 sts.; make 3: work (k.1, p.1) into next st.

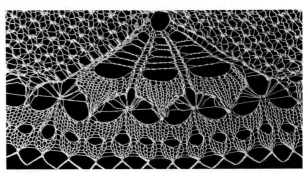

TO MAKE
With circular needle cast on 1035 sts. Join, being careful not to twist sts.
1st row: k.
2nd row: * (make 3, sl.1, k.2 tog., p.s.s.o.) 11 times, make 3, y.r.n. twice; rep. from * to end.
3rd row: k., working (k.1, p.1) 3 times into every y.r.n. twice of previous row.
4th row: * (sl.1, k.2 tog., p.s.s.o., make 3) 11 times, sl.1, k.2 tog., p.s.s.o., k.6 t.b.l.; rep. from * to end.
5th row: k.
6th row: * k.4 tog., (make 3, sl.1, k.2 tog., p.s.s.o.) 9 times, make 3, k.4 tog., (k.1 t.b.l., y.r.n. twice, k.1 t.b.l.) 3 times; rep. from * to end.
7th and following 2 alternate rows: k., working k.1 and p.1 into every y.r.n. twice of previous row.
8th row: * k.4 tog., (make 3, sl.1, k.2 tog., p.s.s.o.) 8 times, make 3, k.4 tog., (k.2 tog., y.r.n. twice, sl.1, k.1, p.s.s.o.) 3 times; rep. from * to end: 1127 sts. (1 pattern 49 sts.).
10th row: * k.4 tog., (make 3, sl.1, k.2 tog., p.s.s.o.) 7 times, make 3, k.4 tog., (k.2 tog., y.r.n. twice, sl.1, k.1, p.s.s.o.) 3 times; rep. from * to end.
12th row: * k.4 tog., (make 3, sl.1, k.2 tog., p.s.s.o.) 6 times, make 3, k.4 tog., (k.2 tog., y.r.n. 3 times, sl.1, k.1, p.s.s.o.) 3 times; rep. from * to end.
13th and 15th rows: k., working k.1 and p.1 into every y.r.n. 3 times, dropping the extra loop.

14th row: * k.4 tog., (make 3, sl.1, k.2 tog., p.s.s.o.) 5 times, make 3, k.4 tog., (k.2 tog., y.r.n. 3 times, sl.1, k.1, p.s.s.o.) 3 times; rep. from * to end.

16th row: * k.4 tog., (make 3, sl.1, k.2 tog., p.s.s.o.) 4 times, make 3, k.4 tog., (k.2 tog., y.r.n. 3 times, sl.1, k.1, p.s.s.o.) 3 times; rep. from * to end.

17th row: k., working (k.1, p.1) 4 times and k.1 into every y.r.n. 3 times of previous row.

18th row: * k.4 tog., (make 3, sl.1, k.2 tog., p.s.s.o.) 3 times, make 3, k.4 tog., k.33; rep. from * to end: 1150 sts. (1 pattern 50 sts.).

19th and every following alternate row unless otherwise stated: k.

20th row: * k.4 tog., (make 3, sl.1, k.2 tog., p.s.s.o.) twice, make 3, k.4 tog., k.33; rep. from * to end.

22nd row: * k.4 tog., make 3, sl.1, k.2 tog., p.s.s.o., make 3, k.4 tog., (y.fwd., sl.1, k.1, p.s.s.o., k.7, k.2 tog., 3 times, y.fwd.; rep. from * to end.

24th row: * k.4 tog., make 3, k.4 tog., (y.fwd., k.1, y.fwd., sl.1, k.1, p.s.s.o., k.5, k.2 tog.) 3 times, y.fwd.,

k.1, y.fwd.; rep. from * to end.

26th row: * sl.1, k.1, p.s.s.o., k.1, k.2 tog., (y.fwd., k.3, y.fwd., sl.1, k.1, p.s.s.o., k.3, k.2 tog.) 3 times, y.fwd., k.3, y.fwd.; rep. from * to end.

28th row: * sl.1, k.2 tog., p.s.s.o., (work butterfly, sl.2, k.3 tog., p.s.s.o.) 3 times, work butterfly; rep. from * to end: 1104 sts. (1 pattern 48 sts.)

29th to 34th rows: k.

35th row: * k.2 tog., y.r.n. twice, sl.1, k.1, p.s.s.o.; rep. from * to end.

36th row: k., working k.1, p.1 into every y.r.n. twice.

37th to 40th rows: k.

TO COMPLETE

Using crochet hook work * 1 d.c. into next 4 sts. and slip off, 12 ch.; rep. from * ending with 1 s.s. into first d.c. Fasten off. Damp and pin out to measurement. Cut circle from linen, with diameter of 43½ in. Turn in and stitch a ½-in. hem round edges. Stitch knitted edging in place.

Acknowledgements

The author acknowledges with thanks the help given with the preparation of this book by the following:

J. & P. Coats Ltd., 155 St. Vincent St., Glasgow C.2.
Emu Wools Ltd., Low Street Mills, Keighley, Yorkshire.
John C. Horsfall and Sons Ltd. (Hayfield Wools), Hayfield Mills, Glusburn, Nr. Keighley, Yorkshire.

Lister and Co. Ltd., Providence Mills, Wakefield, Yorkshire.
Martin Mahony and Bros. Ltd., Blarney, Co. Cork.
Patons and Baldwins, P.O. Box 22, Darlington, Co. Durham.
Robin Wools Ltd., Bradford, Yorkshire.
Sirdar Ltd., Bective Mills, Alverthorpe, Wakefield, Yorkshire.
H. G. Twilley Ltd., Roman Mills, Stamford, Lincs.
Wendy and Peter Pan Knitting Wools, Carter and Parker Ltd., Gordon Mills, Guiseley.
Abel Morrall Ltd. (Aero knitting needles, crochet hooks, Twin-pins and other products).

WOOLS AND YARNS

an important note

It is recommended that wherever possible the brand name and weight of yarn quoted in each pattern is used. Where it is not possible to obtain these particular yarns, the following general equivalents may be satisfactorily substituted. It is essential however whether using the original brand-name yarn, or one of the general equivalents listed below, that you make a careful tension check before you embark on any pattern. Only by achieving the correct tension can you hope to make a successful, well-fitting garment. Remember that the knitting needle size quoted in the pattern is only given as a guide—depending on the yarn you are using and whether you work tightly or slackly, you may well have to use a needle one, two or even three sizes bigger or smaller than the size quoted in order to achieve the correct tension measurement.

Coats yarns
Mercer-Crochet No. 20 should be readily available almost everywhere. In USA substitute J. & P. Coats 6/c Crochet Cotton or 3/Mercerised No. 20.

Emu yarns
For Baby Nylon 3-ply use a standard 3-ply yarn.
For Scotch 4-ply use a standard 4-ply yarn.
For Tricel Nylon Double Knitting, use a synthetic double knitting yarn.
For Filigree use any mohair yarn.

Hayfield yarns
For Courtier Super Crimp Bri-Nylon 3-ply use a standard 3-ply yarn (preferably nylon).
For Beaulon 4-ply use a standard 4-ply yarn.
For Gaylon Double Knitting, Courtier Double Knitting or Diane use a standard double knitting yarn.
For Brig use an Aran-type yarn.

Lee Target yarns
For Motoravia 4-ply use a standard 4-ply yarn.
For Motoravia Double Knitting or Lorette Double Crêpe use a standard double knitting yarn.

Lister yarns
For 2-spun 4-ply Crêpe use a standard 4-ply yarn with a crêpe finish.
For Bel-Air Starspun 4-ply use a glitter yarn which works to a 4-ply tension.
For Lavenda Double Knitting use a standard double knitting.
For Lochinvar Double Knitting use a random-dyed double knitting yarn.

Mahony's yarns
Blarney Bainin and Blarney Berella Baby yarns should be readily available almost everywhere. In USA substitute Blarneyspun for Blarney Bainin.

Patons yarns
For Promise use any Tricel yarn preferably with a 'crinkle' finish.

For Limelight 4-ply or Limelight Crêpe 4-ply use a standard 4-ply yarn.

Peter Pan yarns
See Wendy yarns.

Pingouin yarns
For Madame Pingouin Double Knitting use a standard double knitting yarn.

Robin yarns
For Vogue Double Knitting use a standard double knitting yarn.

Sirdar yarns
For Courtelle Random use a random-dyed Courtelle or similar synthetic yarn.

Twilley yarns
Crysette is a medium-weight cotton yarn; Stalite is a slightly heavier cotton yarn; Bubbly is a cotton with a novelty 'bubble' finish—a thick thread of cotton with a bouclé (or cluster) finish is spun with a very thin thread of the same yarn: for these yarns substitute good-quality cotton yarns of similar weights and finishes, but check tension measurement carefully.
D42 is a medium-weight dishcloth cotton.
For Mohair use any random-dyed mohair yarn.
For Goldfingering use any good-quality medium-weight glitter yarn.
For Cortina Super Crochet Wool use any good-quality medium-weight wool with a firm twist.

Wendy and Peter Pan yarns
For Courtelle Crêpe 4-ply, 4-ply Nylonised or Peter Pan Bri-Nylon Super Crimp 4-ply use a standard 4-ply yarn.
For Peter Pan Baby Quick Courtelle Double Knitting, Tricel Nylon Double Knitting, Double Knit Nylonised, Kinvara or Tricel Nylon Crêpe Double Knitting use a standard double knitting yarn.
For Diabolo use a standard double double knitting yarn.

Ball quantities
Many knitting and crochet yarns are now being sold in 20, 25 or 50 gram balls instead of in ounce quantities. If you are buying balls of yarn to make up a particular pattern, take care that you buy sufficient—i.e. if the quantity given in the pattern is for ounce balls, and the yarn manufacturer has meanwhile gone over to gram measurements, you will need to buy more balls of the new measure than of the old. The exact conversion for one ounce is 28.35 grams which means that a 25-gram ball will be nearest in weight to the old ounce ball, but still slightly under. If you therefore want to buy 4 oz. of a yarn being sold in 25-gram balls, then you should buy five balls to make sure you will have enough. If the yarn is being sold in 20-gram balls, then buy six.